D0851343

POETRY EVERYWHERE

ALSO BY JACK COLLOM

Moving Windows
Arguing with Something Plato Said
Little Grand Island

ALSO BY SHERYL NOETHE

The Descent of Heaven over the Lake

POETRY EVERYWHERE

Teaching Poetry Writing in School and in the Community

by Jack Collom and Sheryl Noethe

Teachers & Writers Collaborative

New York

Poetry Everywhere

Copyright © 1994 by Teachers & Writers Collaborative. All rights reserved. Printed in the United States of America. No part of this publica-
tion may be reproduced, stored in a retrieval system, or transmitted, in
any form or by any means, electronic, mechanical, photocopying, re-
cording, or otherwise, without prior permission of the publisher.

The permissions acknowledgments on page viii constitute an extension of
the copyright page.

Teachers & Writers Collaborative
5 Union Square West
New York, N.Y. 10003-3306

Library of Congress Cataloging-in-Publication Data

Collom, Jack, 1931–
    Poetry everywhere : teaching poetry writing in school and in the
community / by Jack Collom and Sheryl Noethe.
            p.   cm.
        ISBN 0-915924-98-6
        1. Poetry—Study and teaching. 2. Poetry—Authorship.
I. Noethe, Sheryl. II. Title
PN1101.C64 1994
808.1—dc20   93-32351
                                                   CIP
                                                   AC

Printed by Philmark Lithographics, New York, N.Y.
Second Printing

ACKNOWLEDGMENTS

This book would not be possible without the participation of the teachers' writing group of Salmon, Idaho, who put so much of their time and hearts into this program to make it work in the best way for teachers and kids: Dorrie Prange, Dorothy Olson, Betsy Nottestad, Susie Skeen, Eileen French, Chris Casterson, Joy Rebman, Nola Losser, Rose Morphey, Jim Lund, Deb Riggan, Tina Olsen-Cooper, B.J. Mayer, Jim Casterson, Jim Toynbee, Kay Smith, Terry Magoon, Jay Skeen, and Bernadine Berry.

Many thanks also to those teachers and administrators who worked with the poets in the classroom and gave advice for this book: Henrietta Irish, Frances Richman, Rilla Corbett, Dick Hadlock, Connie Livingston, Margaret Gudgel, Elaine Wigginton, Mel Skeen, Jean Hadlock, Liz Lim, Candace Crosby, Clyde Smith, Meridean Bromley, Woo McLean, Gayle Sandborgh, Gayla Gould, Sue Rogers, Sandy Toynbee, Mike Dunphy, George Artemis, Mike Crosby, Martha Edgar, Mary Taylor, Larry Gwartney, Ann Bowers, Bob Cramer, Roy Bossert, Marlys Pearce, Ramona Combs-Stauffer, Gary Foss, James McConnell, Barry Miller, and Matt Weller.

Thanks to Ann Loucks and Linda Scoble, librarians at the Brooklyn and Pioneer Schools, to Jade Hanson, Joy Artemis, Sheila Ankrum, and Anita Stenerson for clerical help, and to Karen Cooper, Claire Wiley, and Dana Newsom. Thanks to Ed Stepanek at the *Recorder Herald* and to KSRA radio station for support and publicity.

Thanks to The Steele-Reese Foundation for asking Teachers & Writers Collaborative to "dream a little." They asked the right dreamers. Thanks to Chris Brady of Steele-Reese for her help and encouragement and to Nancy Larson Shapiro of T&W for putting so much into shaping the program and contributing ideas and support. Thanks to T&W's Felice Stadler, Ron Padgett, Pat Padgett, and especially Chris Edgar. Thanks to Steele-Reese for continuing the program for four years. Thanks to the Salmon Board of Education for giving us a chance and to Jim Smith and his staff for easing us into the system. Many thanks to Bernadine Berry, who helped us to produce annual anthologies, volunteering time and smarts.

*   *   *   *   *

Teachers & Writers Collaborative also expresses its gratitude to the other generous funders of its programs: The National Endowment for the Arts, the New York State Council on the Arts, The American Stock Exchange, The Bingham Trust, The Witter Bynner Foundation for Poetry,

Chemical Bank, Consolidated Edison, Aaron Diamond Foundation, The Heckscher Foundation for Children, Morgan Stanley Foundation, New York Community Trust, New York Telephone, New York Times Company Foundation, Henry Nias Foundation, New York Rotary Foundation of the Rotary Club of New York, Helena Rubinstein Foundation, The Scherman Foundation, and the Lila Wallace-Reader's Digest Fund.

*　　*　　*　　*　　*

Teachers & Writers Collaborative is grateful for permission to reprint the following material. Elizabeth Fox for her "Losing a Goat" and "Wet Hair." George Braziller, Inc., for "Stone" by Charles Simic, copyright © 1971 by Charles Simic. Joe Brainard for excerpts from his *I Remember,* copyright © 1975 by Joe Brainard and published by Full Court Press. William Carlos Williams's "The Last Words of My English Grandmother," "Nantucket," "This Is Just to Say," and "So much depends . . . ," from *Collected Poems 1909–1939. Vol. I.* Copyright 1938 by New Directions Publishing Corp. Reprinted by permission of New Directions Publishing Corp. Denise Levertov's "Pleasures" from *Collected Earlier Poems 1940–1960.* Copyright © 1959 by Denise Levertov. Reprinted by permission of New Directions Publishing Corp. Ezra Pound's translation of Li Po's "The River Merchant's Wife: A Letter" from *The Translations of Ezra Pound* by Ezra Pound, copyright © 1954, 1963 by Ezra Pound. All rights reserved. Reprinted by permission of New Directions Publishing Corp. Robert Bly for his translation of Pablo Neruda's "Ode to My Socks" from *Neruda and Vallejo: Selected Poems,* Beacon Press, 1971. Copyright © 1970 by Robert Bly. "Page from a Notebook" is reprinted by permission from *Blood and Feathers: Selected Poems of Jacques Prévert,* published by Moyer Bell, Kymbolde Way, Wakefield, RI 02879. W.S. Merwin for his translation of "My Sun, the Golden Garden of Your Hair" from the Quechua. The translation of "Arbolé, Arbolé" by Federico García Lorca is reprinted by permission of the translator, William Bryant Logan. "Ballad of the Morning Streets" by Amiri Baraka is reprinted by permission of Sterling Lord Literistic, Inc. Copyright © 1967 by Amiri Baraka. Gary Snyder's "Mid-August at Sourdough Mountain Lookout" is reprinted by permission of the author. Alfred A. Knopf, Inc., for "Ex-Basketball Player" from *The Carpentered Hen and Other Tame Creatures* by John Updike, copyright © 1982 by John Updike. Alfred A. Knopf, Inc., for "A Rabbit As King of the Ghosts" from *Collected Poems* by Wallace Stevens, copyright 1923 and renewed 1951 by Wallace Stevens. Mary Jarrell for "The Truth" from *Selected Poems* by Randall Jarrell. Alice Notley for "Sonnet XVII" from *The Sonnets* by Ted Berrigan.

TABLE OF CONTENTS

PREFACE

In 1987 I left my work in New York City to be the resident poet in a town I'd never heard of, Salmon, Idaho, population 3,308, where local residents Eleanor Reese and Emmett Steele had left their legacy in the form of the Steele-Reese Foundation. I became part of the endowment to the town, going into the schools and working with teachers at all levels to include them in an effort to make creative writing full of opportunity and discovery for students and themselves. We rid ourselves of the notion that student work was to be judged and graded, and instead made it our task to write poetry with honesty and energy, poetry that is wildly true to our dreams. It is, of course, the nature of poetry to shake things up and engage the imagination—the stuff basic to learning anything.

It was as though the children of Salmon had been waiting all of their lives to write poetry. I found myself in the midst of a loosed river of wit and memory and celebration. I had walked into a working gold mine in the Lemhi Valley.

The kids took their excitement home. Everywhere I went parents talked to me about their kids and poetry. In the newspaper we had a "Poem of the Week" that grew to a column of poems every week, thanks to the local editor. The radio station invited us to read poems on their "Voice of the Valley" show. When we held a public reading of children's poetry, it was jam-packed. Standing room only. Who would have thought that on a bitter February night all those people would fill the Salmon City Center to hear one hundred young people read their own poems aloud, hair slicked down, bows tied?

Meanwhile, the extravagant beauty of the landscape raged around us. Hard not to notice. Hard not to write about. Hard not to try to describe. The kids overwhelmed me with information about their lives, adventures at school and play, the names of everything around us. They wrote about their most tender impressions, their earliest memories. They watched the world in its busyness and responded with compassion and humor. Because their parents teach them to appreciate the place, the kids grow up with a keen eye for the country around them, an intelligence about their place in the physical world. Their writing has significant details about everyday occupations—especially those including cattle and horses, rodeos and guns, cats and dogs and bum calves. They have the essential knowledge of mountains, rivers, and love.

The second year, the program doubled when another poet from Teachers & Writers, Jack Collom, joined us. We wanted to give every child in Salmon a shot at poetry. Word of mouth got around so much that children kept asking us, "When do I get a poet?" By the final year we had taught poetry to virtually every student in the Salmon schools—and worked with teachers at all levels.

The teachers of Salmon invested time and serious attention in our poetry program. They wrote along with the students, read aloud, displayed poems, and proved by example that poetry writing is important. The enthusiasm and energy of the Salmon teachers is directly reflected in their students' work.

Each year we made a big anthology of our work. Deciding which poems to include was some of the hardest work I've ever done. Jack and I could have papered Salmon with poems. Eventually the making of the anthology became the responsibility of the teachers. We met in a writing group every Thursday, and they took control of the process of gathering student poems and putting the best into a book using the high school library's desktop publishing system. Our fourth and last year in Salmon, the anthology was done entirely by teachers and students. Teachers also collaborated with us on a pilot version of this book to compile our classroom experiences in Salmon, along with the resulting poetry, so that other teachers could have a guide for using poetry in the classroom. Jack and I have included some student examples from other residencies as well.

The radiant poems of the Salmon students speak for what happened in Salmon better than I can. Salmon, Idaho, is now a town of working poets led by poetry-loving teachers. We had an idea, Jack and I, but we could never have imagined the wealth that would make itself available through the hearts and minds of Salmon's children and their teachers.

—Sheryl Noethe

A NOTE ON THIS BOOK AND HOW TO USE IT

This is a how-to book. It is also a big, many-gated entrance to pleasure and excitement in learning. The substance of this huge claim is the agency of *poetry*—in its broadest sense—in the classroom, not only in literature, not only in "English," but also in history and all the humanities, and even in science and math. Poetry *is* a basic tool of learning.*

More and more, writing is considered the key activity of most school learning. Yet teachers, parents, and other observers note that schoolchildren are all too often turned off by writing. To kids it may seem boring, abstract, arbitrary. Ironically, at the same time their writing is anemic and derivative, their personal speech is likely to be full of verve and originality.

This book centers on writing ideas for a great number of classroom writing activities that are fun for students. Through doing poetry, students find that writing can be lively and absorbing. They find it can express, whatever the subject, how they see the world. Once that recognition is internalized, their sense of enjoyment-while-working can spread into other forms of writing—letters, stories, and even school compositions.

Parallel to this development, students can discover not only that it's fun to write poems but also that it helps them learn about themselves. They will encounter things in their own minds that they didn't know were there. Hidden rainbows of perception arise through the writing act. And while learning about themselves, they also learn in a personal way how interesting it is to look around and see what everything really looks like—an endless study. This sort of curiosity, once aroused, can extend into all areas of learning—and into how learning itself works. Art is a process of exploration, and what we're talking about is the *art* of writing. We feel that the *art* of writing is *central* to the process of learning.

The big organizational change in traditional education we advocate here is this: to reverse the order in which language is taught. Most curricula call first for exercises aimed at the mastery of grammar, and introduce "expressive" language and poetry "appreciation" later. Early on, most curricula allow for stories, word-games, and the like, and individual teachers do much to foster creativity even when faced with an inflexible curriculum. Our revolutionary recommendation, however, is

---

* For the purposes of this book, and to highlight the scope of poetry, we're using the term "creative writing" almost interchangeably with the word "poetry"—though there is little here concerning drama or narrative fiction.

to include the poetic—*as a primary, hands-on writing activity*—from the beginning. We believe that poetry is at the core of language use. This doesn't mean we advocate "poetry only" for grades 1–4; it means we recommend an *overlapping* of ways of learning language. We find that a many-sided approach is both true to the nature of things and easily assimilated by the kids.

Our suggestion is to combine the creative writing ideas here *with* standard teaching techniques. Some of these exercises are discrete entities, but many more blend easily into the entire school curriculum. This combining may well be in the form of different approaches made at different times. In a language arts class, for example, there is no reason not to learn verbs one day and write poetry the next. And so to proceed till the two tend to merge. Each strengthens the other.

What's our working definition of "poetry"? Certainly not "noble sentiments carved in verse." "Magic talk"? Nice, but no help. Poetry, as it works here, is an inclusive term. "Intense language" comes close. Then is James Joyce's *Ulysses* a poem? Sure. And so's this one-line directive (from a dream) which the Australian Kurnai tribespeople repeat to drive away pain: "Show your belly to the *moon.*" Poetry, let's say, is what people may write (say) when their sense of discovery is working well.

The writing exercises in this book combine guidance and openness to allow for the possibility of poetry. Each is necessary to the other, and to the whole, like the "skin" and helium of a flying balloon. The guidance part can consist of: 1) a poetic form; 2) a distinct writing idea; and/or 3) subject matter. Teachers can give their students some additional guidance—toward close observation and original language—without restricting them, and this book contains many detailed hints along those lines. When you do these exercises with your class, think of your leadership as seeking a *combination* of freedom and suggestion: if the students' writing energy is channeled just enough to provide them with a direction to go in—and the direction is large enough to include an infinite field of choices—the working balance should be good.

Oh, it might be possible to walk into a classroom, say "Write poems!" and look out a window—and get a few happy surprises. Mostly, though, the results would be sparse, weak, clichéd. This is because, paradoxically, students (like all people) need *some* direction to become, energetically, themselves. If guidelines are not presented, they will be assumed by the students, but the assumptions students make, lacking thoughtful leadership, are likely to result in some pretty hackneyed, low-octane poems.

On the other hand, just what controls and influences does one impose? Normal directed study—deductive analysis—is too restrictive (as a main approach) for poetry; the art can't flourish. Learning writing without active involvement in writing is not only barren and mechanical but also omits or distorts much that is important. Learning from the doer's standpoint changes the nature of knowledge.

Some popular biases about poetry restrict it to rhyming, to prettification, to an artificial sense of language, to "lofty thoughts" and the like, and associate it with impracticality, weepiness, and solipsism. Perhaps this misunderstanding derives from a fear of intensity. Language is powerful, and poetic language is the most personally derived, intense language one can find.

Here is what we recommend:

1. Read the "Preface" and "My Philosophy of Teaching Poetry in the Classroom."

2. Read the introductory chapter called "Tips on Leading Poetry Sessions." These suggestions are basic to *every* exercise. (At this point, you can if you like jump to step 4.)

3. Read any of the supplementary chapters (which give information on such topics as how to teach different age-groups and traditional poetic forms) that interest you.

The above sections attempt to help you be free and easy about what you're doing *and* at the same time exert the care necessary for good writing.

4. Then pick an exercise from the "Exercises" section and try it out. It will be necessary to familiarize yourself with it, and digest it somewhat, before classtime.

5. If it works, try more. And more and more. Make this creative writing approach a part of your whole educational practice.

—*Jack Collom*

MY PHILOSOPHY OF TEACHING POETRY IN THE CLASSROOM

Ever since the fifth grade, writing has been my better world, a refuge and solace where my imagination is king. This is the opportunity we as teachers of poetry have before us in the classroom. We can offer this sustenance, this self-creation, to children, making their lives richer and happier and giving them more alternatives. Writing is a grip on existence, an empowerment, and a way to listen to the inner truth of the self. The poet enters a dialogue with all previous poets, singers, and writers. You keep great company.

When I read a poem to the class I read it as though it were the most important and only poem in the world. I use the opportunity to hook the students up to the heart of the poet. I use the poem as a force to pull our imaginations into the associative world of words and ideas. I read the poem aloud and make it real for them. Inadvertently, something rare happens when we begin to anticipate hearing a poem; we settle into a dreamy concentration, to sit back and hear the poem in a sort of reverie. Ask the class to daydream and let their minds fill with the images that the poet gives them. Put the world on HOLD for a while and pay attention to your inner life by letting the poem inside.

Eventually you will find a different poem for everyone. If you persist in selecting and then learning wonderful poems to read aloud to the class, you will find that different students will respond to different poems, finally connecting with an idea or phrase that touches them, and they will appreciate that singular thing that poetry does so well. "Ah!" the mind says, "wonderful!" Besides the inherent miracle of the poem, imagine teaching a subject where no one can fail, where the student will achieve some success and then crave more! Turn a child's identity into a respected position—a writer—and have him or her know there is nothing like success. Your job as a teacher is to tell every student what is right about his or her work. This calls for wit, compassion, and a huge frame of reference! Relationships develop with the exchange of history and imagination. Trust and empathy are aroused when you hear someone else's words echo your own feelings, in surprising ways and common ways, and you cannot stay strangers. When you point out to your students where they are at their best in their work—the funniest or the most imaginative or the truest to their vision—you give them success and they in return give you their trust. They write in the only way beautiful things are created—from the heart, without censorship or fear. That's when you get the poetry.

—*Sheryl Noethe*

Tips on Leading Poetry Sessions

In this chapter we list a variety of suggestions to help you take a hands-on approach to teaching poetry. Many other specialized hints are found in the Exercises section, and in the supplementary chapters following it.

In writing these tips, we have opted to take nothing for granted and to be as detailed as possible. We realize that some of our advice may repeat, or depart from, basic teacherly skills and wisdom you have all known thoroughly and practiced throughout your teaching careers. We feel the contradictions are appropriate, since the learning process in a poetry—or other art—workshop is quite different than that in, say, chemistry or grammar. And the repetitions are the price of care. We simply hope that anyone setting out to use our suggestions will find our inclusiveness useful.

In our experience as visiting poets, these suggestions all work and are all important to successful sessions. But there's plenty of room for individual styles to modify or even to go against some of the following ideas.

The tips that we feel are especially important are marked with asterisks, but we don't mean to be dictatorial. For example, we say, "Never tire of pounding home to your class the happy use of *details*, as opposed to generalities." This doesn't mean that language should sound like a seed catalogue when it's poetry time. It's just that it's good to get kids writing intimately of what they know—and this certainly includes their wildest dreams and their imagination of the moment as well as the color of their pet dogs' eyes. Dream is made of detail too. If the students work in an atmosphere of easeful energy, they're likely to "be themselves" in their poems, in ways that will surprise even them.

Our hint categories are organized around the actual classroom "hour":

1. Preparation
2. Manner of presentation and general tips
3. The session itself
    a. Lead-in
    b. Writing time
    c. Reading the results aloud

4. Afterwards
5. Remarks on the poetry of it

1. Preparation

• Planning can be thorough or not, according to the teacher's style. It usually works best when the main points to be made, examples to give, and *timing* of the session have been carefully worked out beforehand, but some poets and teachers do well "winging it." All teachers should be alert to unexpected and serendipitous veerings off from the plan.

• You might try making up poems yourself according to the exercise you've chosen—if possible, just before the session. This may provide you with good example poems, and certainly helps get you "into" the writing.

• Props are sometimes helpful but aren't necessary. Writing to music can be good also. Sometimes with younger students, decor—such as hanging up streamers—can make for a special "poetry time" mood.

• Try things different ways at different times (for example, combine two exercises, or try an entirely new warmup). Let the students know why you are taking a new tack.

• You can use pre-writing (days before the poetry session) and various warmup activities at the beginning of the session to immerse students in a given subject. A caution: there can be too much brainstorming, leading the kids to regurgitate info and to use the same chalkboard vocabulary. (See "On Quickies: Icebreakers & Fillers.")

• Simply reading good books to students is a good preparation for writing.

2. Manner of presentation and general tips

* • Be yourself. You needn't and shouldn't show reverence for poetry by means of an artificially dignified atmosphere.

• "Walking around while teaching, sharing, and especially reading orally grabs *all* the students' attention, involves them as a community" (Chris Casterson, third grade teacher). It also helps lend a physical sense to the poetry.

* • *Energy* is the key—but it shouldn't be forced. It can be "quiet" energy.

• In some ways, you can be less "in charge." Much of the learning in poetry comes from the inside out.

• It's probably best not to "push" your beliefs about the beauties of poetry, but to let them emerge through examples and practice.

• Don't overexplain (as we do in this book).

* • Avoid abstractions. When you speak in concrete terms, it helps bring out better poems. However, stressing "detail," "imagination," and "originality" repeatedly will tend to unify these words with their examples in the poems.

* • Read poetry aloud with energy, expressiveness, and rhythm (this can be the variable rhythm of everyday speech). For example, read or tell the Greek myths as if they happened this morning.

• Make a conscious choice as to whether to read with pauses at the ends of lines (which tends to emphasize the breath, the connection of poetry to the body) or not (which can emphasize the flow of sound and ideas).

• It's helpful to admit your own errors, blankouts, and ignorance. This helps create an open mood in the classroom.

• Presentation of sample material on overhead projectors can help students' visual comprehension (but the reading voice should always "carry" the work).

• When you know a kid, you can criticize his or her poem *if* you include encouragement (and if it's one-on-one, not public). "This part is full of great energy, but down here it just kind of falls apart—you need an image."

• Sometimes a little edge of sarcasm or sharpness in a general sea of kindness and warmth will help the students realize "We're really trying to do something here." It's not goof-off time.

• At any time, you can, if inspired, simply read or recite a good poem aloud to the class—and that poem needn't have an obvious connection to what you're doing.

* • Maintain cheer and confidence if a student reacts negatively. Try to avoid confrontations; often the best approach is to ignore that student for the moment and concentrate on the rest of the class. Your positive attitude and the peer influence of the majority's participation will probably bring the recalcitrant student along.

• If your students seem to have trouble getting going, tell them to flap their elbows and just start scribbling. Urge spontaneity in different ways. "Work it out on paper, don't try to think it all up in your head first." "It can be messy, shows you're thinking; this is a worksheet. We'll make them pretty later." Perhaps suggest that they can copy *topics* from other kids, if their own treatment is original.

* • Never tire of pounding home the happy use of *details*, as opposed to generalities.

* • A brisk pace is good, energizing, as long as you're willing to be flexible and slow down when the situation needs it.

* • Don't worry. Decide thoughtfully what you're going to do, then let 'er rip. Relax and concentrate. Have fun. Freely intersperse humor and seriousness.

* • Be open to children's visions—they really have them.

3. The session itself

A. *Lead-in*

* • A good division of time is one-third lead-in, one-third writing time, one-third reading their pieces aloud (with either you or them as readers), with quick comments.

• Except in special cases, let them know right away what your plans are for the whole session.

• A little smalltalk (such as about their names, if you're new to them) may loosen things up and help direct their attention toward the everyday. A familiar, factual base is good for poetry.

• The warmup need not be tightly organized—an "off-task" icebreaker or poem-read-aloud may fire up imagination, which can then be pointed toward the day's exercise.

* • Read many examples aloud (and then simply tell students not to copy). Point out the "poetic goodies" in the example poems, especially when they channel the students' attention in the direction you want. To focus attention on language, you can ask students for their favorite words in what they've just heard.

* • Get them involved orally by means of questions (based on, or related to, examples) and by working out sample poems or lead-in information on the board with them.

• Say "If you get stuck on one thing, go to another." Even advise them to do the beginning last or to scribble any old thing just to get going (and scratch it out later if it doesn't work for them). Tell the kids not to erase things—they may want them later.

* • Have them sound out difficult words and not worry about it. Tell them not to avoid a word because they're afraid of misspelling it.

• Sometimes you might want to give them a word, sound, or idea on the board (or on tape) and ask them to meditate on it before beginning to write.

* • Often it's counterproductive to let them use the names of other students in their writings. If necessary, simply advise them not to, unless they're positive no embarrassment would result. Allow no cheap shots.

* • If they want to use titles, have them write them *after* their poems are done. A title can be a word or phrase from a poem, or be something related to the poem's subject, or be *anything at all*—even something seemingly unrelated, or playfully wacko. Titles work as parts of poems, and students should consider how a title idea affects the reader's take on the poem. Titles give a perspective to every word in a poem.

• It helps the flow of their writing if they start writing *just* after the sample poems are read.

• Let your students know it's okay to close their eyes and think, visualize, let the poem swim in.

B. *Writing time*

* • Let students talk quietly while they're writing. If any of them seem to be too off-task, you might advise them to "get that verbal energy down on paper before it blows away."

* • While they write, you can walk around the classroom and help them with their questions. Sometimes toss in added hints or nudges to the class at large—sometimes just quietly let them write.

• Early or midway in the writing time, you can ask anyone who's just written something good if you may read it to the class, and do so. This often inspires and encourages the other kids.

* • If you're not too busy, write with them. Jot something on the board. Perhaps read funny sample lines to the class as they occur to you. If they're doing collaborations, join in.

• When it's time to collect the pieces (maybe twelve to fifteen minutes along in the writing time), tell them they can keep writing a few minutes, but if they've finished they can hold their poems in the air (or bring them up) for collection.

* • Stress the idea that they should reread their work before handing it in. We *all* sometimes omit words inadvertently. And an instant revision is likely to be good since one is still in the flow and feeling of the poem.

• You can start reading the kids' work aloud (and tell the class to be quiet and attentive) when all but a few papers are in. (No harm if a few are still working.)

C. *Reading their works aloud*

• Again, read the poems expressively and rhythmically (if *you* read them).

• If the kids don't want their names read aloud, respect this, but in time try to lead them out of their shyness—as long as it doesn't deter them from writing freely. Younger students sometimes like the option of raising hands or standing after their poems are read.

* • It's a definite plus if students practice reading their poems aloud, especially older kids. But use your discretion—the virtues of the poems may get lost in poor renditions. If the students do read, urge pizzazz. Tell them to read "so the termite egg embedded in the far wall can hear it," or something. It's okay if some of them volunteer to read and others don't.

* • It's best not to criticize student work when it's first read; respond with cheer to each kid's piece. Discrimination can be exercised by selective intensity of praise. They'll note this and learn from it. Never give false praise. Be as concrete as you can in each bit of praise. Repeat good words or phrases they've written. You can often praise rhythm or energy or spirit or originality when it's hard to find anything else to praise. But don't let your comments get so long as to impede the flow of their work. A hearty "All right!" will often suffice.

• When students read collaborative poems aloud, try having them do choral readings—divide the class in various ways (blue eyes, brown; even or odd rows). Have them read in different voices—scared, baby, laryngitic, as The Principal, etc.

4. Afterwards

* • Typing up student poems preserves and honors them and makes them available to others. We strongly recommend typing up a selection. Kids love to see their work "in print."

• When typing up, correct spelling routinely (unless it has some special charm) but take grammar on a case-by-case basis. Poetry is always creating its own voice, so "correctness" is relative. In regard to punctuation, suggest—but don't insist—that it be consistent within a given poem.

• Often it's hard to tell whether a student piece is written with linebreaks or not. If there's time you can check with the author. Otherwise, look each piece over before typing and decide the apparent intent, then type accordingly. Sometimes, even if paper-width seems to have dictated the shape, the poem will "feel right," and you should type the poem up the way the student wrote it.

• If a poem or piece is off-task but good (interesting), take it.

• It helps students care for their work if you have them keep it in special folders to which they have free access.

• Then you can have the students bring out, reread, revise, and illustrate their works (see "Two Looks at Revision").

* • In any case, student poems should be kept and can then be typed up, put on bulletin boards, published schoolwide, sent to pen pals,

individually published by the students themselves, and distributed in the community. (See "On Follow-up" for a more complete set of suggestions.)

5. **Remarks on the poetry of it**

* • Give your students a sense of options when they write. Make it clear to them that *they* are the authors of their poems, the ones who will make decisions concerning tone, voice, rhythm, etc. And remember, in many cases kids will invent their own variations on the exercises and poetic forms you give them. (See "Student-invented Styles.")

* • When you choose adult poems to read in class, as much as possible try not to censor shocking imagery, harshness, negativity, "weirdness," low-class language, and so forth.

* • Encourage students to feel free to invent their own syntax at any point, to discover their own ways of handling words. That is, they should be able to decide, "Do I write standard here, or could it be effective to 'make up'?" You might point out how certain example poems you like use offbeat syntax.

* • Initially, it's best to welcome all content and all attitudes (except the "dirty" words not allowed in school), no matter how gruesome or radical or sad or mundane.

* • Any idea is all right in a first draft—or in a journal or in free-writing—or, in fact, in a finished poem.

* • In many cases you can advise students to write like they talk, to base their writings on natural speech patterns. You can demonstrate in many concrete ways how "real speech" is rich in rhythm, metaphor, etc. Pick an example off the classroom wall, or out of their mouths. (Repeating a common sentence several times can show surprising syncopation.)

* • Point out that speaking of emotions by name is abstract and risks cliché and superficiality. Make it concrete ("Write ten *things* you fear"). The clarity of good abstract writing begins with a mental acuity grounded in the concrete.

* • Tell your students that their poems don't all have to be "important" or about a Big Idea. Real significance is everywhere and, in poetry, often arrives on its own.

* • Encourage experiment. Praise it when it comes.

* • Emphasize language. It's their working material; it's a living thing, full of surprises. When the focus is on language, all the personal will shine through.

* • Approve playfulness—as a way of learning and exploring. Students benefit immensely when encouraged to play with language.

* • Speak of the mechanics of poetry as naturally as you'd speak of fixing a broken shoelace (though with a greater sense of options!). "You've rhymed up here but not down here. That makes this word stand out, but do you really want it to?"

• Always "go for the poem." That is, the charms of the language should not be subverted by a larger philosophic urge. If patriotism, say, is the subject, insist that it be expressed concretely or lyrically—not in the same old generalizations. Good poetry does not consist of generalizations.

—*Jack Collom*

Exercises

A NOTE ON THE EXERCISES

Following are the main writing exercises we suggest, arranged alphabetically. The exercises are cross-referenced where it seems useful. *X-ref:* PLACE POEMS means "cross-reference: see Place Poems."

Each exercise description contains suggestions on how to go about it, along with observations on the form described and examples by students. A number of the descriptions include examples by established poets; sometimes one of these forms the lead-in to the exercise (for more on this, see the supplementary chapter called "Using Great Poems as Models").

Also—and this is very important—we urge you to keep going back to the "Tips on Leading Poetry Sessions" chapter. Many of these tips are basic to the successful presentation and use of *any* creative writing idea in a workshop. Although these tips occupy a separate chapter, we'd like you to regard them as fundamental to each of our descriptions of the writing exercises.

There are many more creative writing exercises for class use than the ones given here. Some are indicated in a general way in the following writeups; for example, we note that the DECLARATIONS idea could be applied to almost any subject. Other exercises are mentioned or covered in the specialized supplementary chapters. Untold numbers of good writing ideas have yet to be invented or adapted—and will be, perhaps by you.

We've sought to achieve a balance of specificity and openness in each of these exercises. They will give your students leads but leave them plenty of room to make their writings especially their own.

> *x-ref:* "Using Great Poems as Models"
> "Tips on Leading Poetry Sessions"

You will find additional suggestions in the following supplementary chapters:

> "On Teaching Students of Different Ages"
> "On Inventing and Adapting Exercises"
> "On Collaborations"
> "On Quickies: Icebreakers and Fillers"

A LIST OF THE EXERCISES

Acrostics
Acrostics-from-Phrases
Anatomy Poems
"Captured Talk"
Chant Poems
Collage Poems
Compost-based Poems
Concrete Poems
Creative Rewrites
Declarations
Definition Poems
Dream Interpretation
Earth Poems—Things to Save
"Feelings" Poems
"Fourteener" Poems
Geometry Poems
"Going Inside" Poems
Haibun
Haiku
How I Write
"I Have a Dream" Poems
Internal Rhyme
"I Remember" Poems
"Last Words" Poems
✶ Letters
List Poems
Lunes
Metaphors
"My Soul Is . . ." Poems
Name-Letters Stories
No-Warmup Deliveries
Odes
On Poetry
Origins Poems
Outdoors Poems
Pantoums
Picture-Inspired Writings
Place Poems

Political Poems
Portrait or Sketch Poems
"Primitive" Poems
"Process" Poems
Q & A Partner Poems
Questions without Answers
Recipe Poems
Rube Goldberg Poems
A Run on Imagination
Sestinas
Spanish / English Poems
Spelling List Poems
Talking to Animals
Thing Poems
"Things to Do" Poems
"Thirteen Ways of Looking" Poems
Used to / But Now Poems
Water Poems
William Carlos Williams Imitations
Word Pairs

ACROSTICS

To make an acrostic poem, write a word vertically and then use each letter to begin a line. Example:

M arty,
I love you and like you and
K iss you and go to the park and
E at grapes with you.

    —Michael Busby, 1st

The acrostic is so flexible and delightful a form that we've appended an unusual number of examples.

There's more to say about the acrostic as a form than there is about many of the other exercises, but you needn't explain *all* the following to introduce students to acrostics. Limit your warmup to fifteen minutes or so and bring out some of the points later as they become pertinent.

As part of the warmup, you can name various letters and ask students to say the first word (starting with that letter) that comes to mind. You can move from there to a sort of acrostic "exquisite corpse"—you have a word in mind and one by one write down the letters, getting word-responses from the class as you go. You'll probably end up with playful nonsense, like

B aby
U nleashes
S ilicon
H ands

which encourages associative freedom. Another simple warmup is to use someone's initials: for example, JKH becomes Jelly Kissed Harmonica.

Of course, you may skip these warmups and simply show the class what an acrostic is. Write one on the board. Then write the "spine words" of several more (even a dozen or so) and read the acrostics aloud, pointing to the letters as you go. You might suggest that what an acrostic is is tilting a word on its side and "seeing what spills out."

Talk a little about whatever aspects of the form might be relevant to your students:

• Linebreaks can occur within phrases, at unlikely points; this can lay stress on words otherwise lost in the flow. For example,

C reature who
A pproaches you when it wants
T o

emphasizes the unexpectedness, the independence, of the feline's movements, more than if the poem were only one line ("Cat: creature who approaches you when it wants to").

• There are no requirements for rhyme, meter, line length, or meaning.

• Writers can make their poems relate to the spine word or not, or have the poems "close to" or "distant from" it. Usually the spine word will influence the other words:

P andora	P laying	P opulate the cosmos with
O pened	O n the swing	O dd rhythms from Planet
E verything	E ating	E arth.
T o	T affy	T ake your poems to NASA. They
R ealize	R unning through the	R ead, launch, and make
Y es! But . . .	Y ard.	Y ou an intergalactic seer.

—*Mike Crosby, teacher*

• Since the line is emphasized by the form of the acrostic itself, mixtures of long and short lines stand out musically, and thus semantically. A very short line after a series of long ones, or vice versa, feels different.

Ask the students to pick their own (interesting) words and each write an acrostic or two.

These may well be instructions enough, but here are some additional points:

• With young or beginning student poets, suggest there's a magic to making poems out of one's own name. (See NAME-LETTERS STORIES.)

• You can use a *series* of words for the spine.

• You can use the whole alphabet (for that "encyclopedic" feel).

• You can spell the spine word from bottom to top.

• You can make a "ragged" acrostic by allowing some letters to stick out to the left of the spine word.

• You might skip lines (of paper) when writing down your spine word so you'll have room for long poem-lines.

• It's interesting to have all the students write acrostics based on the same spine word.

• Students can write repeated acrostics of the same word (it's amazing how ideas keep kicking in for this one).

Collect and read. (When reading student acrostics aloud, try announcing the spine word beforehand and reading with gestures and pauses, to emphasize the form.)

*   *   *   *   *

People have written acrostics for thousands of years. There have been many elaborations of the form throughout history—in the Bible, and in works by Plautus, Boccaccio, Chaucer, Ben Jonson, Poe, and others. Poets have also tried having the *end* letters of each line spell something vertically, or even having a spine word down the middle of the poem, or diagonally.

Basically, it's a form with an unusual degree of combined suggestion and freedom.

Is your class studying Lewis and Clark? Electrostatics? Triangles? Sentence structure? Have them make acrostics of key words from the subject.

x-ref: ACROSTICS-FROM-PHRASES; NAME-LETTERS STORIES; "On Quickies: Icebreakers and Fillers"

F ly flower
L ace line
O pened guard
W ild animals
E arth snake
R ound and round.

    —Annah Dahle, 2nd

A
C ord that
R eaches
O ver the
S un
T hat
I s as beautiful as a
C rocus.

    —Jonathan Benton, 3rd

A man, a woman
D umbfounded
U ltimately curse
L ove,
T ime and
S pace.

    —Anonymous

M olehills covering an
O ld
O ptic mass going
N owhere in particular,
S winging around.

    —Jennifer Peck, 7th

e S sence of the
b E st sneaks
a C ross
t O
a N other
a D diction.

—*Michael Smith, 10th*

A nonymous and
N umerous
T urtles
I ntelligently
D evour
I nsects that have been
S earched for, for
E ternity,
S o that they may gain the
    protein
T hat will
A llow them to
B ecome superior to the
L onesome creatures that
    dwell on Earth
I n protecting caves,
S o the Earth can once again
    be
H eld captive by these
M anhunting creatures.
E arth will become a
N atural and more peaceful
    place
T o live on,
A lthough the humans may
    fight until the last
R efugee stands
I n his battle tracks.
A nd on this planet there is
N o possible chance the
I nferior two-legged creatures
    can
S urvive; it is a
M anslaughter.

—*Beau Weber, 8th*

T onight I can
H ear and
E ven

S ense the power
E xpressed in
A wave.

—*Brenda Keene, 10th*

R un
O n the
S ofa even though
E veryone tells you not to.
S ometimes I do.

—*Chris Anglin, 3rd*

R ight is beauty
A nd left is
D read, up
I s art and down is
C onsciousness, forward is
A rranged and backward is
L ard.

—*Forrest Shetley, 4th*

L ooming about the
U nderworld of the moon,
N egative skin near the earth,
A nd everyone seems to be
R iding towards it.

—*Forrest Shetley, 4th*

L abradors are chasing
O xygen toward the
V illage and making an
E arthquake.

—*Aaron Ferrel, 4th*

17

O pen your mind to the
U niverse, and
R un back home and get your
   lunch.

—*Juan Lugo, 7th*

M om
A nd
D ad.

—*Anonymous, 9th*

U nder the ARTIFICIAL me
   which
N o one really knows, I try to
D eliver the message that I
   hope
E veryone will see. What is
R ight or wrong I am
S tarting to find out,
T rying to know which one I
   should do.
A lthough I am confused and
N o one is listening and I am
   almost near
D eath,
I 'm trying to
N ervously tell
G od to fill me with under-
   standing.

—*Jane Martinez, 8th*

T errible,
I mitating
M inutes.
E mbarrassing.

F unny
E mpire—
A thletic,
R ude.

—*Kristy Arbtin, 3rd*

P erson who stands
O utside the
E xit
T o talk.

—*Jennifer Marshall, 8th*

P oetry is like walking
O ut your door into the
E vening with the moon and
T rees. It's like
R unning with all
Y our might to find darkness.

—*Mandy Miller, 9th*

P oetry puts people in an
O riginal state of illusion. The
E nergy will make you rise and
   sometimes make you
M elt.

—*Jeremy Erickson, 9th*

O n a
D irt road going
E ighteen miles to where the

T ules are, on a sunny road
O range sunset over the
   highway.

A bird will sing just like my

C ar sounds, on an
A ugust day as the
R ays hit my shades.

—*Paul Younger, 9th*

P otency
O f
E xpression by
T otal
R elaxation of one's world last
Y earning mind.

P erfection of the
O pening mind
E radicating
T ension and
R estoring
Y outh.

P ressure release
O verwhelming an
E agerness
T o
R emove my soul from this
Y ear.

P revailing
O neness with the
E ternal soul,
T apping a
R eservoir of
Y ellow golden thought.

  —Derek Walters, 12th

S parkling
P earls
A t the
C ompletion of
E ternal life.

  —Travis Holmes, 7th

L ímite. Mi
O jo ve todo.

  —Angela Hobbs, high
  school

O range stripes along the seat
  of it,
D own the road to California
E nding in Los Angeles.

T o that long highway, where
  it is shining range sunset
  over the highway.
O range,

T he gray helmet that he
  wears.
H eather on the back having
  fun,
E very day is an adventure.

M orning falls on the road,
  we drive again.
O ver the winding roads,
T ouring the cities we meet.
O n we go,
R ed helmet on my head.
C oming to the very end of
  the road.
Y ou're so pretty.
C oming to the very end,
  almost to California.
L ooking at the things I see,
E nding in California.

  —Anonymous

S oñar a menudo.
O igo la música.
N ado en la mar de triste.
A dónde? Vamos. Los sueños
  son
R aros y bonitos.

  —Alicia Dahle, high
  school

K ids Creek is kind to me.
I ts water is like my eye,
D ark and dim,
S olid and sly.

C reepy and wide,
R ough and magnificent.
E veryone would agree,
E veryone would try to be
K ind to Kids Creek with a sly
    open eye.

—*Luke Keavny, 5th*

M ajestic view
O verlooking what it was
    possibly
U nder so many years ago.
N atural clean air
T urns to clouds, which turn to
A toms, which
I n turn turn to
N othing.

—*Jeff Robbins, 12th*

H er hair is like the wind
E very hair is silk
A mazing and so wonderful
T he wonderful wind
H it her like lightning
E very time it hit her she
    would
R un away.

D iamonds sparkle
O n earth in
N orth Dakota's
N orthern wind
A nd amazing
N orthern rain.

—*Heather Donnan, 3rd*

M y home is
O ut in the wild. Its
U nspeakable beauty is far to
    the eye.
N obody knows how its
    wondrous beauty grows,
T hough people share the
    beauty.
A bird may fly, a deer may
    run but
I just like to have some fun
N ight hits, the sun goes
    down, and I just dance
    around.

—*Andrea Freel, 5th*

E lastic is
L o-n-g
A nd
S tretches.
T here must be lots of rubber
    bands
I nside the elastic, stretching
    me
C loser to doom.

—*Tara Sorensen, 3rd*

L ike bubblegum
A t noon? I do too.
C lair is my grandma.
Y ellow is my color.

—*Lacy Wiley, 1st*

M ountain moonlight and
    rocks
O r a moose
O n a grassy meadow.
S ee him if you can.
E nd of story.

—*First grade class,
Salmon, ID*

B eaches are
E xciting!
S urely I could build a sand
    castle with
S uch fine sand
I nside there are icicles
E very king is welcome.

B urros
A re stubborn creatures
B ut
I nside
T hem are
S tars.

    —Bessie Babits, 3rd

A gain I go up in the attic
T o find another treasure. There's
T hree shotguns and two twenty-
    twos, boxes everywhere.
I n a corner is Grandpa's old
    whistle and archery gear.
C ould that be my old fishing
    pole? It is but someone's
    calling me.

    —Danny Harry, 5th

A magnificent rainbow
Bellowed the sky with rays of color
Cast the beautiful fairies
Dawned the twilight's mist
Even turned the world to rubies
Fascinating
Gorgeous
Heaps of gold and silver are here
I never heard the music the gold played
Jungle of white ivy—I
Know the world is all turned around
Lovely the perfect place to be by the
Murmuring brooks of crystal blue
Nothing ever would turn the world back—
Open the golden doors
Past the mountains of ice
Quiet place
Running past the silver trees—the
Sun is made of white diamonds
Turning the twilight to dawn
Unicorns made of white rubies
Violets of shimmery purple
White beautiful bushes
eXtraordinary
You will find the magic there
Zap—it's gone forever.

    —Sadie Babits, 4th

ACROSTICS-FROM-PHRASES

A further development for students who've done acrostics is an acrostic variant (see the "On Inventing and Adapting Exercises" chapter for a description of its origin) in which, instead of letters down the margin forming a word, whole *words* down the margin form an intelligible phrase.

Write the capitalized words in the following poem on the board, just as they are printed here. Then write out the lines of the poem. Students will readily see how the form works. With younger kids, you might use the Jenna Helwig poem (below) instead.

> A lovely night for a
> LITTLE thought of how day became day and
> NIGHT became night. Your mind spins and twirls like
> MUSIC coming from an antique phonograph.
>
> —*Dajuana Steele, 7th*

Show them other sample poems (you can write only the "spine phrase" on the board and read the poem aloud, perhaps gesturing to show its linebreaks).

Tell students they will choose their own phrases and can use song or book or movie titles, old sayings, phrases from conversation, or anything at all. With younger kids, you may want to brainstorm a few on the board. Emphasize how the example poems do *not* merely fill out or expand the meaning and feeling of the "spine phrase" but invariably *change* it. Without this change—or at least a strong, unexpected development—it's doubtful whether good pieces can emerge from this exercise.

Then ask the students to write. They should start by writing (in capital letters) their chosen phrases down the margin, skipping lines to allow themselves room, and then compose their poems. They can break their phrases anywhere (not just where a line ends).

Collect and read.

NOTE: *An interesting variation is to have the whole class use the same phrase. In which case, emphasize originality and variation off the spine phrase.*

I'VE had a rotten day. It's
BEEN a tiring, thinking-this-
    day-will-never-end day. I've
    been
WORKIN' so hard readin' and
    writin' I need to lay
ON the couch. Sleep, sleep . . .
    Oh! no—
THE kitchen is on fire. I'm
    dead, dead! No. I'm sitting
    on the
RAILROAD. Is it that late
    already? What an awful
    dream!

    —Jenna Helwig, 5th

WHEN the college alumni go
    flying off into
THE big world, they often
    overlook the fact that they
    are not
SAINTS, merely pawns in a
    grand game of chess, and
    they must
COME to realize this, or their
    glittering glamorous dreams
    of
MARCHING to new heights of
    mental ability will simply
    be thrown
IN the trashcan of life, before
    their potential is discovered.

    —Nick Branstator, 7th

TEARING off a sheet of
    paper can be
DOWNright depressing
    because you know
THE notebook's getting
    thinner like the
WALLS of an old house.

    —Neil Jenkins, 9th

TWINKLING lights with
LITTLE splotches of red seem
    to be
STARS with blood of people
IN them from
THE many wars and
DARK battles we have
    fought,
NIGHT things creeping
    through the
SKY dancing, eager for more
    blood.

    —Annisa Stenersen, 9th

THE men sit, using their
EYE to see the world
OF their mind while
THE children play with the
TIGER of their heart.

    —Cody Jackson, 9th

ANATOMY POEMS

When students are studying the human body, their knowledge can be enlivened by the following exercise.

First, brainstorm body parts on the board; try to include some of the more obscure or specialized human anatomy (within the bounds of classroom propriety).

Next, suggest that the students write a free-form poem showing the various parts of the body interacting. These interactions may combine scholarship and imagination freely. Work out a sample on the board with students. To make sure the sample does not *prescribe* the way their poems go, do two very different samples. In fact, it might be best to compose poems or dialogues of one's own beforehand to show the kids.

Dialogue is a useful technique here, but watch out for a whole bunch of poems in which the femur says to the liver, "Hey, let's go out for pizza!"

Bad Tommy Tongue always broke the laws.
Once he went to a closed river mouth and
screamed, "Help! Here comes Jaws!"
Off to the rescue Sergeant Saliva flew.
He splattered on Jaws and said, "You cruel thing, you."
Jaws cleared his mouth and kind of sagged down,
and the boy outside him had a horrible-looking frown!

   —*Phillip Gilpin, 5th*

The floor is like the skin on a human
and the wood is like the bone
the screws and bolts are like the joints
the rug on it is like the hair on your
skin, the holes in the wood are like the pores
in your skin, the desks are like fingernails
and toenails that grow out of dead cells.

   —*Danny Anderson, 7th*

Starbone connected to the
  milkbone,
Milkbone connected to the
  eyebone,
Eyebone connected to the
  leafbone,
Leafbone connected to the
  bluebone,
Bluebone connected to the
  saltbone,
Saltbone connected to the
  creekbone,
Creekbone connected to the
  bugbone,
Bugbone connected to the
  tonguebone,
Tonguebone connected to the
  starbone.
Walking around!

—A teacher

The heart works perfectly
The colorful eyeball is a smart
  head
The liver can jump with
  excitement
The stomach can hold three
  different foods at the
  same time
The pelvis lets out air
The nose runs slowly
Think before you bite your
  tongue
Suddenly your hair jumps out
  of your head
The color of your teeth
  cannot be put into words.

—Tisha Hyde, 5th

Let's take a walk to. . . .
Mark's going to the Brainy School.
Sarah's going to the Tongue Waterslide.
Chris is going to the Ribs-R-Us Toy Store with Chad!
Amber is going to the Rib Park with Mindy.
Shawn is going to the Jaw Library.
Beth and Tish are going to the Gut Fair.
R.J. and John are going to the Spinal Chord football game.
Mick and Joe are going to Teeth Cruncher.
Sabine and Laura are going to the Stomach Palace.
Jessica and Angie are going to the Pelvis Mall.
Austin and Phillip are going to the Cranium Ballgame.

—Amanda Pearce, 5th

*This piece, like the teacher's above, is technically off-task. As with many
"off-task" poems, its creative sparkle makes it worth the violation.*

"CAPTURED TALK"

Students can do this assignment in or out of class.

As an out-of-class assignment, ask your students to carry around a notebook for a day or so to record bits of language they see or hear—from overheard conversations, signs, TV, printed matter, and so forth. The rough draft of the poem can consist simply of entries taken down, one after another, perhaps one to a line. The poem becomes a collage of the words and phrases that float all around us.

An intensification of this exercise can involve a greater variety of sources. Ask students to seek material from at least six different kinds of "talk," and to list their sources. Seed catalogues, auto repair manuals, grocery stores, babytalk, song lyrics, TV science programs, foreign languages, graffiti, Shakespeare, detective novels, and overheard bus chat are only a few of the possibilities. Students may order their collections for irony, sound, and other qualities, and can put them in any arrangement they want.

Read and discuss various sample poems. Note that the poem can be carefully arranged or random, choppy or long-lined, sense or nonsense, complete syntactic units or fragments. Point out the rhythm and energy of much of our everyday speech. You may want to try one on the board from the material (including talk) in the room. Much of the fun is in the juxtapositions, which may be jagged or unexpected but can point to new meanings.

As an in-class assignment, you might proceed as follows:

• Make sure there are plenty of books and magazines for the students to consult.

• Have the chalkboard be full of writing.

• Bring a tape player to class, with some interesting songs or other material. Play the radio too.

• Ask the class to jot down language they hear and see. Advise them the writing session may be "messy"; they can talk, walk around, and look at things—as long as they write.

• You might stop the music at some point and interject, say, a paragraph from *Tarzan of the Apes*. Or write random words and phrases on the board.

- About five minutes before the end of the writing time, ask the students to stop "collecting" and go over what they have. They can rearrange items, edit them, cross out low-energy sections.

Collect their work and read the best ones to the class—or have the author-collectors read their own.

So I Heard

I'm going nuts!
It's all in your head.
Tell me a story.
I may be stupid once but I won't be stupid twice.
I purty neared seen a snake.
Professional wrestlin' is too a real sport!
Whisper louder, I can't hear you.
If some man expects me to walk 2 or 3 steps behind him, he can also
    expect a few swift kicks in the butt while I'm in the position to do so.
That self-righteous old biddy—I'm glad I'm not like her.
Hi, Sunshine!
If you're going to be in Salt Lake, I'll run you down.
I thought you were the mailman.
I am a male man. I'd look funny if I was a female man.
I can't have my mutts looking like mongrels.
I don't know why I did that.
I'll probably get home and remember I forgot something.
I got so much math to do I can't count it!
Quit complaining, you whiner pup.
I can't slam it any softer!
Sara got grounded because she came to my house on accident and
    she wasn't supposed to.

—*Tammy Baxter, adult (out-of-class)*

Read the following, depend on punctuation. Turning quickly to the left the glass door closed with a soft whush. Dalziel was right in his suspicions, save the environment, it kills Students of the Month, adverbs are good for you. What should I add to Todd ate a bone? Oh oh we got to go, is it alright if I put that on my paper? Say something, my mother was an ape, said Bunnicula, have a most honorable cow. What was that? I was so hungry I started to choke, Kenya says Bulgaria, with a side order of bacon.

—*Tony Sanchez, 7th (in-class)*

I'm just gunna say kina captured phrases.
The native attacked Ellen and packed her notes.
What are you doing.
What.
I'm gunna get me an adverb phrase.
Politicians follow directions.
The stupid jerks.
My father talks in the morning.
Get to work on your orange motor.
I'll sit on dirty pickles.
Can you write down "save the environment"?
I'll write down "gimme that."
This is a 4-letter word.
Oh.
Beef and warm milk for L.C.
How do you do this.
Say something and shut up.
Let's see what you get, Ben.
Can I write that on my paper?
Don't have a cow.
I can see your 4-letter word.
It's not what you think, ape.
You know when it said, "Are you."
What.
I can remember I'm just writing I put my boots out under the sun
     to dry cuz
It was on the song.
I can't find anything to say.
Dip.
There's no words left in Chocolate City.
Let's see if you turn green.
Let me see your bacon.
Just write down "weather at 45."
Shut up, Ben.
That's wrong ha ha . . .

  —James Miller, 7th (in-class)

CHANT POEMS

Chant poems draw on the ancient roots of poetry.

Poetry has been with humankind as long as we've been able to talk. A well-established poetry existed long before writing, as we can tell from the amazing bodies of song and recital preliterate peoples have today. Anthropologists speculate that poetry—as distinct from speech—probably began in religious ceremonies, perhaps around a fire, to accompany dance. Nonsense syllables chanted rhythmically may have been the first poems. These vocalizations grew into song, and song and poem are at base the same—including the use of repetition.

Songs today still use repetition of words and phrases. Repetition establishes rhythm and enchants the listener. But without variety, repetition gets boring. Repetition and variety are a good example of opposites that can coexist and even strengthen each other. Many contemporary poets use this "primitive" form, seeking to capture its power and musicality.

Write the words "Repeating" and "Changing" on the board and let your students know that these are the keys to chant poems.

Read them a few examples of chant poems, energetically emphasizing rhythm (see also the exercise called "PRIMITIVE" POEMS for examples of Native American and African poems). Aim for variety and show the students how the different examples work (how they repeat and change).

Ask your students to pick their own word, phrase, or idea, write it down, and start playing with it on paper, making up their own ways of "keeping it in the air." Simply giving them a range of options and encouraging inventiveness can evoke wonderful spontaneous constructs from the kids.

It's best to have students concentrate on one poem each. Chant poems are usually best fairly long, so the rhythms have some "elbow room." If students have trouble getting started, have them write down a word, take a deep breath, and start improvising on paper (they should feel free to try anything, since they can always scratch it out and start again).

Sometimes kids will find a system and fall into just filling it out ("In the kitchen" repeated thirty times, with all the pots, pans, spoons, etc.). Advise them to keep thinking of new ways to go, to change the structure as well as the items mentioned. If a student feels his or her poem is done, you can suggest a "Part II," starting a new tack.

Collect and read. If the students read, emphasize the importance of loudness, performance values, rhythm.

With older students you can use a more sophisticated example as well, such as D.H. Lawrence's "Bavarian Gentians," a nineteen-line poem in which he uses *dark* or *darkness* eighteen times, nine times in the second verse alone!

x-ref: "PRIMITIVE" POEMS

Cats go crazy
                    Cats go crazy like
Cats go crazy like me
                    Cats like
Cats like to
                    Cats like to go
Cats like to go crazy
                    Cats like to go
Cats like to go downtown
                    Cats like to
Cats like to drive
                    Cats like to drive cars
Cats like to drive a car but bang boom crash
                              Cats like to
Cats like to wreck
                    Cats like to wreck into
Cats like to wreck into you
                              Cats like people
Cats like people to
                    Cats like people to scratch
Cats like kids
                    Cats like kids to
Cats like kids to play
                    Cats like kids to play with
Cats are dead because they got in so many wrecks

—*Crystal Jensen, 4th*

she is beautiful
she is twelve
she is brown-haired
she is tall
she likes me
she is nice
she is smart
she has braces
I know her
we know each other
we walk together
we talk together
we hold hands
I'm feeling great
I think she is too
she looks at me
I look at her
a little kiss under a tree

—Russ LaMont, 7th

I hate
hate strange
strange people
people only
only smoke
smoke little
little lines
lines white
white shades
shades darken
darken shores
shores swish
swish bowl
bowl burning
burning furiously
furiously I

—Lola Benjamin, 12th

The snowflake melted in my hand.
The baby crystal plate turned to
    water.
White turned to crystal-clear
    liquid.
A white piece of heaven turning
    into a lake.
My treasure, into a crystal lake.
A key to the world, a puddle.
A flake makes the world bigger.
A super tiny speck, a speck of
    water.
A white piece.
Water by itself, on my flesh.
A snowflake on my hand.
Melting sadly into water
Sadly, melting, melting sadly.
Another snowflake, melting.

—Anonymous

In the classroom there is a
    desk
and in that desk is a drawer
and in that drawer is a jar
and in that jar is a universe
and in that universe is a
    planet
and in that planet is a
    classroom
and in that classroom is a
    drawer
and in that drawer is a jar
and in that jar is a person
and that person is me.

—Kim Prange, 4th

In my hand
    a stone
cold and hard and then
in my hand
a jewel
sparkling in the sun,
in my hand.

In my hand
    sand
    slips through my
           fingers
    like running water
           in a stream, but it's
in my hand.

In my hand
    I hold
the ability
    to create
    a poem. With paper and ink
in my hand.

      —*Rachel Reid, junior high*

I
I have
I have a
I have a great
I have a great life.
Great, I have a life.

    —*Tara Hopkins, 6th*

COLLAGE POEMS

Bring a supply of newspapers and magazines to class, along with scissors and transparent tape or glue for everyone.

Give the class copies of a collage you've made (or use a sample given here). Make clear to them that their collages do not have to "make sense," but can create associations by feel or whimsy—or be a combination of the real and the surreal. Point out the visual aspect of collage poems—shapes and arrangements of dark and light contribute to their effect as much as the words themselves do. Let students know that the elements of a collage can be ragged or overlapping. Point out the choppy, sophisticated sounds in lively headlines. Headlines are also especially good because of their size and black/white contrast.

Get into the humor of the out-of-context. Advise the students that they may include sub-headline text and even pictures. Direct their attention to the "personalities" of different letters and typefaces.

Turn them loose. (You may want to have the students do their collages on 8 ½" x 11" paper, in case you want to photocopy them later.)

Collect and read, or pass around.

Cowboy LIFE

flaming hair balls

MONTANA

FOOTBALL

—Anonymous

—*Will Russell, 3rd*

COMPOST-BASED POEMS

When students are studying ecology, Walt Whitman's poem "This Compost" can bring some fresh air to the subject.

Any good poem resembles a biosystem in that its survival depends on the interrelationships of its parts—on context. A good poem seems to us a world in itself. The poet weaves with words a network of semblances and distinctions, as nature does. One of Walt Whitman's famous remarks (in *Leaves of Grass*) is: "Do I contradict myself? Very well, I contradict myself. I am large; I contain multitudes." Whitman recognizes, and brings us to recognize, that it's only natural to combine forces that, according to any simplistic notion, don't combine. In "This Compost," Whitman combines rot and beauty, death and life, but expressed in terms of immediate facts rather than high-flown abstractions.

Read the poem aloud to your class, with rhythm and energy. (You might ask students to note their favorite phrases, and ask for them afterwards.)

This Compost
1.
Something startles me where I thought I was the safest,
I withdraw from the still woods I loved,
I will not go now on the pastures to walk,
I will not strip the clothes from my body to meet my lover the
    sea.
I will not touch my flesh to the earth as to other flesh to
    renew me.

O how can it be that the ground itself does not sicken?
How can you be alive you growths of spring?
How can you furnish health you blood of herbs, roots,
    orchards, grain?
Are they not continually putting distemper'd corpses within
    you?
Is not every continent work'd over and over with the sour dead?

Where have you disposed of their carcasses?
Those drunkards and gluttons of so many generations?
Where have you drawn off all the foul liquid and meat?
I do not see any of it upon you to-day, or perhaps I am
    deceiv'd.
I will run a furrow with my plough, I will press my spade
    through the sod and turn it up underneath,
I am sure I shall expose some of the foul meat.

2.

Behold this compost! behold it well!
Perhaps every mite has once form'd part of a sick person—yet
    behold!
The grass of spring covers the prairies,
The bean bursts noiselessly through the mould in the garden,
The delicate spear of the onion pierces upward,
The apple-buds cluster together on the apple-branches,
The resurrection of the wheat appears with pale visage out of
    its graves,
The tinge awakes over the willow-tree and the mulberry-tree,
The he-birds carol mornings and evenings while the she-birds
    sit in their nests,
The young of poultry break through the hatch'd eggs,
The new-born of animals appear, the calf is dropt from the
    cow, the colt from the mare,
Out of its little hill faithfully rise the potato's dark green
    leaves,
Out of its hill rises the yellow maize-stalk, the lilacs bloom in
    the dooryards,
The summer growth is innocent and disdainful above all
    those strata of sour dead.

What chemistry!
That the winds are really not infectious,
That this was no cheat, this transparent green-wash of the sea
    which is so amorous after me,
That it is safe to allow it to lick my naked body all over with
    its tongues,

That it will not endanger me with the fevers that have deposited
    themselves in it,
That all is clean forever and forever,
That the cool drink from the well tastes so good,
That blackberries are so flavorous and juicy,
That the fruits of the apple-orchard and the orange-orchard, that
    melons, grapes, peaches, plums, will none of them poison
    me,
That when I recline on the grass I do not catch any disease,
Though probably every spear of grass rises out of what was once
    a catching disease.

Now I am terrified at the Earth, it is that calm and patient,
It grows such sweet things out of such corruptions,
It turns harmless and stainless on its axis, with such endless
    successions of diseas'd corpses,
It distills such exquisite winds out of such infused fetor,

It renews with such unwitting looks its prodigal, annual, sump-
    tuous crops,
It gives such divine materials to men, and accepts such leavings
    from them at last.

The poem begins with nameless fear; then we find the cause: the foul-
ness and decay that feeds the earth. But Whitman lets "melons, grapes,
peaches, plums" grow out of it, "and all is clean forever and forever."

Note Whitman's long, rolling lines (the nineteenth-century English
poet Gerard Manley Hopkins called his work "prose bewitched"). In the
way he combines prose qualities and poetry, basic fact and strange music,
his writing is like nature—full of surprises, not oversimplified. Point out
some of his most unusual or strongly expressed parts to your class.

The central shock of the poem is that life rises out of "ugliness."
However, Whitman doesn't start the poem with big ideas. He shows us
emotion and the *things* it connects with; then and only then he lets the
ideas arise, out of these details. Poets usually work like this—from the
thing to the thought, not vice versa.

You might also want to discuss Whitman's fear of natural poisons
and its relation to our own present-day fears of poisons of our own
making.

Ask your students to write a poem in free verse, not necessarily in
Whitman's style, based on some harshness, threat, or "corruption" in
nature. Perhaps their poems can "rise," as "This Compost" does, to
praise nature, but this should never be forced, and need not happen at all.

Collect and read, or ask the students to read their own.

x-ref: "Using Great Poems as Models"

An Ode to Allergies

I grope my way
to the medicine
cabinet
behind the mirror
Sine-aid Sudafed
Contac Dristan
Drixoral Benedryl
Allerest Actifed
down a double dose
I feel like Betty Ford
allergies
forsake me please
and leave
yesterday
eight sneezes
in a row
(someone said
you die
after seven)
if it's the
devil inside
that I'm
letting out
(I don't expect you
to bless me
each time either)
I'd rather
be possessed
than congested
why I don't
dare smell
daisies or roses
that poisonous
pollen will
penetrate
my nasal passages

fall is not
falling fast
enough
enough enough
of these
respiratory
embarrassments
and Mother Nature
you're not helping

by refusing to rain
instead whipping
that dreadful
yellow film
off spruce pine
aspen oak
ragweed
and cottonwood
into your
once winsome
now wicked wind
alleviate this
atopy idoblapsis
anon
these purple
crescents beneath
my eyes
are rather
unbecoming
there'll be no
romping and rolling
in a golden field
for me
it's intoxicating
in more than
one way
I'm afraid

ACHOO
that's it
I've had it
I'm heading
west
to the coast
to recapture
the rapture
of the
sea
set sail
on the Pacific
a mistress
of the open
land is
in sight
out of reach
of anything

green
or germinating
call me on
the marine radio
when at last
the first snows
fly and the
dour dust
the frigging flour
of flowers
that damn plant sperm
is finally
frigid in winter's
grasp.

—Rebecca Bush, college

Sledding

Sledding down the snowy slope
    suddenly
I find the tip of my nose froze
in the cold weather looking
down at the world but only
    finding
the deep dream
had been far away without me
    knowing
what was happening "BOOM"
There I go into a tree ouch
I was almost crying
for it had hurt I was moaning
trying to hold it back
but all of a sudden
it came out exploding into the air.

—Shawnee Black, 6th

The   W o o d s

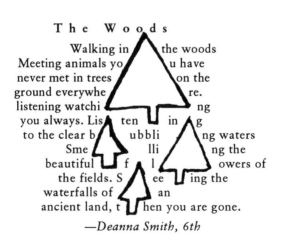

Walking in the woods
Meeting animals you have
never met in trees on the
ground everywhere.
listening watching
you always. Listen in g
to the clear bubbling waters
Smelling the
beautiful flowers of
the fields. Seeing the
waterfalls of an
ancient land, then you are gone.

—Deanna Smith, 6th

CONCRETE POEMS

The visual aspect of language has been alive and well for thousands of years. Early writing was nearly all based on pictorial concepts. For example, "A" was originally a picture of an ox's head, with horns. Chinese writing contains many recognizable visual elements. Poems forming wings and other shapes, the beauties of calligraphy and fine printing, and various combinations of words and pictures, have all been practiced through the ages. In the 1960s, especially, a worldwide movement in "concrete" poetry became popular. Emmett Williams's anthology *Concrete Poetry* (Something Else Press, 1967) displays some of the amazing variety of expression possible.

On the board, show some basic concrete "moves" with words, such as:

The danger is that the students may not see beyond simple visualizations such as the above, so, if possible, pass out copies of complex and various concrete poems—especially examples that are not restricted to making a simple point of one-to-one correspondence. Try making a couple of your own.

A rich pictorial quality to the results may be enhanced by providing the kids with markers, old magazines, scissors, glue, and the like. You can also assign concrete poetry to be done at home, especially with advanced students.

Have the students make their own concrete poems. You might suggest they try an idea out on scrap paper first, then make a big, beautiful version. For easy reproduction, urge them to work big and use thick lines.

Collect their work and pass it around the class.

x-ref: CHANT POEMS; COLLAGE POEMS

My Lolipop

My Lolipop is so nice and sweet. My Lolipop is lusciously Looking Loli. I have my Looking Loli, safe inside my mouth. I call my Lolipop My Looking Lol.. I have my Looking Lolipop because he's a piece of bubble gum. My Lolipop is so nice and sweet. My Lolipop is so sweet. I have the best Lolipop because he is so good to me. I love my Lolipop because he's kind of sweet. My Lolipop is getting smaller every minute of my Lolipop. once opened all hollywood. I love my Lolipop is Fun to Eat. My Lolipop is Delicious.

—Krista Prescott, 4th

CREATIVE REWRITES

We have cast this exercise in terms of a specific lesson in a high school science class, but similar applications of creative rewriting could be made in almost *any* subject (and at almost any age level).

The following exercise is meant to supplement the conventional testing procedures, and thereby help students develop and keep a lively connection to the material.

Read aloud to your students the following passage on the formation of the volcano Paricutín:

> In February 1943, people living in the mountain land 200 miles west of Mexico City were alarmed by frequent earthquakes. Each day for more than a week the number of tremors increased, and on February 19 about 300 were counted. Next day a farmer, Dionisio Pulido, while he worked in his field, heard noises like thunder, though the sky was clear. He saw that a crevice had opened in the ground, and from this narrow opening arose a small column of smoke—actually vapor and fine dust—with an odor of sulfur. That night strong explosions began at the vent, and coarse rock debris was thrown up, some of it red hot. At daybreak the vent was marked by a cone-shaped mound more than 30 feet high, through which in violent bursts large fragments of rock were hurled high in the air. Successive explosions came only a few seconds apart, and a great cloud of fine rock dust mixed with vapor arose continually to a great height. The coarser particles rained down on the flank of the cone and built it up at the rate of tens of feet in a day.

Read it again, but this time ask them to take notes. The notes can include facts, interesting phrases, ideas, and language of their own that has been sparked by the passage. After this second reading, you might want to point out vivid language in the paragraph.

Then ask your students to "rewrite" the material, factually or creatively, in poetry or prose. Suggest going beyond the information given—e.g., to make up stuff about Pulido's family, their responses or adventures, or even his dog. Be sure that students realize that they may invent or choose their own style or forms. Read aloud some of the student examples below.

Collect and read aloud.

The day started as all other days. I was a little tired from the night before. My doghouse kept shaking, and there was a strange odor in the air. Anyway, I went out to eat breakfast, and old Dionisio was uptight. Something just wasn't quite right, and it was my duty to figure out what. I trotted out through the gate to gaze over the pastures. Something was different about the cornfield. It wasn't until I stepped on a hot piece of rock that it dawned on me—I didn't get anything for Valentine's Day. Oh well, dogs usually don't.

All of a sudden red masses of molten earth began falling all around me. I couldn't escape. Dionisio was calling to me from the edge of the cornfield. "It's a volcano—run for your life, Fido!" Aha—a volcano, I knew something was different about this field.

As the relief of the fact that I solved the puzzlement of the day, and that I saved old Pulido, flooded over me, I breathed in my last breath of sulfur vapor and fire, and I went peacefully to the happy hunting ground.

—*Kellie Fraser, 12th*

I was hurtling through the blue space after being thrust out from the pit I called home. Never before had I seen light and open air. Freedom alive with expressive energy. I had discovered my wings of flight and noticed my friends had too. Smoke and fire and lava erupted before us with energy supreme. We, the Ash, flew over a human named Pulido, his family, dogs, and the cornfields. This new-found feeling of ecstasy was ours. At last! Never again will we be caught in desolation trapped beneath the condensing Earth.

—*Angela Hobbs, 12th*

One day I, Earth, had a violent
cold. My sneezing caused many
earthquakes around a cornfield 300
miles from Mexico City. Even though
my conscience, the Moon, said to
quit spinning and revolving, it
was my job so I ignored it. My
cold lasted for one week, then my
cold feet and head gave me the flu.
It got worse and worse and I
could not eat, but the bully, Space,
forcefed me a meteor. This happened,
causing me to throw up, in a
farmer's cornfield. I spit up that
meteor, and ash, gas, and lava, high
into the air. My lip puckered up
like a cone and hardened. Wow,
if you were big enough, you could
kiss me.

—*Jim Miller, 6th*

DECLARATIONS

This is a *sample* exercise. Parallel or similar exercises can be done with other subjects.

In a government class (or any class), read a page or two of The Declaration of Independence. Then point out in detail the rhetorical goodies therein (rolling oratorical rhythms, concrete words balancing the larger utterance, parallel structures, repetition, etc.). Next, ask the students to write "We hold these truths to be self-evident" on their papers. They may substitute "I" for "We." Ask them to follow this with their own *personal* adaptation of this theme—expressed in their own words (*not* a Jefferson imitation). What truths are self-evident to them?

Urge the students to write concretely. If they use a general or abstract word, they should make it come alive through specific, surprising detail ("freedom, like walking around in the park in my blue swimsuit, kicking rocks"). Urge them to avoid clichés. You might try a short sample poem on the board with them.

Read aloud a few student examples to "prime the pump." As students write, encourage them to keep going, adding more details.

Collect and read aloud.

If you use a different source text, try to find one distinct sentence in it that can move the students from the "great work" into their own personal uses of it, a possible bridge to the everyday world of a young person. Charles Darwin's prose, with its dogged use of observational detail, could be used as a model for a class exercise on origins (see ORIGINS POEMS). Freud's writing, with its precise reporting of human behavior, including dreams, could be adapted for a self-analysis poem. Thomas Jefferson was a great stylist—his words have much oratorical power even on the page. Note his rolling rhythms, and the way his expansive statements are peppered with concrete or experiential terms.

The Declaration of Independence (*excerpt*)

When in the Course of human events, it becomes necessary to dissolve the political bands which have connected them with another, and to assume among the powers of earth, the separate and equal station to which the Laws of Nature and of Nature's God entitle them, a decent respect to the opinions of mankind requires that they should declare the causes which impel them to that separation. —We hold these truths to be self-evident, that all men are created equal, that all are endowed by their Creator with certain unalienable Rights, that among these are Life, Liberty, and the Pursuit of Happiness. —That to secure these rights, Governments are instituted among Men, deriving their just powers from the consent of the governed. — That whenever any form of Government becomes destructive of these ends, it is the Right of the People to alter or abolish it, and to institute a new Government, laying its foundation on such principles and organizing its powers in such form, as to them shall seem most likely to effect their Safety and Happiness. Prudence, indeed, will dictate that Governments long established should not be changed for light and transient causes; and accordingly all experience hath shewn, that mankind are more disposed to suffer, while evils are sufferable, than to right themselves by abolishing the forms to which they are accustomed. But when a long train of abuses and usurpations, pursuing invariably the same Object evinces a design to reduce them under absolute Despotism, it is their right, it is their duty, to throw off such Government, and to provide new Guards for their future security. —Such has been the patient sufferance of these Colonies; and such is now the necessity which constrains them to alter their former Systems of Government. The history of the present King of Great Britain is a history of repeated injuries and usurpations, all having in direct object the establishment of an absolute Tyranny over these States. To prove this, let Facts be submitted to a candid world. . . .

The document then goes on to a long list of grievances, using repetition, parallel structures, and strong, passionate, colorful, yet dignified language. Point out examples to your class, especially of such language as "swarms of officers to harass our people, and eat out their substance."

Using such a model as this has a twofold purpose. It may help show a connection between students' own lives and great works, and the great work, met in a new light, may begin to interest them. They may learn they can admire a great thing without having to imitate it.

x-ref: LIST POEMS

I hold these truths to be self-evident:

Yelling, Banging, Screaming, Crying,
Whispering, Speaking, Holding, Knowing

Softly, Quietly, Nicely, Peacefully,
Knowingly, Understandingly, Openly,
Deadly

Understood, Opened up, Kept in, Yelled at,
Left behind, Closed off, Nice Job, Closed up. END

—Margaret-Ann McNab, 7th

I hold these truths to be self-evident—
Diapers will get wet, homework will always be there, my brother will
never turn down his stereo, guys will always be confusing, there will
always be groping, there is always something to do, and life is never
boring.

Part II
There are many truths that are clear:
Mr. Rogers will never be on prime-time television, there will never be an
end to the cola wars, some day your microwave will blow up, beans
are always very likely to give you gas.

 —*Laura Groll, 12th*

I hold these truths to be self-evident:

Freedom is crushing us like a plague

Should we be free to

      destroy?
      annihilate?
      and mutilate?

Should we be free to
 let get destroyed what was once built?
 let toxins get dumped into our seas and oceans?
 let poison gas pollute the air?
 let Brazil cut down the selvas?
Freedom is only in one's mind;
we can all see or we may all be blind.

 —*Mike Gregson, 12th*

I hold these truths to be self-evident:
That no truth I hold self-evident must be a truth which anyone else will hold
self-evident, and that all people's minds should be free thereof to choose
truths for and by themselves. That the essence of life is individual freedom,
and never personal responsibility to someone or something else. That true
love, in all its forms of expression, is the first concrete human value which
will survive forever. That pure evil, in all its forms of expression, is the second concrete human value which will survive forever. That evil and love
shall dance forever in the darkened room outside of which there is no existence. That I like Long John doughnuts.

 —*Charles Ullmann, 7th*

I hold these truths to be self-evident:
My world will end when I am dead. The
sun will shine; the moon will glow. The
feelings I have will fade away. The knowing
and awareness will stop. I will sink inside
myself deeper and deeper. My room will shrink
to nothing. My town will disappear. This state
will crumble apart. Our Earth will travel
    onward.
If all that is left is the universe, when it
blinks out, what truths will be left behind?

    —Brenda Keene, 12th

We hold these truths to be self-evident:
We think we have the world down pat.
Ka-boom! There goes our habitat.

    —Todd May, 7th

DEFINITION POEMS

Whenever a topic or subject is under study, it can be refreshing and revealing to have the students write, either in class or at home, their own creative definitions of the topic. Encourage originality (as always). Tell them it's okay to include negative feelings about the topic, or to be satiric. You might want to bring the results closer to the concision and musicality of verse by the simple expedient of asking them to limit the lines to a maximum of seven words.

Collect and read.

x-ref: ACROSTICS; GEOMETRY POEMS; NO-WARMUP DELIVERIES

Physics is physical is a sign of
being a study
why and how. Physics is
electrifying. Physics is light.
Physics is eruptive, so now
goodnight.

— *Nancy Herrera, 12th*

What is Physics—The Class

Physics is a momentary time
lapse in which many
unimaginable things are thrown
at a group of uncomprehending
students. When the time lapse
is over, all of the students
forget the lapse and continue
unaffected through the remainder
of the day.

— *Melissa Jensen, 12th*

Physics is psychoanalysis of
obscure
and related forces hyperboling
in a
yo-yo fashion, straining to
be understood and compre-
hended, wanting
to be structured and real.

— *Kellie Fraser, 12th*

DREAM INTERPRETATION

This lesson is particularly fun for students because it brings the mystery of dreams right into the classroom. You might broach the topic by describing one of your dreams, or by asking how many of the students have had recurring dreams and how many of them have begun to fall asleep only to awake from a dream of falling. Virtually all of the students will raise their hands. Students are awed (as we all are) by the commonalities of dreams.

The idea for this exercise comes from a guide to dream interpretation called *The Success Dream Book* by one Professor de Herbert. The matter-of-factness of his "scientific" definitions is great for kids to parody. Here is a short example from the professor:

RICE PUDDING—To eat it, signifies great wealth and popularity.
> To see it and not to eat it, denotes failure in business at present.

RICH—To dream that you are rich, when in reality you are not, is a sign of financial success. It also indicates that you will take hold of a great opportunity, which will be the turning point of your life.

RIDDLE—To solve one, denotes that you possess great mental faculties.
> If you are unable to solve a riddle, it indicates that your opportunities will be limited.

RIFLE—To dream of a rifle, denotes robbery and mischief.

RINGLEADER—To dream of a ringleader of any affair, denotes that you will cause a great deal of trouble to one that you love dearly. You will cause this trouble by speaking too hastily, which you will regret.

RIDE—To dream that you ride a powerful horse, indicates great success in business.
> To see others ride denotes that you will invest in a good paying proposition.
> To fall from a horse denotes an unprofitable investment.

RIOT—To see one in your sleep denotes the death of a prominent person.

RIVER—A river of clear water, signifies an honorable career.
> A river of muddy water denotes strife and ill luck.
> To swim in a river of clear water, denotes a brilliant future.

ROAD—To travel over a nice and clean road, denotes great success in business and love affairs.

Students will quickly discern that de Herbert's conclusions often seem either straightforward or relative. Ask them to create their own. For example:

If you dream of stale bread
it means that you have come to a standstill in life.

If you dream of ice
you'll slide out of the grip of those that dislike you.

If you dream of a blind cat
it means friends will unite and go against a cause.

Together you and your students can collaborate on a dream book, or you can have the students write individual poems. The following poems by Elizabeth Fox, a New York City poet, use this technique:

Losing a Goat

When the thunder that's been
kept underground all winter
can't wait any longer
it pops out of the earth
in the form of daffodils and crocuses.
This is what it means to lose
a goat in your dreams.

Wet Hair

It's four in the morning.
The rivers have lost
their sense of direction.
They circle around bridges
and confuse migratory birds
that have just come back to town.
The distance between two streets
is called a block.
You dream of wet hair
when the blocks begin to wander
all over the city.

One way to warm up kids to this lesson is to try a verbal collaboration before writing. Begin by asking questions such as "What does it mean if you dream you left your sister on the bus?"

x-ref: Q & A PARTNER POEMS; QUESTIONS WITHOUT ANSWERS; "On Quickies: Icebreakers and Fillers"

As the eyes appear through
blackened night a sediment of
star sits on the pupil.
While the night encircles
the edges of the eyes the wings
caress the streamlined body.
The fan of feathers tests the
    wind
and directs it high or low,
preparing it to dive at speeds
beyond it. It begins its fight.
The lightning flashes and the
talons grip. Then with the
    sound
of a thunderclap the battle
begins and suddenly ends
    when
the lightning disappears.
The falcon remains with a
    name
that wreaks fear, courage,
acceleration and speed, but
also awesomeness.

The dream's meaning is:
your spirits will soar after a
silent and secret battle.

—Gavin Peck, 6th

If you dream that you go to
    school without your pants
it means you forgot something
    very important
If you dream you are green
    you will break your arm
If you dream you are bald you
    will get lucky and win
    something
If you dream of school you'll
    be a weird teacher
If you dream your cat is a fire
    god then it will die
If you dream of hot air you
    will suffocate
If you dream about riding a
    rat through a field
then grass will grow out of
    your head
If you dream of war there will
    be peace
If you dream of peace there
    will be war
And if you dream of me don't
    tell me!

—Codi Adams, 6th

If you dream of a cricket making little music
and the birds chirp out songs for the rest of the night
like the wolves howl at the moon, the sly fox
sneaking through the forest for food, the big rattlesnake
warning off enemies and the great lion roaring,
the big bear growling while he sniffs for food,
the deer and elk drinking from the cool stream,
it will mean that the next day
will be the greatest day of your life.

—Brad Atkins, 6th

If you dream that a dolphin leaps into your hands
and turns into a butterfly
it means you will start low and reach the top.

—Leslie Gwartney, 6th

EARTH POEMS—THINGS TO SAVE

In and around Earth Day—or, in fact, any time the care of the environment is an issue at hand—here's one way poems can speak for the cause (and still be poems).

Warm up the class by using LIST POEMS (see exercise), including examples read aloud. Then ask your students to write list poems of what they would like to *save* in the world. You can use the occasion to speak briefly of our looming ecological problems.

Encourage your students to be very detailed in what they mention (not just "trees, animals, and the ocean"). You might well also emphasize the power of surprise moves and elements in a list. Encourage them to use a variety of speech in their poems: they don't have to adhere to one tone or style, but can intersperse the items in their lists with various remarks. Urge originality, even humor. And not everything has to be about nature. Mandy King's poem (below) blends nature and civilization, suggesting that it's all interconnected.

Collect and read.

clouds, white shadows in the sky,
cotton candy, white as the lining of
silk, soil black as coal, koala grey
as rain clouds, trees tall as the sky,
polar bear white as ever, dolphins
swimming in the sea.

—*Jessica Flodine, 5th*

The darkness of shadow-like
    wolves
darting across the night like
black bullets, and the moon
shimmering like a sphere of
    glowing mass.
Let us save lush grass, green
as green can be, but, best of all,
imagination glowing with joy aha,
images it is composed of, it is this
that is making the earth grow
with flavor and destination.

—*Fletcher Williams, 5th*

The water running through
    the faucet
The blue birds that fly high in
    the sky
The beautiful mountains
The black sky
The bright stars in the sky
Nice big jawbreakers that get
    smaller
        and smaller
Big libraries that have lots of
    books
Clocks going tick tock
Hot sunny days
All the clothes that I have
My bedroom window
My sweet rabbit
People that I love
My peach toothbrush

    —*Mandy King, 5th*

My black cat
that died,
the light of
the day,
the black
of the
night.
The wind
and the
hot, the
black and
the light.

    —*Alicia Acierno, 1st*

Rainforest

Skyscraper homes way up
    high
festivals of flying and dancing
in the sky, on the snake's
slither, lion's roar, but in
the "oh," that's where it all is,
I mean there is monkeys
that climb way in the sky
raising treetops, snakes
that crawl up and down
the treetrunks, in the
ponds and rivers that flow
    about
fish swim joyfully, frogs
that hop and bounce, in and
out. But when people come,
in and out they take out
all the things that I
think about, and soon will
be nothing left, and
the best thing to say is
that it is as good as
        DEAD!

    —*Christy Rehfeld, 5th*

"FEELINGS" POEMS

People often assume that poetry is "about" feelings. More likely, poetry uses the fuel of feelings to illuminate language and perception. The names for feelings, we tend to forget, are abstract—they merely betoken areas that the reader fills in with already known material. Thus they don't give the reader a new experience, which a poem should do, but merely remind the reader of previous experience. Poems should do more than be repositories of sentiment or memory.

Brainstorm emotions on the board, using adjectives or verbs (not nouns, which induce passivity). Also on the board, work out some sample sentences that mention feelings, especially in detailed situations ("When John Cryan stepped on my toe, moving around like a rhinoceros, I was angry. He doesn't think about me").

Then ask the students to write some sentences of their own, either from their own experiences or from their imaginations. Have them leave spaces between the lines for changes later.

Next, list some adjective categories on the board, such as color/number/texture/sound/size/shape, and below each category list specific adjectives. If you use verbs, make similar lists for them.

Ask the students to substitute adjective phrases (or verb phrases) for the emotions they've already included in sentences. Urge originality, even wildness. Suggest that comparisons can often be a good way to go, as they're highly expressive.

Collect and read.

*   *   *   *   *

This is not exactly a poetry exercise but a "long warmup": simply a way to get emotions out in the open and deal with them in concrete ways—to put them in perspective. It will also tend to further the students' use of images rather than abstractions.

A variant approach to emotions in poetry is to ask the students to write, for example, "ten things you fear," again urging them to use detail.

Right now I'm feeling like a big black hole,
and I feel like 3 big blue blocks.
When I get straight A's I feel like a layer of papers.
Sometimes when I take a test and I don't know the answer
I feel like a tiny green person that no one notices.

 —*Heather Hatch, 5th*

When the first day of school came, I was
21, foggy, 0, and rough.
When Christmas comes, I feel very gleaming,
rising, silk—that I might not get anything.
When I'm going to have a shot I
feel jumpy and gray.
When I got to be in the 5th grade spelling bee
I felt electric and. . . .

 —*Summer Smith, 5th*

SENTENCES ON FEELINGS

I was a pink flower in a foggy day when my parents didn't come home.

 —*Sheri Taylor, 5th*

When I broke Dustin's nose I felt the size of a penny.
When I broke my finger it lost its shape.
When my teacher caught me with a lovenote I felt purple-colored.

 —*Jason Pilkerton, 5th*

When Teacher looked at my empty paper I felt red hot.

 —*Daniel Olson, 5th*

No one knew where Sally was; the poor girl was lost among the ever-
changing living shadows of the sky.

 —*Season Brusch, 7th*

He felt a burst of bright yellow when he finished his homework.

—*Travis Boyle, 7th*

As Meredith wandered hopelessly lost in the woods she felt as though she would explode but did not dare to disturb the silence.

—*Ann Tharp, 7th*

I leaped onto the man like a crack in a dam sending polluted grey sewage down onto a brightly lit city.

—*Tom Anderson, 7th*

The circle spun around, and around, shining off alert colors of yellow and blue. There was laughing in the background.

As he erased the board the blood rushed to my heart. I felt like he erased my big red heart away.

—*Casey Karsh, 7th*

The house in the middle of the plain was a blue-feeling house. The owner had left for a more pink-feeling house.

—*Tiffany Talley, 7th*

The tent was red hot and itchy. A green-black mist swallowed the inside with a deep purple, crashing gulp.

The black granite giants crunched snail-like at the town.

—*Kate Fries, 7th*

"FOURTEENER" POEMS

Ask your students to write a sentence, any sentence. Then ask them to restate it in thirteen different ways.

This restating can go in many directions. It can involve slight permutations in wording, so that the poem becomes an experiment in repetition and rhythm. Or it can expand upon images that lie behind the first sentence. It can also "change" the original sentence by emphasizing any one of the five senses.

Any sentence we might say or write is, out of context, really a form of shorthand for a vast network of feelings, experiences, and contradictions. For example, even the bland sentence "I drove my car to the store" could suggest endless ways of seeing that experience:

> I whipped my battered blue Buick to B & B's for a can of Beluga caviar.
> I rode my rocket to the moon.
> The store to drove I my Chevrolet.
> The distributor parcelled out firepower to the points.
> She'd screamed at me, "Get a pint of real cream!"
> I drove my car to the store under the circle of seductive blue.
> I caressed my car to the slightly opened yellow door.
> I, with dreams of Indian rubies tightening my fingers, drove my car to the store.
> Everything except the car and me disappeared behind me.
> I had eleven cents and a mile's worth of gas.
> I floated toward the center of the American whirlpool.
> The bricks got larger as they approached my face.
> My hand and foot did slick mechanical dances as I rode the wave of metal.

Raymond Queneau's *Exercises in Style* tells a simple anecdote in ninety-nine different ways. You should advise your students that they can explore a single approach or they can mix approaches, according to feel.

Read a couple of student examples to the class. Ask students to write. Collect and read.

> Summer is gold.
> Is summer gold?
> Golden is the summertime.
> Hazy waves of molten gold.
> Heated by the summer sunshine.
> The golden summer sunshine heat.
> The lazy vague seductive heat.
> The golden forgetful don't-care haze.
> The laughing gold.
> The golden laughter.
> The seductive molten golden heat.
> The gold that reaches out and wraps around you.
> The golden heat that turns your body gold.
> Enticing summer gold.
>
> —*Katrina Dalrymple, 10th*

The cat slunk through the darkness.

It crept through the darkness.

The darkness the cat snuck through wasn't illuminated by any moonlight.

No moonlight reflected in the silver eyes of the cat.

The cat stares, unblinking, at the black silhouettes against black.

The cat slinks through the continuous shadow, unilluminated by moonlight.

Without a sound, the cat's paws softly fall as it creeps along.

The cat stalks its unknown prey in the darkness.

The darkness conceals the prey from the stalking cat.

The darkness conceals the cat from the hiding prey.

The prey is as silent as the cat creeping through the darkness.

Creeping through the darkness, the cat passes a deeply shadowed recess,
unilluminated by moonlight.

The prey is still as stone as the stalking cat passes in the darkness.

The cat slinks through the darkness and its silver eyes pass on.

—Vickie Aldous, 11th

Jane, tripping, falls on Spot.

Spot, the shaggy dog, suddenly feels the comparatively large weight of
Jane, as the latter falls upon the former.

The shoelace of Jane's white, new left shoe becomes stuck under the
white, new left shoe of Dick.

Jane's left foot cannot take its place as Jane's weight shifts forward,
expecting a support.

The unfortunate old dog does not anticipate the stumbling person.

Most of Jane's very considerable mass will impact the small body of Spot.

It will snap fragile bones and tear small tendons inside Spot's body.

The very considerable mass of Jane causes Spot to emit several loud, high-
pitched noises, which awaken the old neighbor, who was sleeping.

Jane's fall onto Spot is caused by her carelessly tied shoelace.

The next day Spot is buried, but his tail sticks up, out of the grave.

The blood never washes out of Jane's clothes.

Jane falls on Spot.

Jane's stumble causes Spot's death.

—Micah Prange, 10th

GEOMETRY POEMS

This is mostly an application of the list poem (see the LIST POEMS exercise). Similar applications can be made in nearly any subject.

Give students some background on lists as poetry. Tell them you are going to write list poems on "The Ways Geometry Comes into My Life"—or something close to that.

Brainstorm a number of geometry terms on the board to spur student ideas (and serve as a possible source of words to use in their poems). Students should not feel they have to use these terms, though, nor be restricted to them.

Give them a few tips from the LIST POEMS exercise, as well as some relating to geometry:

- Look around the room for examples of geometric shapes.
- You can mix technical terms with everyday or imaginative language.
- You might try writing in a geometric shape.

Read a few sample poems (such as Carl Sandburg's "Arithmetic," or those from the following pages or the LIST POEMS exercise) aloud. Pass copies around if the poem is visual.

Ask them to write.

Collect and read aloud.

If you have time left in the session, ask them to write lunes (see LUNES) on geometry or science ideas. You can also do acrostics (see ACROSTICS) of "Geometry" or "Mathematics."

x-ref: LIST POEMS; CONCRETE POEMS; LUNES; ACROSTICS

Arithmetic is like sticking your head in boiling water.
Factoring integers and Pie R Squared are like the pins of a
    witch
Doctor that stick in your bean.
If you start with ten thousand, then square it, then
Find the square root, do you know the answer?
If not, wait until I'm dead, then dig through my head.
I feel no pain. Just a pile of jumbled numbers that
Mass together in a universe of pain.

—Matt La Mont, 8th

I
am
not
good
doing
poetic
writing
rhythmic
metricals
ordinarily
undeveloped
compositions
unfortunately
misinterpreted
versifications
mistranslated
contraptions
meaningless
unoriginal
pointless
so these
useless
verses
might
need
use
of
a
"stand to hold them up
before they fall down."

—*Russ Kluge, high school*

A
R otten
I ntellectual
T rouble
H appens to
M e
E very
T ime
I
C ome to math.

—*David Phillips, 8th*

There is a place
with lines I call
my paper. There
are circles made
out of holes. The
corners are hyperbolas
with no pairs to
match. My pencil
makes an axis
going z. My focus
is at this point,
which is dimensionless.
But now I'll stop
before I reach
infinity.

—*Brenda Keene, 12th*

Geometry of Life

The origin is a place to begin
with two axes crossing
    through it
known as the x and the y.
Then add a z,
now it's 3-D.
Life has its origin
with other lives crossing,
    throughout,
continually crossing it in a
    perpendicular way.
Asymptote is the line another
    line will never reach
sort of like the ideas of life
never meeting the full belief
of what you thought once you
    might achieve.
A circle going round and
    round like
many days of a person's life.
One's life is but a small point
in such a terrific graph of our
    universe.
Going forward, staying
    straight,
as if it were just one long line.

—*Will Perry, 12th*

The Way Geometry Affects My Life

Parabola
carlights
Hyperbola
satellites
Circle
tires
Sphere
earth
Ellipse
football
Point
place on earth
Line
road
Vortex
bottom of a bowl where the
    marble rests
Square
block
Triangle
trusses
Infinity
never ending
Asymptote
never-crossing paths
Origin
back to the beginning.

—*Mike Edwards, 12th*

"GOING INSIDE" POEMS

Explain that you're going to try writing that leads the imagination inside things, and that the kids will choose their own things to "go into."

Read the following poem aloud.

Stone

Go inside a stone
That would be my way
Let someone else become a dove
Or gnash with a tiger's tooth.
I am happy to be a stone.

From the outside the stone is a riddle:
No one knows how to answer it.
Yet within, it must be cool and quiet
Even though a cow steps on it full weight,
Even though a child throws it in a river;
The stone sinks, slow, unperturbed
To the river bottom
Where the fishes come to knock on it
And listen.

I have seen sparks fly out
When two stones are rubbed,
So perhaps it is *not* dark inside after all;
Perhaps there is a moon shining
From somewhere, as though behind a hill—
Just enough light to make out
The strange writings, the star-charts
On the inner walls.

     —Charles Simic

Discuss with your class how Simic uses a plain, commonsensical tone, little by little investing the stone with life and interest and movement and mystery (point out the places where he does this), and then surprises us with a sudden plunge into its magical center, full of spooky light, hieroglyphics, and star-maps.

Before your students begin to write, read aloud some poems by children, particularly those that emphasize wild imagination. Suggest to the students that they can talk about the thing first, as Simic does, then describe the process of getting inside, tell of their adventures there and how they got out, and anything else they can invent.

Ask them to write.

Collect and read.

I would like to go inside myself. I would like my brain to be
a table. My heart could be my kid. Inside my hand could be
my husband, and then I could have my bones as a pet.

—*Honey Jackson, 1st*

What would it be like to go in an Indian?
See what would be left. Perhaps some guns or a bow and arrow.
Perhaps they would carry something, perhaps their self.
Perhaps they would leave some treasures, maybe they would
leave buffalo hides behind. Maybe some horns and they might
leave you a note. They might have a secret door.
Maybe they would have a guest room.

—*Jared Pilkerton, 2nd*

I want to go inside Jason as food. I taste so good.
It is dark and warm inside. I go for a ride on his blood train.
I go to his heart, to his brain, and finally to his eyes.
I see the world . . .
I go in a book, I go in a light, I can go in a clock.
I go in a toy. It is tasty 'cause I play in it.
I go in a Jason Wells. It is fun too. I eat the brain.

—*Jason Wells, 2nd*

I would like to go into a rock, shiny walls of color, prisms of light, coolness
of winter, warmth of summer, scenes of water as you splash into the salty
sea of clear crystal water stream, a soft blanket of algae grows green, growing bright, or a slingshot shooting me into the horizon of the mystery, or an
enchanted forest of a secret golden mystery of roses, bright in summer and
vines in winter of golden gold shimmering bright in the middle of the night,
or lightning bolts shocking me, summer picnic smells enchanting me, visions
of clouds oh so high, angels flying hails, and all brightness of day, darkness
of the night, mysterious shadows of eyes looking at me, an old schoolhouse
with farmlands wide and the changing things, history gone by but I stay the
same. Feelings of dungeon close by.

—*Joanna Luckey, 3rd*

Going inside Sheryl's head is like trying to pull
a dog out of the river all you hear is the ice breaking
water rushing and Sheryl screaming at the top of her lungs
it looks like a dark sky filled with stars
she's thinking of the dog she goes after him she
hits a barbed wire fence she falls she screams
the dog leaps out of the water to go help Sheryl
she gets up limps home she sees the blood she screams
it wakes up all the neighbors.

—Donny Anderson, 6th

Walking sadly up the steps into a large building. But inside so beautiful and bright. Chandeliers and pretty paintings, squishy sofas and big plant hangings. There standing sadly gazing into his lifeless face. My grandma weeping. I go over and give him a hug. I'm sure going to miss him.

—Brittney Taylor, 8th

*   *   *   *   *

"WHAT'S UNDER" POEMS

(The idea for this exercise comes from first grade teacher Nola Losser.)

Ask your students to write a series of lines that describe what's under things. This exercise works especially well with very young children, but it's a good warmup for students of all ages. Make up an example yourself, emphasizing a sense of variety and imagination in the movement from one thing to another. Using surprise in the last item helps to wrap up the poem.

Example:

Under the stars is everything.
Five-pointed shadows. From a white wall.
Dust is under the shadows.
Under the dust are worms of light.
A million bones are under the worms of light.
Under the bones is a Tinker Toy—hot to the touch.
A wide green and red country is under that.

Under the country are laws, like squares in the air.
Under the laws are tiny people
Crawling in blue fuzz.
One of them is me.

Loud music is under me.

When your students have finished writing, collect their work and read it aloud.

x-ref: ORIGINS POEMS

Under the moon is
the stars
Under the stars is
the rainbow
Under the rainbow is
a tree
Under the tree is
me and Kitty.

—*Kitty Olendorff &*
   Bekki Fayle, 1st

Under the stars are
cars
Under the cars are
wheels
Under the wheels is
gravel
Under the gravel is
dirt.

Under the dirt is
roots.

—*J.T. Heaps, 1st*

Under the tree is an octopus
Under the octopus is a seashell
Under the water is a mermaid
Under the mermaid is a worm
Under the worm is a rock
Under the rock is a hand

—*Josh Howard, 1st*

Beneath my water skis there is
a clear blue devil called water
trying to suck me under and
when you are as wet as can be
if you get lucky and make it
      back
everyone says,
There is no life like this.

—*Keith Tarkalson, 7th*

HAIBUN

Haibun is a Japanese form that combines prose and poetry. A narrative or description is interspersed with haiku poems that arise from and illuminate the prose. Basho's *The Narrow Road to the Deep North* (see next page for excerpt) is a classic example. Subjects such as travel and nature are "naturals" for haibun.

Explain haibun to the class and read them an example passage or two. Some points:

• It's usually best to call for loose haiku—no syllable count, just free little three-liners in the haiku spirit. (See HAIKU exercise.)

• Emphasize the down-to-image aspect—no generalized writing. Haiku captures a *moment*. (A preliminary haiku session might be helpful.)

• You can use prose pieces the students have already written and "pepper" them with haiku.

• Emphasize that the haiku should add or change something—not just sum up what's already there. The haiku can well be offbeat, unexpected, a "twist" or a passing fancy.

Try one out on the board. Read a paragraph of prose aloud (twice) and then, with the class, compose a haiku to follow it. Here is an example (on Civilian Conservation Corps workers):

> Entertainment for both kinds of camps was basically the same. After-work hours were generally spent playing cards, mainly penny ante gambling. During the summer the men also practiced baseball. Charles Kane noted, "Each camp had a field someplace close by, where they could have baseball. . . ."

CRACK! Bat hits ball
roadbuilder runs bases
dust rises, swirls

Ask the students to write. They can write their haiku on a separate sheet and use circled numbers to show where they fit into the prose.

This exercise is particularly good for a later revision session—mostly getting down to image and "making it new."

x-ref: HAIKU

from *The Narrow Road to the Deep North*
(NOTE: *Haiku are three-line poems; this translator has chosen to make four-line English versions.*)

I went behind the temple to see the remains of the Priest Buccho's hermitage. It was a tiny hut propped against the base of a huge rock. I felt as if I were in the presence of the Priest Genmyo's cell or the Priest Houn's retreat. I hung on a wooden pillar of the cottage the following poem which I wrote impromptu.

> Even the woodpeckers
> Have left it untouched,
> This tiny cottage
> In a summer grove.

Taking leave of my friend in Kurobane, I started for the Murder Stone, so called because it killed birds and insects that approached it. I was riding a horse my friend had lent me, when the farmer who led the horse asked me to compose a poem for him. His request came to me as a pleasant surprise.

> Turn the head of your horse
> Sideways across the field,
> To let me hear
> The cry of a cuckoo.

> —*Basho*
> *(translated by Nobuyuki Yuasa)*

Highway 93 South

> Mountain's shadow falls
> Old cowboy and new girlfriend
> Roll past in red truck.

Every weekend I drive between Salmon and Missoula, about 140 miles. The most interesting part of the trip is crossing Lost Trail Pass, where the state line runs between Idaho and Montana. It is a high winding road surrounded by endless trees and snow-covered slopes where the mountains make their own weather. The rest of the trip always surprises me, however, and every time I make the trip something miraculous happens. Wild animals appear as the river courses alongside us, revealing

> A line of fishers
> in blue coats. Legs and elbows.
> Herons! Ten of them.

So I continue watching the road, craning my neck. Farther on, near Darby,

> Five mountain sheep stand
> curving horn and winged shoulder
> turn like silk and fly.

Once, at the top of the pass, a fox stepped out of the forest and walked up to my parked car to gaze into my eyes as she lifted one paw, then the other, a slow march in place.

My lost pup is here
Green and black eyes of forests
Recognizing me.

I feel a relationship with the wildlife that steps out onto the side of the road to look into my eyes. I got the idea the fox and the mountain sheep had a message, a secret, for me.

Driving pass
Elk appears. I shout, suddenly,
Hear my father's voice.

—*Sheryl Noethe*

(On early school buses)

Ida Egge said, "Charles 'Dutch' Marshall also owned a truck/bus in about 1940. Dutch had a black Chevy truck with a wooden box in back with an emergency door in it, with a hole cut in the roof for the chimney of the wood stove—so us kids wouldn't freeze in the winter. He picked up the kids from about Baker on down to Salmon making a loop on the old highway and around the old back road."

Teeth chatter, children shiver
fire pops, cracks, and clatters
wood and canvas creak

Dr. Frossard, who did not grow up around Salmon, remembered his older brother riding in a school bus "like a crude station wagon, wood-framed, brown in color, with an exhaust pipe running from front to back, to provide heat." He also remembered students having to go home instead of to school because they had fallen and burned themselves on this exhaust pipe.

Bumping into heat
child screams, flesh burns,
brakes screech—oh—cold snow

Don Stenersen had the impression that these early conveyances were makeshift at best. They were privately owned and served other daytime purposes on the farm or commercially after delivering students. Sometimes a different vehicle would transport the kids home at night. These early machines helped speed the development of the modern motor coach.

Motor coughs, sputters
coming to life
—off goes the yellow wonder

—*Annisa Stenersen, 11th*

HAIKU

Write some or all of these poems on the board, preferably before class.

This quietness
The shrilling of cicadas
Stabs into the rock

    —*Basho*

Squatting motionless
The sun-tanned child and the toad
Stare at each other

    —*Issa*

From the plum tree bloom
Is fragrance floating upward?
There's a halo round the moon

    —*Buson*

A sudden shower
And I am riding naked
On a naked horse

    —*Issa*

First, explain to your students that although the Japanese haiku involves an exact 5/7/5 syllable count for the three lines, translation may vary this because the Japanese syllable count and the English syllable count aren't quite the same thing. There are some American haiku that don't follow the 5/7/5 at all, though they do have most of the other characteristics of haiku. Next, mention that the poems are hundreds of years old. Bring out by questioning what runs through each haiku—for instance a connection with nature, generally via a seasonal image. But advise the class not to restrict themselves this way ("We can be a little freer, since we are not Old Masters in Japan").

Haiku use concrete details to ground us in a specific moment, which seems to release a feeling or meaning. In other words, the meaning is subtle, and increases with familiarity.

One good technique is to distribute pictures for the class to base their poems on. This may strengthen the power of the written images.

Write a haiku of your own on the board (and maybe discuss it a bit) or write some with the students. Have them call out lines or ideas or changes.

Read a few student poems to the class.

Ask them to write one or more haiku, with the sense that it's best to concentrate on one good one.

Collect and read aloud.

Later, have a revision session—emphasizing cutting things down to the central image, as well as the value of originality and surprise, whatever is appropriate to the given poem.

    x-ref: HAIBUN

(This group is by students in a social studies class who were looking at pictures from South America.)

The orchestra plays
rhythm of butterflies or
deer bounding over fences.
—*Curtis Peterson, 6th*

Cathedral bells
ringing in rhythm to the
stillness outside.
—*Suzanna Edgar, 6th*

Gigantic turtles
cross the open forest
gazing at the stars.
—*Jennifer Coles, 6th*

Long streams of silk pour
out of weaver's loom on a
blazing summer day.
—*Andrea Blood, 6th*

The mist is rising
because of the water falling
over Angel Falls
—*Jeremy Bolander, 6th*

Night is when
a parked car turns
scary to you
—*Chris Folkman, junior
high*

(The next four followed a study of animals.)

The fox is so sly
and oh so brightly colored
after the rainstorm
—*Heather Hatch, 5th*

A tired leopard
hanging in a shady tree
dreaming happily
—*Matt Lee, 5th*

Rhinos charging rocks
with two horns on their noses
birds riding on their backs
—*Dustin Charlesworth, 5th*

The clock on the wall
ticked like a giant drum
then paced, clock-wise
—*Josh Martin, 7th*

Can't think of a thing
I want to say on paper,
sitting on branches.
—*Shara Sullivan, 7th*

A car hits black ice
Leaning to one side it flips
Water swallows it.
—*Justin Kohl, 12th*

HOW I WRITE

This exercise brings home the fact that writing is a real-life act, and connects writing (thinking) with the world in a multitude of ways. It's also a way to exchange valuable writing tips.

The How I Write exercise works best with students fourteen and older. Students can do it either in class or at home. In either case, the students make an informal list, as exhaustive as possible, of all the habits and practices they associate with the act of writing. Students may include all kinds of writing they do, including letters and diaries.

Here are some leads:

Writing itself

Do you write fast or slow?

Do you make revisions afterwards? When? Do you revise as you write?

Do you think of beginning, middle, end as you write? Or sort it out later, or just let it be?

Do you have an idea before you start? What kind?

Do you start when you have a phrase you like?

Do you start when you've seen or heard something inspiring?

Do you think awhile before starting or plunge right in?

Do you make notes before you start?

Any special techniques (for example, starting in the middle and adding the beginning last)?

Do you write longhand or type?

Do you use scissors and scotch tape ("cut-and-paste") to rearrange your piece?

Do you underline or circle parts?

Any special color of paper and pen? Size of paper?

When and how do you come up with a title?

Do you put a piece away when you've finished, then look at it again later?

Associated things

Dress?

Music?

Presence of people?

Preferred mood?

Place?

Pets?

Time of day?

Warmups?

Nervous habits?

Any oddities?

Where do you look when writing or thinking?

What does your face look like?

Go over these categories with the class; be sure they understand that they are just leads, not limits. Read a couple of examples. Urge the students to be as detailed, full, and frank as possible.

Collect and read a few (with permission).

How I Write

I write during the night.

I write when I'm depressed.

I write when I have the urge to educate the world.

I write when I have the urge to save the world.

I always write prose.

I usually write with my contacts in, because my glasses give me a headache.

I write in sweatpants and t-shirts, but when it's hot I just wear underwear and a tanktop.

I write to entertain my friends.

I write to understand people.

I write to make myself feel important.

I write to sort out my feelings.

I write when I want to kill myself, but I throw away what I have written so my mother won't find it and become hysterical. She did it once.

I write where people won't bother me, if I can.

I write in bed a lot.

I write on notebook paper.

I write to explain myself to people.

I write in different colors of pen, usually blue or black, and sometimes in green, and always in ballpoint.

I write in my study at home so I can look at the wall in front of my desk where I tack up pictures of my friends and family when I write.

I write a lot of stories about myself in different situations for vicarious enjoyment.

I sometimes write in another person's style.

I like to write with a cat on my lap to give me unobtrusive company.

Sometimes I write with the stereo on, sometimes with it off.

I never write with the television on.

I put historical facts and snips of foreign languages into my writing to make it look official.

Sometimes I write about things that are only understandable to me and my friends.

I write with a title in my mind, "Dana Stientjes, world-renowned Pulitzer-winning author, journalist, and photojournalist. Who owns a Porsche."

I write to be me.

—Dana Stientjes, college

I sit on the kitchen table half listening
to the ball game writing my friend in
New York.
I look up across the field. Our neighbor's
horses take off running. I watch for a while
drifting into a different world.
I come back down to earth and the phone
rings and I get out the notepad and
write small, unexplainable words while talking
to my best friend.

How I write
sitting in my room
small unsharpened
pencil in my hand
my Walkman
blaring out
rap songs
making scratching
on a white
notebook paper
not thinking
of the world
around me.

     —*Libby Southwell, 7th*

pencils streaming
brains working "Amazing"
fingers moving
people staring
people talking
cameras flashing
people walking around
wildcats staring at me
heart pumping
blood rushing
people fighting
shoelaces untying themselves
people racing
people humming
people breathing
sun is shining

     —*Josh Martin, 7th*

"I HAVE A DREAM" POEMS

Suggested pre-session activities:

• Watch a video about Martin Luther King, Jr.

• Discuss his philosophy of nonviolence and civil disobedience.

• Roleplay—Rosa Parks and the bus boycott, for example. An informal skit can be worked out in class.

• Do choral readings from King's "I Have a Dream" speech.

Read aloud Langston Hughes's poem "I, too" (in his *Selected Poems*) and the excerpt below. Discuss how Hughes's ideas are expressed, particularly through his use of metaphor and simile. (Note how his ideas are expressed by particular images, and how his repetition of questions has much in common with the oratorical rhythms of Dr. King's speeches.)

Read some student poems aloud. Point out how they work (acrostics with I HAVE A DREAM as the spine phrase, poems with a "Have you ever . . ." structure or an "If I could . . ." structure, etc.).

Then have your students write any way they like, but make it clear to them that their writing should contain specific images, not just generalizations.

x-ref: CHANT POEMS; LIST POEMS

Excerpt from **"Montage
of a Dream Deferred"**

What happens to a dream deferred?
Does it dry up
like a raisin in the sun?
Or fester like a sore—
and then run?
Does it smell like rotten meat?
Or crust and sugar over—
like a syrupy sweet?

Maybe it just sags
like a heavy load.

Or does it explode?

—*Langston Hughes*

Reaching Out

Have you ever reached out to grab
                              something
                              and pushed
                              it farther
                   away. . . .

Have you ever wanted something
                              so
                                   bad . . .
                   you begged
                   too much
                   and
                   never
                   got
                   it. . . .

Have you ever
gone your own way
                              and
                              felt
                              put
                              away. . . .
Have you ever, have you ever done it,
         The way I would?

         —Jody Hennig, 5th

         x-ref: CONCRETE POEMS

I wonder

H ow dreams start do they start like
A n appleseed and
V ary or do they grow big like an
E lephant or do they grow bigger like

A whale or do they shrink down to a

D eer size or do they vary like a
R ainbow or do they run like an
E mu?
A nd run away like
M en or do they disappear POOF! like that

         —Kim Prange, 5th

INTERNAL RHYME

Distribute copies of the following (or a poem of your own choice).

dirt is the absence of a solid (excerpt)

On the east wall hangs a blue shirt;
it couldn't hurt to mention that.
Looks like chickenfat creates the window's yellow—
hello, I hear my clock from Yucatán ticking
in Michael's bookcase, sort of kicking the time
into thinking it exists like a rhyme for something
but, meanwhile, is just umpteen jumps of anything.
There are so many things more against that peeling wall . . .

   —*Jack Collom*

Point out how the rhymes come *within*—not at the end of—each
succeeding line. For instance, *shirt* from line one is rhymed by *hurt* within
line two; *that* from line two is rhymed by *-fat* within line three. The
placement of the rhyming words within lines creates a syncopated rhyme
effect. The objection might be raised that the lines need only be re-
chopped to make a conventionally end-rhyming poem, but if one consid-
ers the line to be a unit of breath and thought (however fragmented), this
technique has its own valid effect.

Read students an example or two. With your class, work out a few
lines on the board, getting into the feel of swinging the line on an inside
rhyme. Ask them to write. Collect and read.

There, going up, I feel my stomachache drop,
then we stop, falling almost to the ground.
I hear sound, clutter, commotion, coming from all.
And then a call, a screech, a start.
Then a fall into a cart of strawberries.
Or it could be cherries, I don't know.
So I fall also. Splash around me.
I'm swimming in a red sea for hours before I reach the shore.
Then we're going up, like before, again.

   —*Alison McMillen, 7th*

"I REMEMBER" POEMS

"I Remember" poems—immortalized by artist and writer Joe Brainard in his book of the same name—make an excellent introduction to a series of classroom poetry workshops. For one thing, they are fun to do and to hear. They're usually vivid, down to earth, and personal. For another, their practice lets the students know that poetry can be made of their own speech patterns and experience.

Especially if this is the first of a series of sessions, begin by reading aloud a poem (or prose selection) notable for its rhythmic energy and sensuous details. Get in a "thing-y" mood. You might use the following excerpt from Brainard:

> I remember the only time I ever saw my mother cry. I was eating apricot pie.
> I remember how much I used to stutter.
> I remember the first time I saw television. Lucille Ball was taking ballet lessons.
> I remember Aunt Cleora who lived in Hollywood. Every year for Christmas she sent my brother and me a joint present of one book.
> I remember a very poor boy who had to wear his sister's blouses to school.
> I remember shower curtains with angel fish on them.
> I remember very old people when I was very young. Their houses smelled funny.
> I remember daydreams of being a singer all alone on a big stage with no scenery, just one spotlight on me, singing my heart out, and moving my audience to total tears of love and affection.
> I remember waking up somewhere once and there was a horse staring me in the face.
> I remember saying "thank you" in reply to "thank you" and then the other person doesn't know what to say.
> I remember how embarrassed I was when other children cried.
> I remember one very hot summer day I put ice cubes in my aquarium and all the fish died.
> I remember not understanding why people on the other side of the world didn't fall off.

Write "DETAIL" on the board, and discuss what it means. Tell the class you're going to ask them to write "I remember . . . ," followed by what they remember—it can be anything, from the day they were born to this morning. And it doesn't have to be "important"; we're just getting some flavor of real life here. Shorthand things such as "I remember my first bike"—period, end of memory—are tedious and generic. Students should flesh out their memories with the *detail* that was part of the original experience—colors, exact names, unusual focuses. They should tell just what it was that made it stick in their mind. Pretend it's a one-minute movie and tell *everything* in it. Make it real.

Try reading an "I Remember" poem of your own. This will help create an atmosphere in which students will explore the personal. Read aloud "I Remember" pieces by kids, pointing out good uses of sound, how poetic language often arises amid common speech, how comparison vivifies language, and any other virtues you find.

Then ask them to write, describing as many memories as they want, but concentrating on each one long enough to bring out its specialness. (You can have younger kids abbreviate "I remember" to "IR" each time.) They don't have to think "poetry," but can pretend they're talking, trading memories with a friend.

Collect and read aloud.

An interesting variation of this exercise is to concentrate on a single memory. In this case you should spend even more time talking up detail. This kind of I Remember is like a family photo, in which one sees not only Aunt Myrt picking pears but also the tree branches, the broken fence next door, half a black dog, the sky, an empty can of Van Camp's Pork 'n' Beans, etc.

Another variant is to draw the students' attention to the possible play between early memories and more recent ones. These memories could be set off in blocks, or interspersed, to cast light on life changes.

I remember when I was in kindergarten my teacher said, "Cut on the lines." I was cutting wobbly. Henry said, "I'm telling 'cause you aren't cutting on the lines." I said, "Who cares?" Then he told the teacher. She said, "You don't have to cut *exactly* on the lines, Henry."

—Patrick Tindall, 2nd

I remember being showered in the wilderness by hot embers from a blazing fire sent into the air by an exploding can of cream-style corn.

—Jim Bates, high school

I remember the forest with trees so thick and tangled the ground was painted with one big, cold shadow.

I remember playing with the skin that hung from my great-grandma's arm and being told not to do it again.

—Phelan Earp, 7th

I remember a wild stallion rearing like magic through the wild river.
I remember a plane taking me through clouds of visions.
I remember a star flashing red and blue in the dark breeze.
I remember a cloud that looked like a beautiful dragon in disguise.
I remember a wolf large enough to ride but it dashed away slicing snow.

—Shauna Goosman, 5th

I remember when I was moving from Wyoming in our gray Blazer. We were about halfway and our Blazer broke down. We stopped at this stinky car shop to have it fixed. They worked on it for a while. It was late at night. We were travelling for a while and I got carsick and threw up all over the place. My mom had an old red sweatshirt on. Our Blazer wasn't working too well again. We were getting tired. My mom and dad brought us to a church to sleep for a while. My dad left to find a place to fix the Blazer. The next thing I knew I saw a dead cat on the side of the road and there was a magpie flying in the bright blue sky. We drove up to the old swampy house. I could not believe that was our old house.

—Tammy Taylor, 5th

I remember being pulled in a little red wagon, watching the leaves flutter on the trees.

I remember my sister stealing a banana from home and running away on her blue bike, up the dirt road.

—Angie Mortensen, 12th

I remember when I was at my grandma's and my grandpa and I and my aunt and my cousin went to a great big pond and fished. I caught a big one and gutted it and digged my hands all in it and saw the eggs and got my hands all bloody and my mom took a picture and I put it in a bag and now I can look at it.

—Terri Christensen, 1st

I remember the time when I was riding in an airplane. And I was scared because I didn't want to wreck. So I looked out a window and I saw blue skies and little islands and it made me relax.

—*Buzz Yohman, 3rd*

I remember going sledding in the mountains. It was fun, the deep white snow was good to eat. My grandpa hitched me up to the truck. I turned over and got a faceful of snow. It was cold. I got back in the sled. We got going fast again. I climbed to the top of the mountain and sledded down. I crashed into a bush. I went flying into the snow face first. The snow was good. I went sledding again. This time I missed the bush. I went down the mountain. Woosh woosh went the green trees. Down the hill me and my dad went. Woosh, we hit the deep snow. Woosh, I'm back sledding again.

—*Michael Parmer, 3rd*

I remember the day my favorite rabbit died.
I picked him up, and he was light and cold and hard.

—*Emma Lewman, 10th*

I remember catching a black and yellow caterpillar. I tried to keep him by sticking two flowers together. But he ate his way through!

—*Michelle Jakovac, 4th*

I remember when I was a flower girl I thought my dress was too puffy. And the bridesmaid, with her pink flowery dress, she said, "Slow down, you're going too fast, you little brat, slow down!" After that we stopped and I said, "Shut up." She didn't shut up, just kept talking. Then we got rice thrown on us. And here comes the bouquet, with all its colors. Now here comes everyone to clobber the bride. Soon we cut the cake, drank punch, finally time to go home.

—*Penny Stenersen, 5th*

I remember a girl with red hair
Heavy red hair
Wrapping a gentle face
   of cream and pebbles
A banana held in her hand
Opening the banana
And the rotten fruit falling on my foot.
I remember going to the Anglican School, Jerusalem
And having my Calvin Klein knickers flushed down
The toilet of the locker room
But I remember it didn't matter
'Cause I didn't like them anyway.
I remember playing house
With 88 cans of baked beans
Beans on the floor and the walls
And telling my mother they were modern art.
I remember dancing and hitting my head
And wishing I had passed out
So Mr. Dish would carry me home.
I remember being chased around the bunny hutch
The bunny hutch painted with a brown rabbit
By Derek
Who had heavy red hair and a face
   of cream and pebbles
And wishing he wasn't so slow
Wishing he'd caught me.

   —Ann Jankowski, 12th

"LAST WORDS" POEMS

Read the following poem to your class:

The Last Words of My English Grandmother

There were some dirty plates
and a glass of milk
beside her on a small table
near the rank, disheveled bed—

Wrinkled and nearly blind
she lay and snored
rousing with anger in her tones
to cry for food,

Gimme something to eat—
They're starving me—
I'm all right I won't go
to the hospital. No, no, no

Give me something to eat
Let me take you
to the hospital, I said
and after you are well

you can do as you please.
She smiled, Yes
you do what you please first
then I can do what I please—

Oh, oh, oh! she cried
as the ambulance men lifted
her to the stretcher—
Is this what you call

making me comfortable?
By now her mind was clear—
Oh you think you're smart
you young people

she said, but I'll tell you
you don't know anything.
Then we started.
On the way

we passed a long row
of elms. She looked at them
awhile out of
the ambulance window and said,

What are all those
fuzzy-looking things out there?
Trees? Well, I'm tired
of them and rolled her head away.

—*William Carlos Williams*

Discuss with your students how Williams portrays his grandmother
through her surroundings and her speech, not by means of generalized
adjectives. You might point out that he liked his grandmother, but was
showing her accurately as she was dying: disoriented and difficult, yet
perhaps with her own particular wisdom and poetry shining through.
Dwell on the last part of the poem, noting how the rejection of trees
("fuzzy-looking things out there") is a perfect metaphor for dying, and
those last words: "and rolled her head away."

Read a couple of student poems as examples.

Ask your students to pick someone, either famous or known personally by them, either dead or alive, and then write a poem, free-form, leading up to their last words. Naturally, in most cases, the material will have
to be invented.

In this exercise, it is easy to fall into clichés and obvious character-ization, so alert your students to these pitfalls and urge them to surprise the reader and to use exact descriptive detail. One good approach is for them to visualize the person chosen and find some aspect they notice that most people don't.

Collect and read.

x-ref: PORTRAIT OR SKETCH POEMS

Goodbye to Mark

Remember last summer—
the great times we had
Can you recall—
when we were ever sad?
Under that warm sun
we laughed and we sang.
Your brown-gold hair
and your brown-gold skin
and your blue-blue-blue-blue
     eyes.
I loved you, Mark,
I really did.
Two whole weeks!
Full of love and happiness.
Remember when we kissed
     goodbye?
You said you'd always love
     me.
What a great big honking
LIE.

—*Katrina Dalrymple, 9th*

He wouldn't go to the
     hospital
'cause he thought he was fine
then they told us he had
     cancer
and he took it with a smile

He said, "I'm goin' home"
even though it was such a
     surprise
He was only thirty-six
when he died in July
His last words were I love you
and don't you dare cry.

—*Matt Stubblefield, 9th*

Last Words of My Great-Grandma

As she was lying in bed she said
Take my glasses, plates, and bowls
and share them with your mother.
Tell your family I love them as well as you.

My Last Words

I am going to say on my last day
I will miss all my grandchildren, trees,
I'm going to miss my favorite food like pancakes, apples,
but most of all I'm going to miss the shiny moon,
stars, and seeing the earth in person when I am going to be in it.

—*Tasha Mitchell, 10th*

My Uncle's Last Words

See you my Sweetie tomorrow I promise
is what he told me.
But he lied, but he didn't mean it meaningly.
I woke up with a happy face and full of grace.
While putting on my clothes my mom came in
and said, with tears in her eyes, where are you going?
I replied, going to see Uncle Tony play piano.
She told me he died in the racetrack stands. I couldn't
talk for a week, stunned with sadness.
I got a balloon for him that said, "I miss you and love you
    forever."
I let it go and watched it as it drifted higher and higher
hoping he would get it. My last words to my uncle will be
"I love you always and forever."

    If you hear me
    hear me loud as you
    float on the highest cloud.

—*Andrea Freel, 6th*

The Last Words of Santa Claus

Said Santa Claus to Mrs. Claus,
"Go bake some of those delicious
Christmas cookies." "OK, but
it isn't my fault if your sleigh
doesn't go up." "I won't leave it
until it does!" And he didn't and
he froze to death. And his last
words were "I don't want to be Santa
any more!" And he threw his hat down on
the floor.

    —*Megan, 3rd*

    I looked at their two
silhouettes in the moonlight. I thought
to myself that their love should never end.
But I heard a loud CRACK.
The love between them had broken and all
I could hear was my father say, "I'm leaving."

    —*Margaret-Ann McNab, 7th*

——
85

LETTERS

Some poems have the intimate quality of a letter to a friend, others feel like a letter to the world. Others are explicit in their form: the epistolary poem. A few suggestions:

- Ask students to write to an animal, to a famous person, to a part of their own body, to themselves, to an idea ("Dear Peace"), etc.
- Have students pretend that they're really close to their correspondent—they can be as personal or "crazy" as they like.
- They can make up names for themselves, to sign with.
- On the board, list things to talk about: inquiries of all kinds (not just the obvious, like "Dear Giraffe, how's your neck?"); little things that have happened to them (the authors), or things they've seen; made-up stuff; the jokes and language play close friends often like to exchange; their hopes and fears (expressed concretely); the weather (of course).
- Whatever students write about should be expanded and, as much as possible, based on the senses. They should remember that their correspondent is away somewhere and they have to make their remarks "real" to him or her or it.
- If they're used to writing,
        "Dear Grandma,
                Thanks for the present. I am fine.
                        Love, Jed,"
get another feel for correspondence going. Get students to look at the letter as a valve for their secret feelings, their imaginations—whatever will help them see letters in a different light.

One follow-up is to pass the letters around the class and have students answer them, taking the roles of whomever or whatever the original letters were addressed to, as in fourth grader Natalie Woodward's:

Dear Sky,
How do you change colors from blue to white to orange to pink? Why don't you pick one color? Do you ever get sick? Is it cold way up there? Do the mountains make you uncomfortable by poking you? How come you're so beautiful? Why are you so high up and not on the ground? Do clouds really feel like pillows? Do birds fan you off on hot summer days by flapping their wings? Do the stars make you squished at night when they appear? Are you made up of air? Is it fun being able to see everyone in the world? Do you like being the sky of the world? Have you ever heard the joke about the bird in the sky? I haven't either. I guess it flew away.
        Sincerely,
                The Ground

LIST POEMS

Lists, or catalogues, have been a common element of both poetry and practical life for millennia. Poetic lists appear in Homer's *Iliad*, Norse sagas, poems by American Indians, the Bible, etc. Many poets have employed lists extensively, including Walt Whitman, Sei Shonagon, and such contemporaries as Allen Ginsberg, Gary Snyder, John Ashbery, and Kenneth Koch.

Give the class a few tips:

- Poems are full of surprises and lists are dull without them.
- Think variety of items, of *kinds* of items.
- Think *specifics*, exact and colorful names.
- Make a BIG list.
- Think variety of syntax.
- Try adding a title *after* the poem's done.
- Rearrange the items in your list.

Here is a list of some sample topics (there are millions):

- Things That Make Me Smile
- What I'm Afraid Of
- Stuff That Drives Me Nuts
- Animals That Should Exist but Don't
- My Favorite Things in [name of a place]
- Things I Want to Toss Out of [name of a place]
- Rock Groups I'd Like to Start
- Where I'd Like to Go in My Time Machine
- What I'd Like to Have in My House
- Things I Wish People Would Say to Me

Read some of the example poems aloud, with feeling and rhythm.
Ask students to write one or two list poems each (no more). You can suggest a topic, but it's good to have them decide on their own.
Collect and read.

See *The List Poem: A Guide to Teaching & Writing Catalog Verse* by Larry Fagin (New York: Teachers & Writers Collaborative, 1991).

x-ref: "CAPTURED TALK"; CHANT POEMS; EARTH POEMS—THINGS TO SAVE; GEOMETRY POEMS; HOW I WRITE; "I HAVE A DREAM" POEMS; PLACE POEMS; "THINGS TO DO" POEMS; USED TO / BUT NOW POEMS

In the night my pajamas ripped off in the breeze.
In the night a pink ghost drove to the cemetery.
In the night I ate four jellybeans.
In the night my eyes pop open when I hear a snow owl feeding her babies.
In the night my dolls grabbed my bowl of Froot Loops.
In the night bubbles of Miss Piggy swayed over the sea.
In the night my barrettes scratched my head.
In the night my underwear danced through the sleeping home.
In the night the moon came out and up and down and rolled around like a
    lighted bowl.
In the night the stars sparkled like a glittery dress of snowy eyes.
In the night car lights slid through my walls.
In the night Donahue whispered into my ear.
In the night my teeth glow like gorgeous flowers.
In the night my blankets turn into little shortcakes.
In the night my sheets wrap around my head like a fireball.
In the night my mother goes to the bathroom.
I am not afraid of staying alone.
In the night I have faith in my father.
In the night the quiet deadness filled a truck.
In the night flowers faint and die.
In the night seven ghosts visited the bathroom and ran into my mother.
In the night I crawl in bed with a spider.
In the night scissors of glue clip and clip.
In the night my sister sticks my feet with toothpicks.
In the night I tapdance in front of Sammy Davis, Jr.
In the night the peaceful ballet came into my dressing room.
In the night the clouds cannot leave the room.
In the night the river carries many frogs.

    —Kelvin Moncayo, Candice Robinson,
      & Ananie Noel, second grade, New York City

(See CHANT POEMS, EARTH POEMS, GEOMETRY POEMS, "THINGS TO DO" POEMS, "THIR-TEEN WAYS OF LOOKING" POEMS, and USED TO / BUT NOW POEMS for more student examples.)

Haircuts

butch
Afro
naps and peas
flathead
jeri curl
mohawk (Mr. T)
cameos
vees
finger waves
corn rows
french roll
Shirley Temple
pineapple waves
extensions
pinhead
mushroom
Congo
seesaw
punk rainbow
Don King fright wig
ponytail
pigtails
cocktail
bucket-cut
bowl-cut
chitlin cut
Kojak
Buckwheat
chicken cutlet
Patty Labelle aircraft carrier
Tina Turner static control
Alfalfa state of shock
crewcut
box
braids
Medusa
Watusi
grape soda
Eiffel Tower
conehead
uh-oh
coconut
bullethead
burr cut
egghead

—Eighth grade group,
New York City

LUNES

To make a lune, write three words in the first line, five in the second, three in the third, and you're done. In counting words rather than syllables, the lune is more flexible than its ancestor, the haiku. Also, lunes have no necessary association with nature or season or even images. It's just eleven words arranged 3/5/3; anything goes. Any class used to haiku should be apprised that lunes may well "feel" entirely different than traditional haiku.

Write the following lines on the board:

> Think of me
> as a beautiful ballerina twirling

At this point, pause and conjure up the implied scene—a big star on stage, spotlights, an audience of thousands, etc. Then write the third line:

> around the block.
> —*Shirley Marc, 5th*

The shorter third line in lunes helps snap off surprises. The first line in this one has set the stage, the second contains multisyllabic rhythms and alliterative music to bolster the fancy image, and the third flips it down to a poignant picture of a little girl practicing on the sidewalk.

Read aloud a goodly number of lunes. Read each one twice, pointing out the variety of tone and the characteristics of each. As always, emphasize originality. These little poems can have an astonishing range of tone and style.

Ask students to write their own lunes, as many as they like. Advise them to look around if they're short of ideas.

Collect and read aloud.

Another good warmup is to write a few lunes on the board with the class; you can write lunes "born" from parts of other lunes (i.e., using lines or fragments from the lunes you find here or elsewhere).

Let your students know that lunes are great to tinker with. In a very short poem every little thing stands out; exact wording can make or break a poem.

A raindrop falls.
It falls on my nose—
delicate, light, transparent.

    —Anonymous, high school

You write with
a pencil tip bending lines
into your thoughts.

    —Bill Gee, high school

As darkness unfolds
the man with the knife
cuts his potatoes.

    —Anonymous, high school

Load the ship.
Go out to the sea.
Don't come back.

    —Anonymous, high school

Remember me, remember
me. Put it all together
and remember me.

    —Nora Llerandez, 3rd

When a cat
waves I wave. He lays
on my grave.

    —Reinaldo Aguino, 4th

Go to Heaven.
If it's nice, call me.
I'll be there.

    —Jennifer Leyden, 3rd

Double Lune

Fantasies are floating
images of silver that make
life more interesting,

creating mirrors that
ripple away at a touch
of a finger.

    —Suzannah Edgar, 5th

When you look
at a snowman too long
it comes alive.

    —Ian Gott, 1st

Here I am
for you to see me
and that's it.

    —Jeremy McFrederick, 1st

Here I am
in the dark purple tulips
riding a horse

    —Angela Prange, 2nd

I want to
be a valentine but my
mom says no.

    —Sonja Roland, 1st

Something bothers me
but I don't know what
it is yet.

    —Michael Parmer, 3rd

My new car
blows a tire. Over the
cliff I go.
      —Stacey Davis, 11th

March: grass brown,
ground numb, but dandelion
      sparks
jump the gun.
      —Terry Magoon, teacher

I am a
nice person and so is
my shadow, hee.
      —Zane Selph, 3rd

Think of me
as a rock sitting in
a big museum.
      —Scott Pruett, 3rd

I think I'm
dancing with a fish but
I'm not sure.
      —Patrick Darrah, 3rd

My cat and
me were playing in the
sunshine and ebony.
      —Sarah Wade, 1st

I know my
times tables. That's why I
feel like X.
      —Micah Bandurraga, 3rd

The leaves fall.
You pile them up and
then *you* fall.
      —Lisa Gilpin, 2nd

The curious sightseers
slam the door and chipmunks
explode all over.
      —Tim Pepper, jr. high

Think of me
as an interesting young lady
while I sing.
      —Katie Milan & Mich-
      elle Lyons, elementary

Picture my dog
as a perfect little angel
who never lived.
      —Shanna & Raina,
      elementary

Double Lune

From across the
street I saw the perfect
little parking space.

After the most
beautiful speech was made, a
period ended it.
      —Jennifer Peck, 7th

¡Claro que no!
No tengo mucho dinero
      ahora.
Tengo un coche.

Una vaca gorda
nada en el mar y
da leche mala.
      —Rosa Miller, high
      school

METAPHORS

Talk with the class about how important and useful comparisons are in writing, and spend a few minutes brainstorming some. Write a number of them on the board, including some that have become clichés ("clouds like cotton balls," "strong as an ox," etc.).

Let the class know unmistakeably that what's desired is not these stale oldies but fresh, new ones.

Ask the students to call out some original similes or metaphors—you can suggest that they only look for one similarity—a roll of toilet paper is like the sun; a telescope is like a freight train. Teacher Jim Casterson says, "It is important to stress originality and creativity. Encourage the students to think of 'weird' comparisons. This helps them think freely and avoid clichés. I hear some students say, 'I just thought of a comparison, but it's too weird to write down.' I tell them to be brave and write it down, because it's those that are the best."

Then have the kids each pick something and compare it to something else they feel has a resemblance to it. Next, ask them to write as many qualities or associated words as they can about the first thing. Then ask them to see how many of those qualities might fit the second thing, and to make a freestyle poem pointing out these connections. And you can, if you like, simply ask them to remove the "like" or the "as" and have it be a pure metaphor. "My dad's laugh *is* a train" has more impact than "My dad's laugh *is like* a train."

Collect and read.

My dad's laugh is
a train coming down
the tracks,
whistling and chugging
from the pit of his
stomach,
soft at first, then
full blast.

Ha. Ha, Ha. Ha, Ha

ANNIE GRAY, *7th*

A tiger is a flashing light, fur, madness, strong glare,
a flashing bullet, all in one body.

   —*Anonymous, 7th*

Night is a bear
roaring and going around in circles
chasing ants to gobble them
up.

   —*Anonymous, 7th*

Night is a black stallion
Running between us and the sun
Casting a shadow on the earth
Snorting thunder
Casting sparks when steel hits a star
Pounding hooves
Destroying some
Saving others.

   —*Anonymous*

Dialogue with Comparisons

Aaron, the Beaverhead mountains look like huge ghosts watching over us.
And the tree branches look like weeds in the field.
The weeds are scattered, like hair on an elephant.
Which reminds me, your shoes look like the fur of a groundhog or a
    beaver.
Oh yeah? Yours look like a couple of old snowballs.
Well, this school looks like a world of hurt, let alone some of the teachers.
This one room is like a tiny box of matches.
But outside the field looks like a minefield with all those cowpies laying
    around. . . .
But now my mind is as blank as a dark room without any windows.
And suddenly an idea breaks in, like a crowbar through a brick wall.
Say, I'll bet if you were to gather up all those cowpies in the field and
    plant seed in them you would have yourself quite a beanstalk.
Yeah, a beanstalk as power-packed as the planet Jupiter.
And with the water supplied by the cattle it would never die, unless it
    drowned.
Like a giraffe in the middle of the ocean.
Time to go. So long.
Adiós.

   —*Aaron Beasley, high school student, & a teacher*

"My Soul Is" is a favorite writing assignment for many younger students. Once they've done it, children will frequently ask for it again in writing workshops.

When you tell your class about this exercise, suggest that they not use the first word that comes to mind. Instead, have them think about writing *around the word.* For example, instead of saying simply "bird," Crissy Adams wrote "hollow-boned/ winged creature" in her poem. Instead of just saying "horse," Amanda Bagley wrote "wind/through the waves nostrils open wide/running onto the beach at Georgia/pounding hooves flapping mane/sweating all over but soft." Have your students reflect upon their own secret ideas about themselves—what animal they are most like, for instance. Or use yourself as an example and say, "My soul is a typewriter that drives eighty miles an hour through the night." Think about what makes each person different and mysterious.

Sometimes a single line is enough. Remind the class (and keep stressing this) to write *around the main idea,* using description and suggestion. On the board, write:

My soul moves like _____
     dreams about _____
     smells and feels like _____
     has been seen _____

and so on. Have the class offer ideas aloud to get their minds going and keep their ideas rolling.

When you collect and read the poems aloud, try to pace your voice to the best advantage of the line, whispering some words, drawing others out slowly.

My soul is a hollow-boned winged creature
with feathers soaring through the blue skies
sometimes losing a beautiful colored feather

   —*Crissy Adams, 4th*

My soul is a rabbit walking inside of me.
I like it when the rabbit catches my food.

   —*Jackie Barrett, 2nd*

Maybe my soul moves like a
  fish
Maybe my soul can glide
Maybe my soul sleeps on a
  sofa
Maybe my soul dreams
There is one thing—my soul is
  beautiful

—Sammie DeCora, 4th

My soul is a chair. It feels like
  sitting stiff
and quite hard and it never
  wants to get out
I come over to my soul chair
  to sit in it
but when I sit in it it fades
  into the sky

—Amanda Vermaas, 4th

My soul moves like wind
through the waves nostrils
  open wide
running onto the beach at
  Georgia
pounding hooves flapping
  mane
sweating all over but soft
its hair grows in the winter
it's leaving
help it stop it
from dying help help
going going gone the black
is turning to red from blood

—Amanda Bagley, 4th

My soul is jumping fences
sleeping through the winter
  winds
chasing cars
and roaming in the wilds

—Crissy Adams, 4th

My soul is a cartoon flying
in the air like humming in the
  world
and flying on a cloud.

—Katie Sperl, 1st

My soul is a wild wild wild
  horse
swimming across the ocean in
  his own body.

—Michael Shippy, 1st

My solar system
is I like
that the war stopped.

—Liz Russell, 1st

My soul is mountains
the beautiful sights
It loves the birds
It loves the deer too

Mounds
Of beautiful sights
Up in the still
Nights
That's where
All the animals live for
Infinity
Nothing moves everything is
Still

—Nathan Thompson, 4th

My soul was last seen in a bar
drinking wine and beer
It smells like garlic
It travels like a car out of gas
It sleeps very loudly

—Daniel Chaffin, 4th

My soul is a chicken dancing with a jellybean.
My soul is a chicken dancing with a rug.
My soul is a chicken dancing with my cells.
My soul is a chicken who's scared of the dark.
My soul is dancing with my brain.
My soul is a chicken dancing with the dirt.
My soul is a chicken dancing with a toad.
My soul is a big fat frog dancing with the bog.
My soul is a caterpillar dancing with a butterfly.
My soul is a gingerbread man dancing with the cookies.
My soul is a bell dancing with the railroad.
My soul is a shoe dancing with you.
My soul is a bowl dancing with a mug.
My soul is a reindeer flying in the rain.
My soul is a snowman dancing with the end of the world.
My soul is a floor dancing with the door.
My soul is a rug dancing with a bug.
My soul is dancing and singing.
My soul is a house dancing with a mouse.
My soul is a dog dancing with a cat.
My soul is a Christmas tree dancing with a bee.
My soul is a net dancing with a jet in the air.

—*Adrienne Vincelette, 2nd*

My soul is a cowboy he is all dirty
His horse is so fast with his muscles
Just if the horse was my horse. . .

My soul is a girl who is so cute
I kissed her this morning
Everybody wants to go out with her

—*Rustin Stephenson, 4th*

The Ad for My Soul

My soul looks like cauliflower.
It was last seen by a grocery store, where it
once was is now air
If you find it there will be no address
just look around and you will find me
there is a tiny hole in my stomach I call a belly-button
where my soul escaped
DO NOT EAT IT

—*Craig McCallum, 4th*

NAME-LETTERS STORIES

Write the following example on the board (or invent one using your own name):

  C is a lake on the moon. No water, just
      liquid dust. In sunshine it turns
      reddish-brown and starts to sizzle.
  H is a sneeze while you're climbing up
      a ladder. The sky says "Ooo" as you fall
      into your lemon-sauce lawn and swim
      to New York City.
  R is a musical instrument used by caribous.
      They make it out of arctic bushes and it keeps
      growing as they play. It sounds like a computer
      covered with silk, but it smells awful.
  I is a frozen snake, very peppy, who runs
      around looking for blue honey. Every day
      at sunset its ears fall off.
  S is a very grateful old woman who can
      hardly stand up but nobody cares because
      she's a dancer. She sings and dances
      about the letters R-I-C-H and
      her voice is like fighting mice.

(You may want to write just the five letters and read the rest aloud, or pass out copies of the piece.)

Mention to your students that the author just let his imagination run, usually beginning with ideas derived from the looks of the letter (but *not only* looks—*any* association is good: the sound, the "personality" of the letter—emphasize the free imaginative takeoff). Talk about letters with your students. See if they have "favorites."

Mention the *variety* from one "letter-story" to another. This is the sign of a lively and creative mind.

Read a few sample poems by other kids.

As they write, urge them not to cut their letter-stories short, but to go on and on.

Collect and read aloud.

This exercise is superficially similar to—but quite different from—ACROSTICS. It may freshen up your students' approach to letters if acrostics have become a knee-jerk way of making poems.

T is a two-sided swing that rocks its way to New Jersey and on the way he stops for a pop.
A is a lake that has a little magical stream going out of it. It passes my house and it goes through the town past the barbershop.
R is a rambunctious riding rowdy rocking-horse.
A is an ant pile that gets carried by ants.

—*Tara Sorensen, 3rd*

K is a mountain leaning against another mountain kissing.
A is a rounded leaf falling from a tree high high high in the sky.
S is a snake trying to kill another snake.
I is an igloo where four Eskimos are playing poker.
E is an egg that is playing a keyboard, singing "Oh where is my darling?"

—*Kasie Buhler, 5th*

S is like a snake coiled on the ground.
H is a sideways I standing tall and proud as the American flag goes by.
A is an original apple appealing to my intestines.
N is a no-nonsense nauseating nobody.
N is a Z sideways smoking a cigarette in the wind.
O is the tire of my Lamborghini speeding down the road chased by a police car.
N is one of the three N's in my name that makes me so awesome.

—*Shannon Taylor, 7th*

M is a robber who squeezes himself up to a straight line when he's robbing the World National Bank.
I is a boat with four oars and he goes fast.
C is cool as a cucumber because it looks like ice cream.
H is weird, he catches the M, and the H bends his legs and his arms. He squeezes the M up and puts him on his head and runs around pretending he's a giraffe.
A is a mad bull ready to charge.
E is a Chinese restaurant.
L is a driver's seat ready to take off.

—*Michael Parmer, 3rd*

W is a ray that escaped from the sun eleven years ago.
E is hair that was cut from my head.
S is a dollar sign that robbed a bank and got its stripes cut off.

I is a lazy H that is never awake.
V is a tent that got blown over by a fox.
A is a bullet from a thirty-ought-six.
N is a ZZZZZZZZZZZZ that tries to sleep but never can.

W is an upsidedown M that is looking for money.
O is a dirty, slouchy, and ugly head.
O is a dull, old, and stupid brain.
D is half of a butterfly.
W is a headlight of a car.
A is a mountain with snow on the peak of it.
R is almost a B but it doesn't have the courage.
D is a lake where all the animals eat dogs.

—*Wes Woodward, 5th*

Z is a percent sign that got hit by two arrows.
A is an arrow point that an Indian lost.
N is a mountain and a half mountain.
E is a magnet that sucked up one needle in the middle.

—*Zane Selph, 3rd*

NO WARM-UP DELIVERIES

Especially with an experienced group, it's interesting to give them a simple assignment with no explanation and no examples; e.g., write "What is a hammer?" or "Write about questions you can't answer" on the board and say no more. At most, explain to the students that you're saying no more.

Ask your students to keep writing the whole fifteen minutes.

Collect and read.

The class will largely enjoy the independence of this exercise, going without hints and examples. For any who don't, it's good to be "forced" to construct one's own response from the ground up.

The head of a hammer is shaped
like a rabbit's head. They are used
for building houses, shelves, cabinets, and
telephone poles.
The trunk
is like a
treetrunk.
They are
used for
putting
pictures
on your
wall. They
pound nails
into walls.
Don't miss
the nail
because
if you do
you will
have a
good mark
on your
wall.

—*Wes Woodward, 5th*

(*x-ref:* CONCRETE POEMS)

How many telephone poles are there in Idaho?
I-D-N-O.
How many molecules of
skin are on a grown-up's body?
Hard question!

    —Chris Anglin, 3rd

My brother said, what is Heaven like? I said I don't know.
I asked my brother, why don't you like your hair sticking up?
He said, I can't tell you.

    —Heidi Hugunin, 3rd

Well, I can't answer how God first got here or how was music made.
Or even how do people grow or how was the alphabet made.

    —Gayl Kramer, 3rd

Buffalo, Buffalo, you run so fast through the air. Your silver red rose hide,
it sparkles as you run through the air. Almost blinds me, and an Indian kills
him. Is there a buffalo with silver red rose hide?

    —Emmett Black, 3rd

A question is a question.
What is a question? Do you know?
I do not know.
But I will some time.

    —Darin Schneider, 3rd

ODES

The ode is a song or lyric poem that celebrates a thing or person. The Greek poet Pindar (522?–443 B.C.) first used the form to describe athletic glories. Usually, an ode addresses a person or thing not present. Traditionally, an ode exalts the qualities of its subject, illustrating it with elevated praise, but modern poets have come to use odes to describe everyday things.

The examples below, by students in Idaho, celebrate the details of morning, potatoes, joy, dogs, and cats. Before students wrote their odes to potatoes, fourth grade teacher Rose Morphey taught a unit on spuds. Students brought tiny Idaho blues into the classroom, and sculpted bakers and yellow potatoes, then took photographs of the sculptures. They learned that the Spanish explorers took potatoes back with them from the New World and gave a gift to their people more lasting than gold.

The students combined facts and romance to get the feeling of the ode. It's good to read an ode or two in class before the kids write. Among the great poets who have written odes are Pindar, Horace, Keats, Shelley, Wordsworth, and Alexander Pope. We give one here by the twentieth-century Chilean poet Pablo Neruda:

Ode to My Socks

Maru Mori brought me
a pair
of socks
which she knitted herself
with her sheepherder's hands,
two socks as soft
as rabbits.
I slipped my feet
into them
as though into
two cases
knitted
with threads of
twilight
and goatskin.
Violent socks,
my feet were
two fish made
of wool,
two long sharks,

sea-blue, shot
through
by one golden thread,
two immense blackbirds,
two cannons:
my feet
were honored
in this way
by
these
heavenly
socks.
They were
so handsome
for the first time
my feet seemed to me
unacceptable
like two decrepit
firemen, firemen
unworthy
of that woven
fire,
of those glowing socks.

Nevertheless
I resisted
the sharp temptation
to save them somewhere
as schoolboys
keep
fireflies,
as learned men
collect

sacred texts,
I resisted
the mad impulse
to put them
into a golden
cage
and each day give them
birdseed
and pieces of pink melon.
Like explorers
in the jungle who hand
over the very rare
green deer
to the spit
and eat it
with remorse,
I stretched out
my feet
and pulled on
the magnificent
socks
and then my shoes.

The moral
of my ode is this:
beauty is twice
beauty
and what is good is doubly
good
when it is a matter of two socks
made of wool
in winter.

(translated by Robert Bly)

Ode to Air

I'm glad you're there
in my ears and under my
 chair.

 —*Daniel Chaffin, 5th*

Ode to the Piano

Plink here plunk there
black licorice color shines
in the light. GREAT BALLS
 OF FIRE!
She's playing it again. Plink
 plink plunk.

 —*Marian Turner, 5th*

Oh potato I see you hanging in the sky. You are as big
As a raindrop. I like the way you grow out of the ground.
You are as purple as a milkshake.
You are like a ladybug. I love what you do.
I like how you can be more than money.
I think you are pretty as a kitten.
You are as fluffy as a cloud.
You are as rough as a piece of wood.
You are as cool as Spuds McKenzie.
You like all the women in town. I know that for sure.

—*Samantha Edwards, 4th*

Ode to My Cat

His name is Buddy.
He has a heart shape on his
    leg.

—*Ayla Johnson, 1st*

Ode to the pizza and the rose
Ode to the flower and to the
    doggy
Ode to the whale and to the
    cat.

—*T.J. Herzog, 1st*

Ode dog and ode
mom ode dad ode sister
ode horse and ode me
ode cat ode roses
ode sun ode crayons
ode grass ode tree
ode friend ode moon
ode to flowers and hearts
ode to crayolas

—*Lea Rieffenberger, 1st*

O h! You shine like the moon
D ark yellow like
E veryone has never seen such a

T hing but
O h! You shine so yellow.

T he sun isn't so bright as you.
    Every
H ead is watching.
E verybody wants to see you.

P otatoes aren't as good as you.
O h! Please help the dark yellow
    potato moon
T rembling with
A
T errible fright the potatoes keep
    calling
O h! Please help! but nobody
    comes.

—*Troy Herman, 4th*

Ode to Wind

The wind comes in on
    running horse feet
Blowing so hard through the
    trees
Blowing through my hair
But moving so fast over the
    town.

    —Kristi Fisher, 5th

Ode to My Cat

My cat Vanilli's eyes
are like blue lakes
shining in the dim soft night.
Her paws are like a long piece
of white yarn, and her nose
is like a bright red rose in
    sunlight.

    —Jessica Sprute, 4th

Ode to Fishing

Running water in a mountain
    stream,
a sudden burst of wet dew
    splashing
against my jeans.
Near a rock lies a perfect
    hole.
I toss my worm toward the
    rock
I hear a splash I wade
a few seconds then I feel a tug
on my line.
I set the hook, the brookie
    jumps viciously
out of the water struggling for
    his life
I twist my feet making a
    squealing sound.
There is no other life.

    —Shannon Taylor, 6th

Sometimes in the morning
I feel the wind
I look my window's open
Then I feel whiskers
My horse, Big Willie, leans his
    head
Into the window and wakes
    me up.
His whiskers are soft and
    tickly.

    —Bessie Babits, 3rd

ON POETRY

This is a good final exercise in a series of workshops. Tell your students that since they are now practicing experts of poetry, today you're all going to write poems about poetry.

You can do this exercise in many ways. The important points seem to be to urge originality and to offer the students a lot of options, so that the remarks they write on poetry are themselves poems. The type of poem is not important; they can write in any form they like, or in a variety of forms.

Tell them *not* to rely on general terms ("Poetry is nice," "Poetry is boring") but to make poetry into something alive, something that moves, something they can see-hear-touch. Or encourage them to make a story with poetry as its main character—poetry as a creature that knocks on the door or something. Emphasize comparison as a good way to go ("Poetry is like—" in a chant string). Also, let them know that they are free to include, if appropriate, negative feelings about poetry—it can be or seem tiresome, difficult, upsetting, as well as exciting.

Read them a *large variety* of student works about poetry, and then tell them to forget all that and write their own.

Collect and read.

Teachers of music, art, biology, etc. can also use this exercise to get their students speaking poetically of their subject.

x-ref: ACROSTICS; CHANT POEMS; DEFINITION POEMS; "MY SOUL IS . . ." POEMS

I'm a fearless bounty hunter and I'm hunting down part of a dangerous gang called poems. I have already captured some of the men. I'm hunting for the men named words, letters, phrases, sentences, and paragraphs. I found them, my thoughts are surrounding them, there's too many of them, they're trying to escape where they will be safe on my paper, too many words trying to escape onto my paper, they're scattering in my head, too many words, too many letters, they're overtaking me, there's too many words, too many, too many, too many.

—*Aaron Thompson, 7th*

Poetry is frying in the oven, toasting in the toaster, even smoke coming out to the clean fresh air, because really air is an ocean of our yes yes yes.

Poetry is like a Wonderful Mistress Dream Blowing against the window in the moonlight and the tumbleweeds outside roaring with fear and the wind gliding and screeching. And the shingles on the roof flapping and the trees with pinecones gleaming with fear.

—*Shawnee Black, 4th*

I

Can't
And really
aNd truly can't
Think

That
He (poetry)
Is
Nuts.
Kids

Often
Find

Ants
iN the
Young
True
Head of
Intelligence
Never knowing where it's
Going to strike.

Right now poetry
Is
Getting rather too
Heavy
To handle.

—*Nichole Nardella, 5th*

Poetry is like wind blowing
 you away
and rain hitting you on the
 head and riding
horses in the rain and snow.
Roping cattle in the mud
and throwing hay in the
 thunder
and lightning.

—*Mark Tracy, 5th*

Poetry is a
bowl of thought whizzing
 through
the air, crash.

—*Ben Gould, 4th*

Poetry is like
having a snake
in your room
and you don't know what to do.

—*Lisa Colon, 6th*

Poetry is like a lake full of glares of the stars.
The texture makes me like a beautiful woman.
I like that when I dream.
I always dream of the lake I see before my eyes.
Oh-oh-oh-oh I love lakes like that.
Maybe it'll be a magic lake or stars.
When you think of lakes or rivers or swimming pools or
    oceans
be careful of the ocean if you dream of there.
I can't stand when I drowned in the lake.

The lake said, "Oh, did she have to die?"

I can't stand people who die.

The lake spits me out and I come back to life.

Oh I am beautiful when I get out of the lake.
He dresses me up beautiful.
How can I repay?

    —*Katie Helm, 2nd*

Poetry is like chickenpox
that invades everybody
and everything. It's almost
like having poetry pop out of
your skin and then it gives you
the itches, but if you itch it too
    much, more might pop out of
    your skin, and if you keep
    itching it
you might just turn into a chicken
pock of a poem.

    —*Donny Anderson, 7th*

Poetry Confusion

You stir and stir my emotions.
Sure they all come out on paper,
But what's the use if no one can
Experience or even image them?
Sometimes you get me so confused
All I can do is take a bubblebath,
While other times I can write all
Night. Why are you so difficult
But so easy, so complex but
    simplified,
So unique but common? Wait a
Minute, this sounds like me.

    —*Tiffany O'Dell, high school*

Poetry is like the alphabet all talking at once.
    —*Kristina Lacognata, 4th*

There is a jungle of words
as the elephants walk through
it BOOM BOOM BOOM
the coat is changed to diamonds

The hunter's poem is the deer
bounding off the page
The elk being chased by the hounds
Why why do they hunt, chase
the elk as he bugles to his mate
She is standing by the fence with spikes
Who is the gun? Winchester is his name
No time-outs in hunting or poetry
Hey! That's not fair! says the deer
Who said hunting is fair says the hunter
So I quit! says the deer
No way! BOOM!

—*Theo Vanderschaaf, 6th*

Poetry is a squirrel running across the fence teasing your dog.
Your dog will never catch it but he tries anyway with all his heart.
Poetry is like someone leaning back in their chair then falling back-
    wards and cracking their head open.
Poetry is like a shotgun blowing away the side of your head.
It's like a pit bull tearing away your throat.
You tell it to sit but it keeps thrashing and thrashing and thrashing and
    thrashing and thrashing.
Poetry is all-colored and turned around and overlapping.

—*Mike Swanson, 6th*

My life is a poem. I love my little poems, tiny words shattered in a sort of
system in my heart, in a sort of little voice, could be to me. A poem is like
little suns in my face when I shatter the words that appear in mind that I put
in a sort of dangerous associated system I love.

Poems should be positive and strong, raising and raising. When words appear in a system it could be positive or an accident or nature sorting it to life,
if you put it that way.

—*Melissa Kawecky, 3rd*

ORIGINS POEMS

The dictionary defines the word *origin* as ancestry, or derivation of source. This exercise asks students to go backwards in time, going all the way back to the inception of something. Sometimes the opposite of a thing will be at the end of a trail. Think of the image of a film running backwards, retracing evolution to the seed of an idea or an object.

The following poem is a good starting point:

Page from a Notebook

Two and two four
four and four eight
eight and eight make sixteen
Repeat! says the teacher
Two and two four
four and four eight
eight and eight make sixteen.
But lo and behold the lyre-bird
passing in the sky
the boy sees it
the boy hears it
the boy calls to it:
Rescue me
play with me
you, bird!
Then the bird with joy
flies down and plays with the boy
Two and two four
Repeat! says the teacher
and the boy plays
and the bird plays . . .
Four and four eight
eight and eight make sixteen
and sixteen and sixteen what do
    they make?
Sixteen and sixteen do not
    make anything
and especially not thirty-two
in any way
and they go away.
And the boy has hidden the bird

in his desk
and all the children
hear the music
and eight and eight in their
    turn go away
and four and four and two
    and two
in their turn clear out
and one and one make neither
    one nor two
one and one like a shot go off
And the lyre-bird plays
and the boy sings
and the teacher cries out:
When will you stop being the
    clown!
But all the other children
listen to the music
and the classroom walls
collapse quietly.
And the windows turn again
    to sand
the ink to water
the desks to trees
the chalk to cliffs
the quill to a bird.

—Jacques Prévert
(trans. Harriet Zinnes)

Read this poem to the class, stressing the simplicity of Prévert's language; use the drama and mystery of the poem to hypnotize your students. Ask them first to imagine the classroom walls tumbling away, then to watch as the rest of the room returns to its original forms. They get a feeling of freedom and chaos, and they love it.

Ask your students what the connections are between chalk and cliffs, desks and trees, windows and sand. Have them consider other connections, other roots. Then read some of the student examples below, pointing out the terrific variety of ideas in them, which go far beyond the conventional images of chickens and eggs, babies and parents. Some of the poems contain bits of historical truth, some logic, while a number combine scientific fact and fantasy. Encourage your students to reveal (and create) relationships that are not readily apparent, or that exist only for mysterious and unknown reasons. As always, *anything goes*!

Have them write.
Collect and read.

A map becomes Idaho again.
Monday Friday again.
Mad Math St. Patrick's Day
    again
with T. Rex.
Dad a dinosaur with wings
    again.
2 becomes 4 again, with 5.

    —Lisa Sandborgh, 2nd

The horses become the grass.
The grass becomes the field.
The field becomes the
    mountain.
The mountain, the rock again.
The rock into meteorite.
The meteorite turns into
    nothing.

    —Shaun Donnan, 2nd

The cassette turns round and
    round
rocks and sticks make a
    rhythm
that only people pounding
    understand
the heat of the heartbeat gets
    you in
rhythm of the beat in the
    pounding of the
canvas over the rock, hitting
    it with a
crooked narrow stick.

    *—Cindy Morgan, high
    school*

Women become witches.
Men become skeletons.
Donald Duck becomes an egg.

    —Tommy Goddard, 2nd

The floor became the door
and the doors became sea
and the sea became a tree
and the trees became a dream.

    —Zach Settle, 1st

Your teacher turns into an
      ant.
You squish your teacher.
Your teacher goes to heaven.
In heaven she falls out of the
      sky.
Your ant-teacher comes back
      into the classroom.
She has knives. She throws
      one at you.
It shatters against the side of
      your head.
She throws another knife at
      the other side
of your head. You have a
      Mohawk.

      —Ricky Mann, 2nd

Bus is a fuss hustle muscle
tussle must. Rose is a hose
doze hose rose pose is a rose
nose hose
sky high tie
is a kite is a fright

      —Sam Wing, 2nd

And as the romance shatters,
      shockingly gone,
the hate becomes love again.
The pain, kisses again.
The tears, smiles again.
The fear, security again.
The memories, his again.

      —Stefani Matteson, 11th

And the war scene
      becomes alive again
The smoldering becomes
      chairs again
The bones become mammals
      again
The metal becomes cars again
The dust storms become
      lawns again
The bombs become whole
      again
And the lawns grow
The cars roll
The mammals go
      and go and go.

      —Bob Miller, 11th

The music teacher
becomes music.

      —Shaun Severson, 1st

The beautiful sun rises with
      1/4 of it gone
the seagull flies in an egg
a machine turns into a big
      metal plate
the wind turns into wind in a
      jar
a squiggle turns to a gas
the elephant turns to a
      fingernail
the poem turns to a famous
      poem
the end turns to the end.

      —Schuyler Drummond, 3rd

113

1. The grease spot on the highway becomes a grotesque mass
of fur and blood again. The mass of fur and blood becomes
a gopher about to be mowed down by a Mack truck again.
Then a gopher safe in his hole again. The gopher's hole fills in
and becomes solid ground again. Too bad the gopher was
still in it.
2. The soil becomes ashes again.
The ashes become a circus fire-eater again.

     —Schroeder (a.k.a. David Phillips), 8th

Disneyland turns into flat ground again.
Mickey Mouse fades away.
Donald Duck goes back to his farm.
Pluto turns back into a planet again.
Goofy becomes a globe again.
Daisy Duck floats away into a white and yellow daisy.
Minnie Mouse turns back into a miniature doll again.

     —Nancee Feagans, 4th

The mustache becomes a mustache again.
A 1000 becomes 900 again.
Yelling becomes talking again.

     —Jeffrey Cummings, 2nd

OUTDOORS POEMS

"I *am* what is around me," said poet Wallace Stevens. First grade teacher Nola Losser says that when she was in school, writing was anti-descriptive—concentrated in summaries and "meaning"—and that this was a great loss.

One of the basic functions of poetry is to lead us to a *closer look* at our surroundings. Take the students (with writing materials) outside, preferably a place with varied views. Have them look around and chat a bit about the details of what they see. Shapes and colors can be quite challenging to put into words, so try comparisons ("The white picket fence is the teeth of the Brown family"). Note variations in distance. Read aloud sample poems strong in observational details and discuss how their details create an effect: a little world rich in detail.

Ask the students to write about what they see, beginning at any point and proceeding round in a circle. The circular movement and shape can give a form to the poem, and provide an ironic or otherwise meaningful "ending."

This is an exercise in the very tough task of verbalizing one's powers of observation. Our usual articulations of what we see are allowed to lapse into a kind of oral shorthand or into generalizations. "Y'know those cliffs out back of Hayward Stables? Well, there were some goats on 'em last week." What, exactly, the cliffs are, or look like, doesn't come to light; the mere reference locates them sufficiently for surface communication. But there's an important human loss in experience involved in this sort of skimming over our sense data; we take our senses for granted, using them only pragmatically. The complex, amazing wonder of the goats gets lost.

Not every poem, of course, delves into the minutiae of sensory experience, but if the poem doesn't do that it should be by choice, not by default. Looking closely at our environs helps create love for them.

Collect and read.

One variation is to take a walk and write while walking. Then the "form" is likely to be more linear than circular. Another variation is to do this 360-degree observation in the classroom instead of outdoors, noting the light on the desks, the crack in the wall, pictures, words, people's clothing, what's out the window, and so forth.

Bikes look like blueberries.
Rides are heaven.
Skies look like spirits.
Cars are like red shiny apples.

—*Christifer Kammeyer, 2nd*

Staring camera
Flying paper
Green pencils all over the
     place
The gorgeous sea
Dirt balls
People jabbering
Things blinking
All different colors

—*Gayl Klemmer, 2nd*

Huge rocks break the majestic flow of mountains ages old. Scattered tree limbs lie all above me. Almost a contrast to all the plants and animals alive. Living, dead, and "never-been-alive" in harmony. I sit on a moss-covered rock and write this journal. Little tufts of grass and weeds spurt out of the ground in a splendid random pattern. The clouds lie about me, offsetting the ice-blue sky. It reminds me of a swirling patchwork quilt. On a hillside nearby the vertical tendencies of the trees breaking the sun-highlighted horizon of the hill. It looks like a glowing pin cushion. The cool breeze hits my face and it feels good. The sun hides behind the clouds. A chill runs up and down my spine. The snow no longer glistens. Rocks are miscellaneously strewn about the golden sand. The trail is no more. Logs no longer guide the way. It's only us and the map. . . .

—*Phelan Earp, 7th*

A bright flash of lightning through the sky
Tiny raindrops glimmering past my face
Intricate blades of grass winding through each other
The tall majestic pine tree sways uneasily in the winds
A woman strolls and looks at the stormy sky
Another flash of lightning.

—*Meredith Menk, 7th*

Weather Poem

It's raining lightly
and the wind is blow-
ing. The trees are whishing
from side to side while the
litter is being thrown
around. The clouds
are darkening and
the sun is
down
I need
to
go
inside
now.

—Kelly Wagner, 7th

Mountains
are
blue
and
with
trees
with
green
leaves
and
animals
bears
and
deer
and
birds
and
raccoons
and
elk
and
rivers
and
cabins

x-ref: CONCRETE POEMS

*—Jillian
Martina
Miles, 2nd*

PANTOUMS

The pantoum is a poetic form from Malaysia. It began, centuries ago, as an oral folk form. For our purposes, a pantoum is a poem of indefinite length made up of four-line stanzas; the lines get repeated in a pattern like this:

1
2
3
4

5   (same as line 2)
6
7   (same as line 4)
8

9   (same as line 6)
10
11 (same as line 8)
12

and so on.

Closure of the poem is an option. That is, the last stanza can include, as its second and fourth lines, lines 3 and 1 of the first stanza. Thus the circle is completed. Or the pantoum can be open-ended.

Constantly repeating whole lines in this interwoven way often gives pantoums a hypnotic or dreamlike effect; the challenge is to use this repetition so that the elements of the poem remain fresh. In a good pantoum, whole phrases (lines) continually reappear in surprising new lights.

Show the class how pantoums basically work, as outlined above. By reading aloud or passing out copies of an example (and leaving the above graph on the chalkboard), you can make sure that students understand the pattern.

You might advise students (unless you want to be very strict) that they may change the words a little when they repeat lines ("walk" to "walked," "dog" to "dogs") or add a couple of little words. Another thing to know about pantoums is that they're easier to write if each line forms a self-sufficient, modular unit.

For advanced students, one device is to use a phrase or word whose meaning changes with the context.

With younger students, you can take dictation on the board in a class collaboration. With hesitant students, a good way to start is to provide an opening line.

Because birds are gliding across your brain,
I rise into the shadows
And the mist is rolling in
Because my breath is rolling out.

I rise into the shadows
Like a pond that went to sleep:
Because my breath is rolling out
You hear doorbells in the woods.

Like a pond that went to sleep
And woke up inside a dream,
You hear doorbells in the woods
Though the woods are in the dream.

And woke up inside a dream!
Although the air is filled with blue and white clouds,
Though the woods are in the dream,
A good idea can smell like pine trees.

Although the air is filled with blue and white clouds,
I am filled with ideas about dreams.
A good idea can smell like pine trees
And a dream can grow like a cloud.

I am filled with ideas about dreams.
The stars don't know what they mean
And a dream can grow like a cloud:
You can't explain this bigness.

The stars don't know what they mean
And the mist is rolling in.
You can't explain this bigness
Because birds are gliding across your brain.

—*Anonymous*

The Black Horse
ran so fast
the wind
was jealous

Ran so fast
the storm
was jealous
forever

The storm
the wind
forever
jealous

    —Missy Amster, 5th

Black tron aliens take
Over the Earth.
They eat all the candy
And do not say please and
    thank you.

Over the Earth
They fly sky high
And do not say please and
    thank you,
Which is not very polite.

They fly sky high
And shoot lasers,
Which is not very polite.
Then they leave in a rude,
    exciting attitude.

    —Brian Anglin, 5th

The wind
blows
through
the trees

Blows
real soft
the trees
the blue grass

Real soft
is
the blue grass
as it touches my face.

    —Missy Amster, 5th

PICTURE-INSPIRED WRITINGS

Try this exercise to help ground poetry in observation, as well as to demonstrate how imagination can arise from simply looking.

Bring copies of a picture to class and pass them around. The picture can be of anything but should be complex enough to stimulate close observation and/or various interpretations. Surrealist paintings work well. Ask the students to look closely at the picture and let ideas start to swim in.

Give the class some options:

• To write a story-poem of how this scene came to be, or what's happening, or what will happen.

• Pretend to be something in the picture.

• "Walk into" the picture and see what happens.

• Create a wild fantasy.

• If the picture is abstract, describe what is suggested by its shapes, etc., as with clouds.

• Create a dialogue between elements or persons in the picture.

• Use poetic forms you know already (such as the haiku and list poem) to comment on or take off from the picture.

• Use comparisons to connect the picture with other things.

To get students focused on details, do a sample chalkboard workout from a picture hanging in your classroom. Advise them to look closely at the handout picture again if they run out of ideas, to uncover some previously overlooked detail.

Ask the students to write.

Collect and read.

x-ref: OUTDOORS POEMS

(The following two pieces were inspired by a photograph showing items salvaged from sunken ships, with a boat on the left, and some men in the distance looking at the "treasures.")

Photograph

Time is frozen.
The plates lie still.
The men stand motionless.
Without breath.
Water does not flow.
The boats do not move.
The shadows motionless like their casting figures.
Everything is frozen in time.

—*Richard Anderson, 12th*

The Suits

"But I don't have the money," the bald guy
was saying.
"You wrecked my flea market,"
he insisted. The suits
didn't care. They wanted their money
now.
They took the bald guy, Harry,
on their boat
docked next to
Harry's Flea Market.
"No, no!" yelled Harry. No one heard his
pathetic cries, and
no one saw him again.

—*April Tibrow, 9th*

(The following poem was inspired by a picture of a kitten in the arms of a gorilla.)

Surrounded by black,
The orange mammal cautiously, smoothly
Slips out of the arms of the black.
He tiptoes away
Tingling from the static shocks.
The orange mammal leaps into the black again.

—*Leslie Gwartney, 6th*

(The following two were inspired by a painting of a woman on a beach.)

A woman walks along the wet, sandy beach
In her tattered old clothes.
Her burlap scarf wrapped around her.
The birds hovering over her.
The frigid waters collapse
Onto the fungus-covered waxy rocks of the coast
As she elevates her hands
To admire the tangible, tepid sun,
Then walks on.

    —*Jody Hennig, 6th*

As I rode my horse along the shore,
I stopped to give her a rest.
I turned my back to pick up a delightful shell.
When I turned back around my horse was gone.
Again and again this happened.
Then one day as I was walking along the beach
I heard the roar of the ocean.
I looked around and nobody was on the beach.
So I placed two fingers in my mouth
And whistled as loud as I could.
Then the roar grew louder and louder.
I turned my back to the ocean to sob.
Then hearing the ocean grow louder I stopped,
Wiped my eyes and turned around.
I blinked once, then twice—
I couldn't believe it!
Nearly forty-one horses were racing toward me from the water.
The waves chased them to shore.
But then out of the water grew a huge demon,
A bull, and chased them back to the midst of the ocean.
That is my story.

    —*Misty Winterowd, 6th*

PLACE POEMS

Write PLACE in huge letters on the board. Tell the students that they're going to write about places they know intimately, using any style of writing they like.

Discuss place: how the sense of place is probably our most basic memory; how the new-born baby probably knows its mother first as a collection of physical qualities—temperature, texture, shape, etc.; how we get to know our special places extremely well—crib, rug, yard, street, world. Each student knows, for example, his or her own room in tremendous detail—with deep and complex emotions tied in—but nobody ever comes up and says, "Tell me all about your room."

Suggest a variety of places likely to be known intimately—backyard or street frequently traveled, a bathroom, a kitchen, a favorite hangout, a secret den of some kind, a fishing hole, a rooftop, etc.—even places not often visited but indelibly etched in memory, such as a particular vacation spot.

Urge students not to take on a place bigger, say, than one can see all at once—Nebraska, for example, is not a place but a complex of millions of places. Advise them to write about one place only. You might ask the students to draw a map of their chosen place first—this helps direct attention to the geography (even of their bedrooms!). Let them know a good way to make a place immediate is to picture themselves in it, with something happening that evokes the feel and fact of that place.

Urge detail rather than generality. They *know* the details of their special places, and that's what makes those places special.

Show them a poem you like that is, in particular ways, evocative of place, and discuss how the poem works. For example:

Nantucket

Flowers through the window
lavender and yellow

changed by white curtains—
Smell of cleanliness—

Sunshine of late afternoon—
On the glass tray

a glass pitcher, the tumbler
turned down, by which

a key is lying—And the
immaculate white bed

—*William Carlos Williams*

Note how the poem works not by trying to describe the whole island of Nantucket but rather by picking one small view within it—a view that seems to capture the quiet, light, elegant, homey essence of the place. Williams simply but formally mentions the items he sees, all pale, ending with something mysterious.

Read aloud some student examples, pointing out how each takes its own approach to the place it speaks of, how each is unique and particular.

The following little poem works about the same as Williams's does. It concentrates on one small but characteristic aspect of a whole scene:

Baseball Diamond

CRACK! You lay the bat down and gaze up at the ball in flight.
It flies over the green green grass so smooth, so steady.
You look at the fine line of brown dirt with a snow-white base
at the end. CAUGHT! You're out.

    —Julian Hitchcock, 5th

A list poem, such as the following, is a condensed, high-energy, rhythmic way to write about places, by simply telling what's there.

A Dark Alley in New York

Bolts	rocks
garbage cans	drug deals
bums	murders
screws	bullet shells
rusty cars	fights
dirt	darkness
nails	broken bottles
ants	rabid dogs
garbage	and—Boom—
hippies	it's daytime.

    —Adam Arthure, 5th

And here's a beautiful poem that captures the loneliness of an abandoned farm by focusing on sound.

Deserted Farm

A deserted farm is a lonely place.
It gives you a deep cold thought.
As the wind blows through the tall weeds
the trees bend and crackle
and the windmill squeaks
while the door wildly claps against the barn.

    —Fred Beanblossom, 9th

In the Rodeo Arena

The announcer puts on a country tune.
George Strait sings, "Don't Call 'im a Cowboy."
The arena is filled with horses and people.
Everyone is laughing and talking about the last rodeo,
or the party last night.
"Please clear the arena, we will start the rodeo in 5 minutes."
A dust rises as everyone moves toward the gate at the same time.
The grand entry and salute to the flag all take place.
Bronc riders' nerves are building.
Breakaway ropers tie on their ropes.
Lope the horse one more time.
Get off, tighten the cinch—
before you get back on the horse, you hear the announcer say,
"All he'll get is your applause, no pay today."
The audience's applause rings in your ears.
The next thing you hear is
"One more bronc rider, breakaway ropers, start thinking about it."
Now your nerves are building, you're the first one up.
Will your horse scare?
How will the calf move?
Will he move to the left or move to the right?
Take a deep breath, ride in the box. They've called your name.
Back the horse up, nod your head.
"Go!" someone yells as you leave the box. The barrier snaps back.
"You're out!" your pusher yells. "Throw! Throw!"
"All she'll get is your applause. . . ."

      —Sheila Betz, high school

Against the Rock

Sitting on the bank of Wallace Lake
A feeling of coolness and peace arises.
The waves beat and splash against the rock.
In the distance, a roar begins to build!
The pines come alive with movement,
Crashing and thrashing by the force
Of the wind beating their tops.
As it approaches, all stop to listen,
Waiting for the crash to reach them.
But silence—the wind hits the lake,
Where no trees carry the sound,
But water waves and beats
Against the rock.

      —Kevin Stokes, 11th

Livingroom

The afternoon sun shines on the livingroom floor.
It is broken by the shadow of a cat walking across the slick floor.
The shadow of a plant stretches across onto the now-sleeping cat.

—*Zack Belish, junior high*

R ocks
O n top of the
C liff
K rackle as
I f they are
E xcited
S tones.

—*Davin Livo, 3rd*

Rodeos are fun.
They smell somewhat like
cotton candy.
There are lots of colors.
All you can hear is the
        announcer
and the horses' feet.

—*Gayl Klemmer, 3rd*

Sitting by a lake of blue and green with clouds as white as
marshmallows, sitting on a tuffet of green peppermint sticks.
The fish were jumping up and down and swimming through their
little town. By went a little red car. The water was shimmering
like diamonds. The Indian paintbrushes paint this summer scene.
The butterflies fly like flying ribbons from my hair. I smell
the air. It smells like a creampuff donut that we are all
trapped in. It's time to go. The summer sun is going down
and the big lamp is coming along with millions of glowing
flower petals.

—*Sabine Moats, 4th*

There are stars above the arena
Glowing like the eyes of a young cowboy
As he gets off
The bull safely and wins the buckle.
There are stars above the town
Like the fireworks on the Fourth of July.
They hang in the sky
Like the lights on Main Street.

—*Craig Stoddard, 8th*

POLITICAL POEMS

This is a two-day procedure, partly because political poems tend to be flat or exaggerated in their initial drafts. On the first day, brainstorm with your students, on the board, some political issues or questions. You might bring in a newspaper for ideas. Introduce or evoke topics from school or town politics to make sure that students understand that politics is not just international or far away.

You might read them a political poem or two (for example, see the anthology, *Against Forgetting,* edited by Carolyn Forché).

Have each student pick an issue and write a poem about it. Advise them that the best way to do this is not merely to state an opinion but to make it come alive, reify it with detail, perhaps bring it down to an individual case. Recommend free verse, at least as a start (if students "find" a form as they go, fine).

Collect the poems and tell students you'll bring them back tomorrow so they can work on them further.

Before the next meeting, go over the poems and write suggestions on each as to how it might be improved or developed. Point out good phrases, rhythms, etc. You might also note down any general remarks to pass on to the class as a whole.

The next day, relay your general remarks, writing some on the board. Here's a sample list:

• Remember, we're not concerned with agree/disagree here, just effective writing.

• Focus on DETAILS—illustrate your points—make word-pictures—examine every abstraction and replace or illustrate it with something concrete—or use it in an altogether new way.

• Make comparisons.

• Consider using repeated phrases or parallel structures.

• Cut, condense, and fine-tune language.

• Define the parts of your poem—consider rearrangement.

• See if the ending is strong (an image is often better than a statement).

• Consider picking your best phrase or image, developing it, and throwing the rest away.

- Find more unusual verbs, more exact nouns.

- Rewrite slowly, questioning each word as you go.

- Try rewriting without looking at the original.

With the permission of the authors, read aloud or pass out copies of the most interesting pieces and discuss ways the poems could go.

Hand back all the poems and ask the students to reread them and to read your suggestions for several minutes. Invite any questions.

Then ask them to work on the poems. They are of course free to go counter to your suggestions—"*Don't* just 'satisfy teacher.'" Consult with students as they write, if they desire. However they go about it, they should rewrite their poems on separate sheets of paper. Ask that they work the whole time—if the poem seems finished, suggest writing "Part II"—take it in a different direction, add a different formal idea (lune, acrostic, etc.).

Collect and read.

x-ref: "Two Looks at Revision"

Why War?

Why must there be hate in the world?
What makes us long to destroy one another?   *good phrase*
Must we resort to the primitiveness
that our ancestors strived to overcome?   *Too wordy & explanatory. Find an image.*

maybe develop this picture.

Like enraged beasts   *Not bad.*
they face each other   *What kind*
for reasons they say   *of beast?*
they understand.

Their technology is   *Too general.*
truly awesome.
But still they
resort to the
way their primitive ancestors   *Repeats.*
followed

Why
he invaded
I defend
he wants more
So do I

Why War?

Why must there be hate in the world?
What makes us long
to destroy one another?
Is our ancestral hatred too much
too much to overcome?

> Like enraged apes
> they attack,
> their hidden savagery
> exposed.
> Yet they don't really
> understand why.

Their weapons have advanced.
Missiles and planes,
no rocks and bones.

> Why war?
> He invaded.
> I defend.
> He wants more.
> So do I.

—*Josh Fuellenbach, 12th*

PORTRAIT OR SKETCH POEMS

The idea here is to catch some essence of a person, as an artist's quick sketch does.

Read aloud "The Last Words of My English Grandmother" by William Carlos Williams (see "LAST WORDS" POEMS exercise), or poems of your own choice. Discuss how these poems portray a person effectively by describing in detail the objects surrounding the subject, and then showing the subject doing or saying something that illuminates his or her character. No generalized adjectives ("mean," "nice," etc.) are used. This point may well need heavy emphasis.

Have each student pick a person he or she knows well, and then list things, using exact names (e.g., "broken-down blue GMC pickup" rather than "truck"), associated with that person. You might want to work out a sample list on the board using someone every student knows.

This poem can go several ways. Usually it's good to pack a lot of visual or sound details around the person—but sometimes a stark, single glimpse will work well. Usually it's good to stress compact language, but you can leave things open for an "aerated" syntax or a series of events, in which case the piece would be more like a thirty-second movie than a snapshot.

Mention the lively characterization possibilities of particularized verbs ("shuffled" as opposed to "went"). Then ask the students to write a free-form poem (or prose piece) using some or all of the associated objects from their lists, perhaps catching the person portrayed in a revealing act, event, or bit of dialogue.

Collect and read.

A variant or warmup is to have a person (perhaps a stranger to the kids) walk in the room at the beginning of the session and do a few things, then leave. Then ask the students each to write a little piece describing that person. Compare results.

x-ref: "LAST WORDS" POEMS; THING POEMS

Upon Julia's Clothes

Whenas in silks my Julia goes,
Then, then, methinks, how sweetly flows
The liquefaction of her clothes

Next, when I cast mine eyes and see
That brave vibration each way free,
—O how that glittering taketh me.

—*Robert Herrick*

Santos

Bristly shaven, with tobacco
    breath,
cigarette butt on the ground.
Cussing his age and poking
    jokes.
The windiest-speaking man
    I've ever known.
Lifts up his black hat and
    scratches
his bald wrinkled head.
And dreams about shooting
a 12-point buck.

    —*Joey Caywood, 10th*

My grandma with grey hair
cleans house, goes shopping,
bakes cookies and pies,
goes to church and plays
    cards.
She gets lonesome a lot.
"You don't love your
    grandma anymore,
you never come visit," she
    says.
She plays dice and games with
    us
when we go visit her.
She wants things to be her
    way.
When she goes for walks she
    walks slow.
"Take time to smell the
    roses," she says.
She plants her flowers
in the spring and watches
    them grow,
then arranges a bouquet of
    flowers for me.

    —*Tami Neyman, 10th*

Wylie

Achoo!
There's no way I could forget
    Uncle Wylie's sneeze.
It sounds more like a sonic
    boom!
I can see him with his full black
    beard
and stomach sagging over his
    Bermuda shorts.
He's always worry-free,
always whistling a tune.

When he showed up to Yellow-
    stone four hours late,
his comforting voice said simply,
"We took the scenic route."

    —*Jeremy Casterson, 10th*

My Grandma Josie-May

Silky, flowery, bright
'60s-style grandma clothes
Bell bottoms
Set in her ways, she knows how
    to get what she wants
Innocent? Not really
"Don't ever put up with a man,"
    she's told me
"They're all pond scum."
A shuffling walk
A bent, sturdy back
Absolutely crazy but loving every
    minute of it
"Well shit, honey. I'm just fine,"
    she tells my mom.
"I've just got so many ailments in
    this old body I don't know
    what to do with them."
Then she sighs and walks away,
    contented.

    —*Britton D., 9th*

Slumped in an antique kitchen chair stroking his black handlebar mustache with his crooked dead finger and cigarette in hand. Legs crossed and beer sitting lightly on the table. Rambling on about unknown things. Cussing every word. Taking off his multi-colored ballcap and scratching his square half-bald head. Finally while smothering his cigarette he mumbles a few words resembling "Good-bye" and stands up with a grunt and lumbers out the door.

—*Aaron Schlueter, 7th*

Drizzle bom bom bom the sound of a drill
giving the screw a new home. It goes silent as
he sets down the drill. He stands back and looks
at a job well done and a wounded thumb. His face
red & sweaty. He goes to the radio & asks what
he is to do next yet not really listening &
when he finally gets a word in edgewise
he simply states, "I'm taking a lunch break." Soon
a yelling voice calls out, "At 9 A.M.? You're out
of your mind!" "OK," he says, "I'll take a coffee
break instead."

—*Kym Amar, 7th*

His head is under the hood of a beatup old Ford.
He bongs his head on the hood and cusses as someone
calls his name, but his Indian features relax into a smile
as he recognizes
his granddaughter.

—*Andrea Blood, 7th*

Bernardo

"Run faster!" "Hit harder!" "Get mean, baby!" yells Bernardo as he gets out of his brown Ford pickup truck at football practice. He's carrying his two-year-old son in one arm and he's wearing muddy hiking boots from his city work. He struts over to us and then a big smile grows on his worn-out, dark face and he says, "I love you guys."

—*Drew Turrill, 9th*

"PRIMITIVE" POEMS

In his anthology, *Technicians of the Sacred,* the poet Jerome Rothenberg says there are no half-formed languages, no underdeveloped or inferior languages. People who don't have the wheel may have a language with more complex grammar than our own; hunters and gatherers without agriculture have vocabularies that distinguish the things of their world down to the finest detail. For example, the Eskimo vocabulary for snow is incredibly precise, with a huge number of words to describe its various qualities and forms. Hopi Indians can, with a flick of the tongue, make subtle and exact verb distinctions to show different kinds of motion. As outsiders, we may consider other people(s) "primitive," but once we begin to understand their cultures, their intelligence and creativity and complexity become apparent.

"Primitive" poems are carried by the voice, chanted and sung. The poet becomes what the occasion demands—a dancer, a singer, a musician, or a shaman. Likewise, the form of the poem is open, ready to serve as praise, or prayer, or celebration.

This lesson works very well with any class that's studying a "primitive" culture. Students are often put off by (to them) bizarre customs. If they understand how appropriate these customs are within that culture, they will realize it is only to them, as outsiders, that things appear odd or unusual. For instance, the last line of this Bushmen poem is quite startling:

Hunger

Hunger is bad
Hunger is like a lion
Hunger is bad
It makes us eat locust.

But once students know about the life-threatening climate of the Kalahari Desert, they can come to grips with the notion of locust-eating.

Read the example poems to the class, then ask your students to consider and write about their own lives with the same tone. Have them praise nature or describe acts of bravery. Before the kids start writing, suggest that they try using comparison, repetition, and variation. Remind them of CHANT POEMS and ODES. For example, the following poem is both a chant and an ode. It's entitled "The War God's Horse Poem" and comes from the Navaho.

I am the Turquoise Woman's son
On top of Belted Mountain beautiful horses
Slim like a weasel

My horse has a hoof like striped agate
His fetlock is like fine eagle plume
His legs are like quick lightning

My horse's body is like an eagle-feathered arrow
My horse has a tail like a trailing black cloud
I put flexible goods on my horse's back

The holy wind blows through his mane
His mane is made of rainbows

My horse's ears are made of round corn
My horse's eyes are made of stars
My horse's head is made of mixed waters
                          (from the holy waters)
                          (he never knows thirst)

My horse's teeth are made of white shell
The long rainbow is in his mouth for a bridle
With it I guide him

When my horse neighs
Different-colored sheep follow
I am wealthy from my horse

Before me peaceful
Behind me peaceful
Under me peaceful
Over me peaceful
Around me peaceful
Peaceful voice and when he neighs

I am everlasting and peaceful
I stand for my horse

    —*Tall Kia ahni*

Another sample is this Bushmen poem:

Prayer for Rain

New moon, come out, give water to us
New moon, thunder down water for us
New moon, shake down water for us.

Here is one from the Quechua:

My Sun, the Golden Garden of Your Hair

My sun, the golden garden of your hair
Has begun to flame
And the fire has spread over our cornfields

Already the green ears are parched
Pressed by the presence of your breath
And the last drop of their sweat is wrung from them

Strike us with the rain of your arrows
Open to us the door of your eyes
Oh Sun, source of beneficent light

(translated by W.S. Merwin)

Note the lovely use of metaphor: burning hair, rain of arrows, sweating fields, the doors of the sun's eyes opening.

In this last poem (from the Cherokee), note how the word *listen* begins each of the threats and keeps pulling us back to the beat of the poem:

The Killer
(after A'yu'ini)

Careful, my knife drills your soul
          listen, whatever-your-name-is
          One of the wolf people
Listen   I'll grind your saliva into the earth
Listen   I'll cover your bones with black flint
Listen   I'll cover your bones with feathers
Listen   I'll cover your bones with rocks

Because you're going out where it's empty
          Black coffin out on the hill
Listen   the black earth will hide you, will
          find you a black hut
          Out where it's dark, in that country
Listen   I'm bringing a black box for your bones
          A black box
          A grave with black pebbles
Listen   your soul's spilling out
Listen   it's blue

x-ref: CHANT POEMS; ODES

Black cat
Like night
Brave as hunter.

　　—John Logan, 2nd

My horse sounds like thunder
when he runs
and when he walks he sounds
like a river.

　　—Jenny Blake, 2nd

Animals watch out because
　　I'm coming
I will praise you but watch
　　out
or you will be my dinner
　　watch　　watch
here I come on my horse
　　hey you
Lion come back I want to talk
　　to you
all right I praise I praise you
But the golden corn
You are peaceful　　peaceful
　　in a way.

　　—Camille Goddard, 2nd

Horse　　horse your mane like
　　a cloud
pretty and white
your tail gently in the wind
your legs like stilts
your ears like tepees on solid
　　ground
your wings like flags
your eyes like buttons.

　　—Crystal Davis, 2nd

I praise deer and mountains
I like deer fur　　I like to eat
　　deer
I like to watch them run
I like to look at their tracks
I like the mountains because
I like to go sledding and jeep
　　riding
I like the white tops they got
when I go sledding
I like to watch the animals
　　and deer
run and hide in the mountains
　　and it
looks like a jigsaw puzzle in
　　the sagebrush
and grass and the fur and skin
of the deer is brown
that looks like the brown
　　ground.

　　—Joshua Tabor, 2nd

"PROCESS" POEMS

The following exercise leads students through a fairly intricate process in order to get into language in a way that is partly personal and partly aleatory. Many schemes can be invented (and have); you can easily invent your own.

Ask the students to write as fast as they can, pencil never leaving paper, for two (or three or five) minutes, urging them to free-associate, to scribble any weird stuff that comes into their heads, or "just words."
Then have students pick nine words from what they just wrote and list them vertically under the freewriting. Meanwhile, write the following on the board (or any nine words of your own):

perfect
head
jump
three
air
slow
think
suddenly
word

Ask your students to write these words in a vertical column *alongside* their own list of nine. Then ask them to write, on a separate sheet of paper, a poem in which the first pair of words appears in the first line, the second pair in the second line, and so forth. The pairs of words can appear in either order, with other words between and around them. The students can vary the form of the given words, e.g., *slowly* instead of *slow*, *heads* for *head*, *thought* for *think*.
You may want (depending on the class) to try at least part of a sample poem on the board with them first, to make the process clear.
Read a student example or two aloud.
After they write, collect and read.

The random element of this exercise helps students view language as a "material" they can do a lot of things with. You might want to tinker with introducing other ways in which chance can play a role. Picking, say, the fourth word on pages 20, 40, 60, etc., in a book and "juggling" a poem out of these words is one of thousands of possible methods.

The perfect touch
of a unicorn's head.
A splash of sand when you jump in a crystal
stream, when you ride triumphantly on a unicorn through
the three golden gates you feel that springy thought
jump through your head. Leaving a trail of silver
in the air. Slowly having a tiny silver crown
on your head. Thinking you will fly through
the moon. All of a sudden the wind will
rise, sending through a shower of tiny golden words.

     —Sadie Babits, 4th

Look at the perfect tools
with black heads and
silver joints even though
they can't jump they've got
gold stamps three on each
tool they sparkle like stars
in the air above the sky
slowly moving behind the
    bushes
thinking about landing on the
    floor
all of a sudden it begins to
snow falling in the shape of
    words.

    —Jacie Green, 4th

I love this perfect world, I thought,
as I climbed a tree locked in my
    head.
There was also a plant jumping so
I tried to climb that also.
Here I live my three lives
with the slow clear white air.
The blackness slows me down as
the sun starts to think
about the pictures that suddenly
appeared in its head.
My last words helped him.
I cried, "Shine, sun, shine!"

    —Staci McComb, 6th

The following two poems by high school students were written using the first word from each line in W.H. Auden's "Nocturne."

With Love

Make the days longer, with the
Moon overseeing the earth and by
Looking for the one that will
Bless me with
Finding the single person.
And will love stay in the air?
It's like sharing with another—both in a dream
Surrounded by a background with caring, and the
Innocent babies looking as if they were watched by
An eye of the great white god looking down with
A great shine upon them.
The motion was in a sense that was there already.
Then I was awake
Looking around wondering what it was
To really be there, maybe just wishing it was and
Someday will be true.

    —David Merritt

Make this shuttle arrive at the
Moon, and keep the Ruskies from
Looking at us with bad intent.
Bless those on board,
And this time let them come home.

With a new O-Ring
Surround the once troubled spot.
Innocent be the crew who
Watched the last one fall with
White ashes that covered the sandy beaches.

Shine, as a falling star
In the midst of a cloudless night.
Wake with this goal in mind,
To keep the American people
Wishing on this far-off planet.

    —Clint May

Q & A PARTNER POEMS

The experience of second grade teacher Dorothy Olson is similar to ours:

> My students love to work with partners (as I'm certain all second graders do). One student gives a statement and the other person says the first thing that comes into his or her head. The kids really like doing this. Then we do question and answer in role-playing. There's lots of giggling! They're ready to write! I will use this method again and again. In fact, the kids ask when they'll do it again.

With very young children, try posing interesting and provocative questions, such as:

Who are you?
Who am I?
Why is the sky blue?
Will you marry me?
What are we living for?
What's outside the universe?
Who named the numbers?
What is the tiniest thing in the world?
What is electricity?
What do you see?
What's inside the color pink?

Write a few on the board, with the kids' answers. Try to choose the answers that are imaginative and various in form, not just the obvious. Humor is good, but shouldn't be the only mode of thought going.

Arrange the students into partnerships and ask *each* student to make up and write a question. Then have the partners trade papers and answer each other's question. Continue this process until they've written enough for a piece of good length.

Collect and read.

This exercise works well with older students too, although with them the example questions and answers should be more complex and sophisticated. Remember, though, that questions and answers combining simplicity and originality may be the most poetic responses of all.

Why is March so green?
St. Patrick's Day!
Why did St. Patrick's Day come?
Because it's green.
How will we get pinched?
If you don't wear green.
Does your body turn green?
Yes!
Does your hair turn green?
Yes!
Does an elf or a leprechaun come?
A green Santa Claus comes!
Do we get green toys in a green bag?
YES, YES, YES, YES, YES, YES!

 —Janie Stoddard & Kory Vanderschaaf, 2nd

What is time?
Time is the sections of the day and night.

What is life?
Life is the movement of bodies and forces relating, taking, and moving
 around other people, places, and things.

What is education?
Education is the transition of the mind.

Why is Earth round?
The Earth is round because it bounces off the sun and Mars, forming a
 ball.

When was Earth born?
The Earth was born in the Andromeda Galaxy. It was mentally born at
 the beginning of time and its mother was a blue-white star named
 Zeta Oridani.

What is inertia?
Inertia is a star-like form, near the end of the universe.

Why do people meditate?
To relax their mental needs.

 —Rhian Horgan & Lindsay Baldwin, 7th

The following is an excerpt of a Surrealist game called "Dialogues." As in children's "foldover drawings," participants collaborate on a series of questions and answers (or parts of sentences) without knowing what their partner is writing. These were written by the Belgian poet Achille Chavée and his friend Raymond Dauphin, a café owner, in 1938.

D. When time stands still
C. The forces of nature turn into laboratory jokes.

D. When a concept becomes obscure
C. Trees shed their leaves and buy themselves a wig.

D. When the individual is drowned in collectivism
C. Chance finds its nest in the ear of a poor and
   beautiful woman.

D. When a dictator dictates
C. The anachronistic law of gravity is peopled
   by silence.

D. When a star dies out
C. The eyelashes of anger flip coins.

C. What is pot luck?
D. It is the destruction of concrete data.

C. What is an attempted crime?
D. Truth bland as an English tune.

C. What is sleeping sickness?
D. It is the hot beam of the hallucinatory triangle.

C. What is the eighth wonder of the world?
D. It is the Danube peasant.

C. What is communism?
D. It is a fever.

(translated by Nicole Ball)

QUESTIONS WITHOUT ANSWERS

"Questions without answers" is one good working definition of poetry. "Without answers" means that the mind *keeps on seeking*.

Brainstorm some questions without answers with your students. It helps to prepare a few beforehand ("How high is up?" "Why is the sky?" "What are thoughts made of?" "Where is at?") to stimulate this kind of thinking.

Read a few student poems to the class, pointing out the various ways they can go, such as responding to the lead question (which can become the title of the poem) with other questions. Emphasize that, since the question is unanswerable, any response may be poetically good. The point is to get students to open up rather than just give information.

Then ask your students to invent their own questions and to write responses to them. (A variant is to pose one question for the whole class to work on.)

Collect and read.

Especially with very young children, a preliminary session may help create the right mood, such as reading a book to them that evokes cosmic questions and answers them with legends and the like. You might also try a class collaboration.

x-ref: Q & A PARTNER POEMS

How come I can't think of a
    word?
What is a word?
Wait, I do know,
Oh I know, but what is a
    word?
Wait, I do know but
what is a word? Do I know?
Wait, I don't know what is a
    word.
Do I know?

—*Jeremy, 1st*

How Low Is Low?

Is low beneath my
feet? Is low dancing
at the bottom of
my life? Or is low
dancing around me?
Did it come from
the devil? Or did it
come from me?
Or did it die
at my feet?

—*Melissa Olson, 4th*

What is Normal?

What is normal?
What is strange?
And who are you to judge?
Strange is normal
Normal is strange
Which are you?
I hope you're weird
Do you know
a normal person?
I
feel sorry for them
Never
anything crazy, anything
    weird
No hot pink windowpanes
    under purple curtains
They have white
on white
or some tasteful cream
Uggh
They drive brown station
    wagons
Why be normal
when I can be ME?

—*Katrina Dalrymple, 10th*

Where Do the Noises Go?

Where do the noises go?
Throughout the world and
    back again?
In the sky with all the stars?
Is there a big sponge that
    gathers them all?
Or do they go into all of the
    airheads?
Do the birds suck up all
    noises and give
    them back again?
Do they have a world of their
    own?
Or is life just one big noise?

—*Mindy Blayden, 10th*

What Is in the Mind?

In the midst of the hollow
something scratches as though
    it were the wind,
beating the door, tearing the
    soul.

Like a sealed box:
nothing may enter;
nothing may leave.

Like an empty skull
it pulls the sea.

—*Rhonda Webb, 10th*

How Far Is Heaven?

What does it look like?
What do angels wear?
Ballet clothes—
or suits of bright aluminum?
Do they have wings—
can they fly—
do they die,
bleeding thought?

—*Arlene Rice, 9th*

Who Am I?

Maybe a piece of
baloney with
wobbling skin
and if you bend
me I will have
wrinkles!

—*Jenny Blake, 2nd*

What Is inside the Moon?

A floating baboon.
What's inside Mars?
Two valuable cars.
What's inside night?
A little starlight.

—Heidi Hugunin, 2nd

What is inside a cat?
Who knows, maybe some-
        thing he ate,
like a mustache.

How fruity is fruit?
Maybe as fruity as fruit juice.

Who am I?
Maybe a rat or a cat
or a pizza or a bottle of
        bubblebath.

What is a shamrock?
Maybe a big pile of grass
        shaped like a leaf,
a funny leaf.

—Jenny, 2nd

Who Is the Devil?

I don't know. Maybe you
do. I don't think anybody
does. I'll find out some
day when I die or I might
not. How should I know?
I'm still alive.

—Andy Snook, 2nd

How long does space go?
It goes forever.
Where is the moon?
It is in space.
Does the moon have a face?

I don't know.

—Chris Anglin, 2nd

How Loud is Loud?

Is it a rocket in a whirl?
A quiet whisper from a girl?

Maybe a car with loud pipes
Or a child that gripes.

Could it be bright-colored
        shirts?
Checkered neon skirts?

An opera on a high note?
A dainty lady clearing her
        throat?

—John Blood, 10th

RECIPE POEMS

Discuss with your class the language used in cookbooks. Note the concision of recipe language. On the board, brainstorm a list of words from recipes, especially verbs (sift, dice, broil, sprinkle, sauté, ladle, pinch, etc.).

Read the following piece aloud, explaining that it was put together from writings by many children:

> Cut into lengthwise slices: one earful of darkness.
> Salt with cold snow falling at night.
> Sing your heart out till you break a window. Sprinkle it on.
> Add and brown slowly:
>> green pearls upon your blue eyes
>> bees flying near
>> fifty stars like your mind.
> Simmer.
> In the meantime take a trip to: Japan, the future, the sky, the sun.
> Blow electricity through a telephone. Fold briskly into:
>> the flow of going backwards and the motion of going forward.
> Beat until stiff but not dry:
>> one-at-a-time raindrops
>> falling stars when you don't expect them
>> a sign on a store window that goes off and on.
> Preheat paper to a breath in the air.
> Sift the heart in your mind that beeps into a rainstorm just standing there.
> Cover the whole thing with a zoo of heads.
> Dust the top generously with:
>> cherries in the ears
>> flags blue and white
>> the sky scraping the skyscraper.
> Bake the alphabet all talking at once until heated through
>> but don't allow the snake in your room to know what to do.
> The movie star with no fans may be cut into squares.
> The dirt rushing in your face is used to line the pickup truck dish.
> For dessert, peel the words shattered in a sort of system in your chest.
> Play music from a black bear's winter den and serve.

Write the following categories on the board (modify them if you like):

ingredients
action
tools
containers
temperature
how long to cook
accompanying music

setting or decor
serve it to whom & to how many
dessert

Then have your students write their own poems. It seems to work best when you give them (or have them choose) a non-food topic—recipes for planets, animals, boyfriends, emotions, etc. When they're done, ask them to add imaginative titles.

Collect and read.

• You may want to ask them to have the recipe be a recipe for a poem, keeping in mind that anything from typewriters to stars to love and hate can go in a poem.

• Let them know that greasy green gopher guts, fried eyeballs, and the like have already been "overdone."

Sample poems from students follow; however, the very presentation of them may be overprescriptive. Use your judgment.

The Universe

First you start with a black bowl,
And put a letter in it and stuff
And a bear and other things.

Then blend on slow,
Then add a can of mystery.
Put it in a dark window,
And wait for six hours.

Then take out the window,
Put in nine panda bears
And two mice, then one school.

Then put in a cake tray,
And bake for twenty-two days.
Afterwards glue to a wall.

—*Nickie LaMothe, 5th*

My Very Own Recipe

I have a recipe
A very small recipe
But I just can't get it right, you see, for this is what it is
Mix together a tree with a bumblebee
And all the zoos in the world, with cow moos
Dessert is very oblong
With a very weird sour sour taste
A computer is best, but don't forget a vest
With polkadot spots on it
Blend together, mix together, everything you can think of
Add a blob of grass, a big glob or blob of grass
But wait
You need music, tons of low but soft music
When do you serve it? I don't know, but first
Make a deer napkin, with a lot of dishware
My tools with leaves are very tasty, but
Don't forget the cheese
The temperature is very fast, only 10,000 for 1 hour or 2
My brother hates it but I serve it to him anyway
My sister says she loves it but after she eats it
She goes to the bathroom
It has dirt and mud in it but I like it so very much
BUT my mom won't let me make it, my recipe—
    Add pennies, nickels, toenails, dimes, grease, gas, a
    bass, grass, puzzles, muffins, bottles, quarters, fire,
    tabasco sauce, fried pears and lemon cores, and add
    25,000 pieces of chalk. Cook for the longest time. Enjoy.

    —Jenny Hawkins, 4th

How to Cook Something for a Clayfish or Two

Put in half a cup of stars along with 1 teaspoon of grassroots
and boil in water for 1 second.
When done add 2 gallons of red melted lava mixed with tree trunks,
snow, rain, and 1 quart of chopped-up waterfall.
Then get in your Corvette and drive up to heaven and get a chunk
of cloud. Then drive down to the ocean and get some sand.
Bake the following ingredients:
chimney sweep, dead flowers, and two cut-up power lines.
Then blend all ingredients together.
After done, serve to clayfish.
Also put some melted earrings on the side of the dish.

    —Jacie Green, 4th

RUBE GOLDBERG POEMS

Make photocopies of the Rube Goldberg cartoon below (from 1928) and pass them out so that each student can appreciate the intricacies of the contraption and the humor and style of the drawing.

The introduction to Goldberg's sequence begins with, "Professor Butts walks in his sleep, strolls through the cactus field in his bare feet, and screams out an idea for a self-operating napkin." This gets the kids into the whimsy of the writing. Read the rest of the caption aloud while the students follow the diagram. The machine is, of course, entirely fantastic—shooting off a small rocket and using the flight pattern of an enticed parrot to tip a perch and thus a bucket of seeds!

Ask your students to invent a gadget or machine that makes their lives "simpler and easier." (Their machines don't *have* to be wildly unusable, they can be practical too.)

You might encourage them to use numbered steps, like an instruction manual, and to illustrate their pieces with diagrams.

This lesson is similar to the recipe poem and the "how-to" poem. It invites kids to explore their (and our) fascination with gadgetry, to play with cause and effect, and to poke fun at the human tendency towards over-complication and self-importance.

x-ref: RECIPE POEMS

Professor Butts walks in his sleep, strolls through a cactus field in his bare feet, and screams out an idea for a self-operating napkin. As you raise spoon of soup (A) to your mouth, it pulls string (B), thereby jerking ladle (C) which throws cracker (D) past parrot (E). Parrot jumps after cracker and perch (F) tilts, upsetting seeds (G) into pail (H). Extra weight in pail pulls cord (I) which opens and lights automatic cigar lighter (J), setting off skyrocket (K) which causes sickle (L) to cut string (M) and allow pendulum with attached napkin to swing back and forth, thereby wiping off your chin. After the meal, substitute a harmonica for the napkin and you'll be able to entertain the guests with a little music.

How to Get Rid of Cattle in Your Yard

1. Let ants loose in attic 2. ants chew wire releasing dynamite falling into bedroom 3. pesty mouse freaks 4. grinds teeth, causing sparks to fly 5. lights dynamite 6. causing it to fly to the moon 7. blows up moon 8. causing sparks to fall on cattle 9. cattle run away.

—*Benjamin Miller, 6th*

Chopping Wood

When my dad screams
the cow jumps off the scale
and pulls a string
which flings a Chinese star
that cuts a rope
that drops a boulder
that hits a catapult
that flings a cat
that clings onto a sheet
the cat pulls the sheet off the wall
that releases the missile
that hits the wood
that blows it up into a pile
then an escalator picks it up
puts it by the fire.

—*Jaimos Skriletz, 7th*

Eating Dinner with Dirty Hands

1. Pull string dangling about your head
2. String triggers electric shock to shock cat
3. Cat runs frantically from room
4. String attached to cat's tail lights blowtorch
5. Blowtorch burns through chain holding 100-pound weight
6. Weight falls onto wooden plank
7. Plank flips up and hits a blind bird on a perch
8. Bird flies into a wall, gets knocked out, falls and lands in bucket
9. Bucket lowers and causes spoon or fork to rise to your mouth
10. You must wait about ten minutes or so to take another bite because the bird is still out cold.

—*Aaron Schlueter, 7th*

A RUN ON IMAGINATION

A good way to begin this lesson is to tell the kids, "Just close your eyes." When kids close their eyes, it enhances a very natural quality in children's writing—the ability to take an idea and run with it, changing the time-frame, playing with possibility and the fantastic, and exploring the magical realism that seems to come so easily to kids. It comes so naturally, in fact, that this lesson doesn't have much more structure than simply reading the sample poems and allowing the class to pick up and continue with the concept of pulling the reader into the race of images and narrative—almost like falling down the tunnel with Alice in Wonderland. The following example condenses a lifetime into a single running sentence:

> I'm walking by a river it sounds like it's screaming 'cause the waves are rough and I hear him singing a song and he's saying a poem and a boat comes by and I jump in the boat and the wave gives me a ride and we are so happy to be friends and I say thank you for being my friend 'cause I have no friends and I'm about to go over the cliff and my father comes, flings a rope around the boat, and brings it back and my dad says I can't come any more and I got a little older like twenty and I came back and the river gets slower and slower and I say hi and I have to leave and I come back when I'm like forty-five and I remember when I was young and I saw a boat again and this time I jump in it and this time I fell off the cliff. . . .
>
> —*Edward Rivera, 6th*

Fifth grader Jake Jacovac wrote another type of "run on imagination." In his poem he switches from the reality of being bucked off a horse into a sudden dream and then back again, pulling us with him. Notice the freedom he feels moving from the hard compacted ground to a starry night years earlier:

> It was the end of 1989. I had just got done breaking
> a little horse and I was out riding her.
> I went to lope her and she started bucking.
> I didn't stay on very long. I fell on compacted dirt.
> That split second I hit the ground I was thinking
> of when Ty Cole and I were young and Ty and I were
> wrestling those darn goats. We were racing across
> the lawn. Ty and I were sleeping under the dark blue sky
> and some bright stars.
> Then my dad came over and shook me until I woke up.

It's best to discourage the kids from concluding with the old and tired "It was just a dream." Point out to them that in this particular poem, it fits—it's not just a pat ending, a convenient answer to a bad situation, but instead brings us back to where we began—the end of 1989, loping a little horse.

Here's another example from a fourth grader:

> Driving downtown in the night I go
> faster and faster all of a sudden
> a corner so sharp it was like a knife
> I go zooming off the road I'm falling
> into the ravine. Then lights start to flash
> I fly out of my car. I feel weird inside
> so weird I can't explain it. Blue lights
> and white things surround me. Then I'm in this
> strange world. Then a voice said, "You must
> go back you are not ready to die yet."
> I felt mad at that because being there feels so good and peaceful.
> All of a sudden BOOM I'm back in the old wrecked car
> screaming for help.
>
> —*Aaron Hardinger*

Like the Jakovac poem, Aaron's poem involves a "flashback" technique, but uses it in a deft and startling way. Note how his narrative switches from present tense to past back to present. Aaron seems to be constantly asking himself, "What happened next?," creating a vivid, condensed (and dream-like) chain of actions and events; encourage your students to do this too, to feel that they are "experiencing" rather than "writing."

This next poem (by a teacher) displays a similar freefall of associative connections and unraveling fantasy:

> Dreaming of an open window, dark and empty,
> the bird of paradise caught me in time from a
> fall down an endless staircase and saved me from
> a disastrous love affair, and set me down
> beside a dinosaur hitchhiking his way to becoming a
> successful poet. From his scaly pocket he withdrew
> an ancient mirror, tinted deep blue and cracked in
> one corner. There I saw myself riding a black-winged
> steed chasing, chasing something dark and gloomy.
> In the cracked corner I caught a glimpse of moving
> clouds, and singing there were all my ancestors,
> waiting for me to join them. But not yet,
> for I was running down a dark and dirty alley—
> running for President of the United States.
>
> —*Jim Casterson*

Note how "free" association and language (e.g., "running" in the poem) redirect the narrative, taking it in unexpected directions. Encourage your students to use whatever comes into their heads, and to stay with it even if things start to get a little weird. At the same time, remind them that they must "make it real" for the reader (which is not hard, if it's real for the author).

Here's an example of some of the things we say to the students just before they begin to write.

"You'll notice that all the poems you've heard are like going inside a film or a long dream. The narrator's voice creates the scenery as you go, and there are no rules in this place. People and things pop up out of nowhere and behave mysteriously. The impossible becomes possible, and what happens next is entirely up to the imagination of the author. Now you try pulling me into your stories, running head over heels into whatever situation you can describe and flesh out. Let the momentum of the run pull us along. Let the words keep our pace strong, and write your poem like a river of words. Let's see where we end up together."

* * * * *

Another approach to the "Run on Imagination" lesson is to have students work as partners. Let the kids share a poem, taking turns controlling the impetus and events of a poem. Try asking and answering questions like "Last night guess who was pounding on my door?" with replies like "A bear wanting to borrow my hat." One student can end a sentence midway through and his or her partner can pick it up and continue. Here's an example, a collaboration between a first and a third grader:

I went in to the refrigerator
I saw a bear in the kitchen eating
a black widow spider out of a jar
and I took his hand and ran
outside at 12:00 A.M. and got away
outside in a forest. So the guy went in bed.
I saw a dog and it was a black shepherd.
He had aunts in his pants.

—Danny Compton, 3rd, & T.J. Broome, 1st

The unpredictability of this style is terrific, like two different people grabbing your hand and saying "run with me"—in two different directions. And then we all end up in the same place at the end. (At the end of the poem!)

x-ref: "On Collaborations"

SESTINAS

The sestina is a traditional poetic form, and a demanding one. For school purposes, it is probably best to do it as a class collaboration with young children (a veteran class, with ample time to work on it) or individually by older students as a take-home assignment. In the latter case, it might help to run through it as a class collaboration first.

To make a sestina (assuming you do it as a class collaboration), first choose six key words with the class. These will be used over and over as the end-words for each line in the six six-line stanzas of the sestina form. There are no rules for picking the key words, but it helps if each of them can be used in a variety of ways. *Zygote* or *puissance*, for example, would tend to stand out too much (though such words can be used for comic effect).

Next, begin composing the first stanza. Ask students to come up with six lines that somehow go together, each ending with one of the six key words. Once the first stanza is composed, the order in which the key words will appear is set for the rest of the poem. Here is the order for the six end-words for all six stanzas:

	1		5
	2		3
1st	3	4th	2
	4		6
	5		1
	6		4
	6		4
	1		5
2nd	5	5th	1
	2		3
	4		6
	3		2
	3		2
	6		4
3rd	4	6th	6
	1		5
	2		3
	5		1

There is also a three-line stanza at the end, which utilizes the six key words in this manner:

1st line—1 appears within the line, 2 ends it.
2nd line—3 appears within the line, 4 ends it.
3rd line—5 appears within the line, 6 ends it.

Notice that the key words are now back in their original order.

You can check this rather complicated scheme against the example below, and it will become clear. Elizabeth Bishop's "Sestina" is a good example, even though she scrambles the order of the end-words in the final three lines.

As chalkboard secretary, you can give the kids an idea of the form, and then simply manage it as the students call out lines. One of the kids can take down the poem on paper, if necessary. Read a sprightly example or two before beginning to write, or pass out copies. Point out how each example poem gains its variety and liveliness. At any point, you can read the whole thing aloud to help everyone keep track. Once again, the thing to emphasize and strive for is variety and liveliness in the face of the necessary repetition. Versatile end-words will help you in this, as will varying line-lengths (the inclusion of very short lines combats turgidity). Insist that the poem progress and not settle into a repetitive rut. You'll probably need to devote two class periods to the composition of a sestina. Whether the finished poem is a masterpiece or not, students will have gained some understanding of what it is to create a poem using a challenging poetic form.

High school teacher Terry Magoon suggests trying a reduced version—the tetrina, which uses four key words to end the lines in four four-line stanzas.

Sestina

Today's a special holiday
for King Kong, that special gorilla,
who jumped in the ocean,
took a mermaid and went up the mountain.
He heard the soft music
that reminded him of a black color.

The mountain was a blend of many colors
that reminded him of a holiday.
He growled the soft music,
what a famous gorilla!
He fell off the mountain
and rolled into the middle of the ocean.

Floating in the ocean,
they splashed the blue color
onto the snowy mountain,
sprinkles of joy on a holiday,
on the beautiful day of gorilla.
They floated to the beat of the music.

Roaring and singing the music,
swimming in the shining cold ocean,
the tender gorilla
with the fresh brown and black colors
covering his skin like a holiday,
floating and watching the mountain. . . .

Taller than the ivory mountain,
with his ear in the wind's music,
jumping around inside the holiday,
stronger than the radiant ocean,
bursting with color,
went the sorrow of King Kong the gorilla.

Out of the ocean came the gorilla,
coming back to the mountain,
and the mountain changed color
as it changed the music.
He let the mermaid float back into the ocean;
that was the end of the holiday.

The holiday of a magic gorilla
may flash and crash between ocean and mountain,
crash of soft music, flash of fresh color.

—Fifth & sixth grade class

157

SPANISH / ENGLISH POEMS

If your class is studying Spanish (or is already bilingual), pick a poem by Federico García Lorca, such as the following, and read it (or have it read) aloud first in Spanish, then in translation:

Arbolé, Arbolé ...

Arbolé, arbolé,
seco y verdé.

La niña del bello rostro
está cogiendo aceituna.
El viento, galán de torres,
la prende por la cintura.
Pasaron cuatro jinetes
sobre jacas andaluzas,
con trajes de azul y verde,
con largas capas oscuras.
"Vente a Córdoba, muchacha."
La niña no los escucha.
Pasaron tres torerillos
delgaditos de cintura,
con trajes color naranja
y espadas de plata antigua.
"Vente a Sevilla, muchacha."
La niña no los escucha.
Cuando la tarde se puso
morada, con luz difusa,
pasó un joven que llevaba
rosas y mirtos de luna.
"Vente a Granada, muchacha."
Y la niña no lo escucha.
La niña del bello rostro
sigue cogiendo aceituna,
con el brazo gris del viento
ceñido por la cintura.

Arbolé, arbolé.
seco y verdé.

Tree, Tree ...

Tree, tree
dry and green.

The girl with the pretty face
is out picking olives.
The wind, playboy of towers,
grabs her around the waist.
Four riders passed by
on Andalusian ponies,
with blue and green jackets
and big, dark capes.
"Come to Córdoba, muchacha."
The girl won't listen to them.
Three young bullfighters passed,
slender in the waist,
with jackets the color of oranges
and swords of ancient silver.
"Come to Sevilla, muchacha."
The girl won't listen to them.
When the afternoon had turned
dark brown, with scattered light,
a young man passed by, wearing
roses and myrtle of the moon.
"Come to Granada, muchacha."
And the girl won't listen to him.
The girl with the pretty face
keeps picking olives
with the grey arm of the wind
wrapped around her waist.

Tree, tree
dry and green.

*(translated by William Bryant
Logan)*

Discuss the dreaminess, the colors, and the musicality of the poem with the class, pointing out what you like, and have the kids point out the things they like.

Read aloud some student poems that mix Spanish and English, making the most of the sonorities of the poems.

Then ask your class to write their own poems mixing Spanish and English. Suggest to your students that they may want to create a dreamland, to write romantically, to include a lot of colors, to have mysterious strangers ride by, or whatever you feel will aid them to free up their imaginations.

Collect and read aloud.

This exercise is based on one in Kenneth Koch's *Wishes, Lies, and Dreams*.

Sea of Gold

The dove flutters softly
across el mar del oro
The playa was como lace
y la luna rises despacio
so that la arena glitters softly
alrededor de la muchacha y su
    hombre
by el mar del oro.

> —*Lynette Goddard, high
> school*

Dreamland! Dreamland! So
bright and colorful, azul,
amarillo, blanco, rojo, plata,
naranja, verde, y rosado.
The colors are so beautiful
they form a planet full of
wonderful things. That I
wish I was there. La cosa es
que yo estoy aquí con los
    colores.

> —*Jasmine Figueroa, 3rd*

B andidos
O rgullosos
Y
S abertodos!

> —*Tracy Charles, high
> school*

My house is bright blanco.
It is especial for me.
The beach is brown. I said,
Brown, Brown, you get
around. Esta tierra es
muy rojo. Como
    Chimachirichibel.

> —*Belgica Ramos, grade
> unknown*

Piedra   blow
Piedra   blow
Piedra de corazón   blow the man down.

> —*Elias Zambrane, 5th*

Bonk! Bonk! Allí viene el
    carro. Come on, move
    your car.
Cayese, dice el hombre que
    viene en
su carro rojo. Allí viene el
    carro azul.
Watch it, you dingbat! Ahh,
    we're going
to crash! Cuidado, allí viene
    el viejo borracho en su
    carro blanco!
Boom!

    —David Vasquez, 3rd

Lunes we dormir
Martes we ir
Miércoles we metir
Jueves we decir
Viernes we salir
Sábado we drink beer
Domingo we sentir enfermo.

    —Ramon, Matayo,
    Nardo, & Francisco, high
    school

Mi soñar es bailar
en rosa vestir
to float and move freely
across the floor
sentimento solo
sentimento un ángel
feeling free

    —Beatriz Bills, high
    school

Princess, Princesa, es mas
    bonita.
I'll take your heart y tu
    cabezita.
Mato el monstruo que ta te
    guardiano
y me caso with you, my love!

    —Federico Barona, 5th

SPELLING LIST POEMS

Take the current spelling list for your class and extract a dozen or so of the more interesting words from it. If the list seems too specialized, you may add some more commonly used words.

Write the list on the board, vertically. Ask the students to write poems in which one of the listed words appears in each line. A line can be of any length. Ask them to use all the words on the list, but in any order. Let them know that they may vary the form of each word from the list—by making it plural, adding *-ing* or *-ed*, adding or removing prefixes and suffixes, etc.

Read an example or two aloud. If you can make a poem yourself beforehand from your list and read it aloud to your students, all the better.

Collect and read.

A variant is to ask students to use all the words, but not necessarily one in each line.

x-ref: "PROCESS" POEMS

The following example uses words from a sixth grade spelling list. The list words are in italics only to help clarify the procedure.

Old Love

It seemed like sunshine was *illegal.*
The vast, *irregular* shapes of
midnight blotted every spark; even
the *semiprecious* stones we call stars
that sometimes *compile* themselves into a
superpower of sparkle across the
immobile, marble sky in skeins of dream
were *unseen.* It was perfect
darkness but *imperfect* life,
unlike the light that lifts all imperfections
to a messy, "perfect" day. *Inhuman* memory
among the shadows of the heart, and still *unsung.*

  —A teacher

The Perfect Mouse

I want your semiprecious mouse.
I would like to see your unseen mouse.
Does it have superpowers,
or is it immobile?
It should be illegal for me not to have it.
It would be inhuman for you to not
give me the mouse. Unlike you,
I would keep it if I were going back to Colorado.

—*Jason Linger, 6th*

The semiprecious feel of this imperfect it,
of this inhuman feeling unlike the feel of something
new and irregular, this, its unsung midnight feeling,
it's unseen to hear of compilings of words like this,
I sit here in my immobile stage feeling as if a superpower
is coming over me
. . . unsung by
anyone but me. . . .

—*Curtis Peterson, 6th*

Is it illegal to skip school?
Well, it's irregular.
I know, but it's inhuman.
You can sneak away in the midnight moon,
go into the bathroom and open up the window, crawling out
    unseen.
If someone glances your way jump into a shadow perfectly
    immobile.
It's semiprecious to go slow, go fast,
unlike a turtle.
I'll compile all these ideas and try them, maybe.
The school has a special superpower that
as soon as you walk
in it sucks your brain out.
I'm so imperfect.
So I'm unsung at school.

—*Danny Harry, 6th*

TALKING TO ANIMALS

Kids love animals and write about them with ease, wonder, and first-hand knowledge. Animal stories weave through their poems no matter what the topic. This exercise is good for all ages, but works especially well with younger kids.

You can introduce this lesson by using two model poems: William Blake's "The Tyger" and Wallace Stevens's "A Rabbit as King of the Ghosts" (see next page). First, read the Blake poem aloud. You might bring up Blake's "archaic" language and say a little about the evolution of language as well as that of poetry—how some words and phrases fall out of use and new ones are created, and how in Blake's time nearly all poetry rhymed, but not so now. Then point out some of the images in the poem—"When the stars threw down their spears/And water'd heaven with their tears" and "In what furnace was thy brain."

Blake asks the tiger how it came to be. Students can ask animals what they've always been curious to know: Where does the cat go at night? What's it like to see in the dark? Can a snake really hypnotize a chicken? Third grader Katie Ellis asked a snake,

> Are you a slithering slimy avalanche?
> How come Kitty and Everett are afraid of you?

Second grader Crystal Davis simply remarked to the buffalo,

> I can hear you breathing
> and then you walk away.

Follow "The Tyger" with Stevens's "A Rabbit as King of the Ghosts." In his poem, Stevens describes the thoughts of a rabbit watching a cat; his vivid language delights students. The language softens the tone of "The Tyger" and opens up another angle for the writer—not only asking questions of an animal but seeing things from the animal's point of view.

Writing about animals allows students to discover how much they really know about them, and how to detail their own powers of observation.

This exercise is derived in part from Kenneth Koch's *Rose, Where Did You Get That Red?*

The Tyger

Tyger! Tyger! burning bright
In the forests of the night,
What immortal hand or eye
Could frame thy fearful symmetry?

In what distant deeps or skies
Burnt the fire of thine eyes?
On what wings dare he aspire?
What the hand dare seize the fire?

And what shoulder, & what art,
Could twist the sinews of thy heart?
And when thy heart began to beat,
What dread hand? & what dread feet?

What the hammer? what the chain?
In what furnace was thy brain?
What the anvil? what dread grasp
Dare its deadly terrors clasp?

When the stars threw down their spears
And water'd heaven with their tears,
Did he smile his work to see?
Did he who made the lamb make thee?

Tyger! Tyger! burning bright
In the forests of the night,
What immortal hand or eye
Dare frame thy fearful symmetry?

—*William Blake*

A Rabbit as King of the Ghosts

The difficulty to think at the end of the day,
When the shapeless shadows cover the sun
And nothing is left except light on your fur.

There was a cat slopping its milk all day,
Fat cat, red tongue, green mind, white milk
And August the most peaceful month.

To be, in the grass, in the peacefullest time,
Without that monument of a cat,
The cat forgotten in the moon;

And to feel that the light is a rabbit-light,
In which everything is meant for you
And nothing need be explained;

Then there is nothing to think of. It comes of itself;
And east rushes west and west rushes down.
No matter. The grass is full

And full of yourself. The trees around are for you,
The whole of the wideness of night is for you,
A self that touches all edges,

You become a self that fills the four corners of night.
The red cat hides away in the fur-light.
And there you are, humped high, humped up,

You are humped higher and higher, black as stone—
You sit with your head like a carving in space
And that little green cat is a bug in the grass.

—*Wallace Stevens*

I'm going to Africa in the
  middle of school.
I'll ride a flying monkey.
When I get there the people
  will kiss me.
And the birds will teach me to
  fly. And the animals
Will make me stand on my
  head. And the water
  will throw
Fish at me. And the ground
  will make me dance.
And everything will sing to
  me.
So let's go, monkey.

  —*Bart Bateman, 4th*

Farewell Ratso farewell.
I hope you like your new
  home.
Farewell. Well, there goes
  your favorite dessert,
water skippers. Farewell
  you're going to see
something ten times bigger
  than you.
A doberman. Farewell. Adiós
  amigo.

  —*Rusty Swanson, 3rd*

G od is up there, Boris
O utsmart pheasants and
  ducks
O utrun the wind blowing the
  green grass.
D og, you are great
B ye dog bye
Y ou are the best.
E very day I think of you
D o you have fun up there in
  heaven?
O utplay me.
G oodbye I miss you a lot.

  —*Jon Green, 3rd*

A raccoon gets
chased by dogs
and people. And when
they're up there
they take pictures of em
and we developem
and my mom's a taxidermist
so that helps a lot
cause she mountsem
it's a lot like stuffinem.

  —*C.J. Tracy, 2nd*

Big cow all fat
and heavy let you soon
have a calf. What will
the big cow do. It will be
  mad!
Here comes the owner with
  some
medicine to eat! And some
  with
shot! Oh no! The worst part!
An ear tag! "Moo," says the
  calf!
The cow is mad!
She is breathing snot all over
  the owner!
And the owner was mad at
  the time.
"Grrrr," the cow says!
She is kicking!
Be careful! She might get
  worse!

  —*Carrie Loudy, 3rd*
  & Cameron Thomson, 2nd

A rattlesnake is what I'd be.
I could go in the rattle and see what
makes the noise and if I could see the air
compressor that makes them hiss
and the garden hose that shoots the poison
and the green mirrors that hypnotize a chicken. . . .
He has to put lotion on his stomach because he blisters.
He gets mad when he walks into a room
and girls scream.

  —*Mitch Jones, 5th*

Open up your door
Metamorphosis amazes me
And I want to watch you become Monarch

Open up your door
Fuzzy orange young one
You'll soon be breakable and flighty

Open up your door
What changes you this way?
Do you cry with pain when wings sprout from your body?

I'll open up your door
My curiosity is too great
You are asleep and there is nothing special

You've opened up my door
I'm dead and still larval
I'll never see the world as a king.

  —*Greg Hardinger, 12th*

The unpopular bird is a mixture between a scribble, a bird, a camel, a Cheshire cat, a deformed leaf, a pig, a dead teddy bear and that's the way the unpopular bird is made.

—*Liella Derrer, 5th*

THING POEMS

Talk up the wonders of common but relatively unnoticed objects—hand, floor, egg, sky, hair, river, piece of bread—and ask your students to write in any form they choose about one of these everyday things. Encourage them to write something that no one ever has written about this object; the point is to see the thing anew.

One potential pitfall with this exercise is that clichés tend to accrue around common objects. Talk about clichés with your class. ("Don't write, 'My hands help me to work in life.'")

You can preface this exercise by reading aloud an original "thing-oriented" poem, such as "Pleasures" by Denise Levertov (below).

Read a few student poems to the class. After your students' poems are done, collect and read.

Pleasures

I like to find
what's not found
at once, but lies

within something of another nature,
in repose, distinct.
Gull feathers of glass, hidden

in white pulp: the bones of squid
which I pull out and lay
blade by blade on the draining board—

tapered as if for swiftness, to pierce
the heart, but fragile, substance
belying design.   Or a fruit, *mamey*

cased in rough brown peel, the flesh
rose-amber, and the seed:
the seed a stone of wood, carved and

polished, walnut-colored, formed
like a brazilnut, but large,
large enough to fill
the hungry palm of a hand.

I like the juicy stem of grass that grows
within the coarser leaf folded round,
and the butteryellow glow
in the narrow flute from which the morning-glory
opens blue and cool on a hot morning.

    —Denise Levertov

Poem about "the hand"

It's got veins, it's dirty.
Knuckles like balls.
It can move, it has fingers and it has fingernails.
It has bones in it.
It has little lines and dots.
You can wear marriage rings on it.
The lines look like lightning.
Your hand can look like a spider.
The fingers can look like snakes crawling in the grass.
It can look like a pumpkin with a stem.
It can look like a starfish.
It can change different colors when you squeeze it.
It can look like sandbars when you squeeze the two together.
It can wear clothes and be Spuds McKenzie.
Blue veins like rivers with boats sailing down them.
Your hands can move with muscles.
You can make cookies with them.
You can tie strings around your fingers.
You can wash them.
You can grab cookies and things.
You can grab grass.
You can break things, like punching paper,
    styrofoam, sticks, cups, cookies (in half).
You can clean fish.
You can break a pig, or a piggybank.
You can break a counter.
The hand has blood.
Purple veins like thunder.
Like rivers splitting up.
You can read.
You can rip things. Paper, cardboard, shirt material.
You can build houses, clocks, snowmen.
You can hold things—cups, snakes, toys, babies,
    the flag, pictures, calendars.
You can build doors, fences, windows, curtains.
You can chop trees.
You can feel things—paper, wood, a baby.
You can cut paper.
You can move clocks.
You can make puppy dogs.
You can pick up snow and throw it.
You can push heavy boxes.
You can comb your hair.
You can write.

—*First grade class, Salmon, ID*

My hand is a train
that is stopping
at a red light.

My hand is a
monkey swinging
from tree to
tree.

My hand
is holding
the American
flag. I am
proud of my
hands for
doing all of
this writing.

My hand looks like an
    anteater
that is looking for an ant.

When I get my hands cold
they feel like they are going to
    explode!

My hand is a bouncy ball
    bouncing
all the way out of Idaho.

My hand is a bus taking
    everyone to school.

My hand is a genius at work.

My hand is a
beautiful flower
blooming.

My hand is a kitten purring
    for food
but my owner won't
give me any food!

    —Megan Bills, 2nd

My hand

my hand
has blood
and bones
my hand
has a river
in that
river there's
blood and
bones in
that blood
there's a man
floating in
the bloody
water in
my hand.

    —Joe Ganske, 4th

Clouds are like a never-ending
    filmstrip
of animals and things like
    hamburgers,
ice cream, yogurt, islands, and,
    best
of all, weapons. But if you
    understand,
it will come after you to tell
you what it is. You grab the
food but it turns to water
and drenches you.

    —Shane Jensen, 7th

It's about five inches long, three inches wide, covered with an elastic sheet bearing many fine, dark, yielding blades. Underneath the sheet are four hard ridges spanning its length, ending at four hard knobs. Stuck to the underside of the thin sheet is a network of green tubes. When the sheet is pulled, the tubes are pulled with it. Etched out of the surface of the sheet are thousands of lines criss-crossing as though it were an intricate jigsaw puzzle. In one corner, opposite the knobs, is a tiny red dot. Closer to center is an equally small brown dot. It is neither hot nor cold to human touch, and it feels neither dry nor damp, though rubbing it reveals many more grooves and ridges between the four visible ridges. It is utterly without taste, though the sheet lends itself easily to being sucked between teeth and tongue. When they're wet, the fine spikes rooted in the sheet become pasted to it. A thousand times larger, it could be mistaken for a semi-arid landscape, especially with its shallow cracks and sandy color. At that size its flatness, coupled with its grooves and bumps, would make it a good candidate for a typical, neglected street.

—*Ted Dace, college*

A rock is like a big pretty hill
all bumpy and round that you can
throw and break a window and glass
will shatter.

An egg is like a big breakable rock
that you can throw and it will break
into little pieces like glass in the
beautiful green grass.

—*Karen Bradley, 5th*

"THINGS TO DO" POEMS

The basic idea of this exercise is quite simple: title a poem "Things to Do . . ." in a particular place (the bathroom, Indianapolis, the Milky Way) or time ("at midnight," "while following fox tracks in the snow," etc.) and then write the lines as simple directives.

Naturally the things in the poem should express the place or activity—but not exclusively, and not just what the reader expects. Any thing or act is full of odd mysteries or offbeat connections for poetry to bring out, so urge students to get beyond the typical, and to consider their language—whether it should be plain or fancy or both.

Read a few examples aloud, pointing out their variety and the keenest surprises.

Ask the class to write. You can have students think up their own subjects, or you can have everyone work on the same one. Collect and read.

x-ref: LIST POEMS

Sandpoint

Pick a gallon of huckleberries up on Bald Mountain for pies and pancakes.
Go to Schweitzer for skiing.
Jump off the Pack River Bridge and do a bellyflop.
Fish for a gigantic brook trout from a pond a mile away from my home.
Gape as a bullmoose runs through the school field.
Watch the Bulldogs rush a long run at Bulldog Stadium.
Go jump off the dock at Sandpoint City Beach.
Win the beauty pageant. Now I'm a Snow Queen.
Get knocked over by a jumping white-tailed deer.
Play video games at Squatty Bodies.
Watch a moose eating moss from the creek by our house on Sunnyside Mountain.
Trot up to Lost Lakes, Idaho, on my Shetland pony named Christy Christmas Renee Barnes.
Rollerskate on the refinished rink at Bonner Mall.
Drive to Sunnyside to see an eagle's nest of sticks with little birds inside.
Take pictures of fantastic snow sculptures.
Crash the snowboard on a ski run.
Go camping and watch an eagle flip over to attack and claw a bird.
Break an arm at Lincoln School and faint.
Jump my bike off the docks at Lake Pend Oreille.

Swim underwater to get it.
Watch elk drink and swim in our beautiful lakes.
Go to Klondike Mike's Frozen Yogurt and ask for samples.
Get tired as heck on a 15-mile bike-a-thon.
Go to Cavanaugh's Casuals and look at the neat skateboard stuff.
Have more fun in Sandpoint than anywhere else.

—*Fifth grade class, Sandpoint, ID*

Things to Do on the Plane to Austin, Texas, from Denver

Wish you could spit out the window.
Wish the person in the bathroom would hurry up.
Wish they had comic books instead of airport info magazines.
Wonder what's in the so-called food.
Have any kind of soft drink you want.
Wish we could "buzz" the capitol.
Look at the clouds that seem to look like things.
Wonder why the pilot had the hiccups and was walking funny and had bad breath.
Wonder why the cloud we are about to go through is steel and has wings.
Wonder what the co-pilot meant when he said, "Ahh, we're all gonna die!"
Wonder why the stewardesses were passing out parachutes.

—*Jamie C. Jack, 6th*

Things to Do at My House

sit in my chair
watch a little TV
break my horse Spike
get bit by my dog
spit in a cup
watch the dust blow by
shoot my guns, my bow too
throw a lariat at a bale of hay
chase a few chickens, break a few eggs
tease my brothers
fight with my mother
run over some cats
shoot a few cows
ride up in the hills on Spike with my dog
get bucked off
horse runs away
long walk home
to find Spike eating hay
my house is boring
I want to move away.

—*Hoke Morton, 10th*

"THIRTEEN WAYS OF LOOKING" POEMS

Using Wallace Stevens's poem "Thirteen Ways of Looking at a Black-bird" as a model poem makes for an exciting exercise that really challenges students to look at things in new and different ways. Stevens's poem (see excerpt below) focuses on a single subject and reexamines it in a series of imaginative leaps. Here are some of the different approaches Stevens uses:

- comparing and contrasting
- making plural and giving motion to
- suggesting the mysteries of a thing
- telling the story from multiple perspectives—taking on differing roles, positions, and personae
- using free association: making dream-like moves and images, moving around freely in time and space
- discovering the unseen beauty in things

Thirteen ways of seeing something is like having thirteen different subjects. Have the students imagine their object in many different places and roles. The common theme of the object (like the blackbird in Stevens's poem) can tie together a very diverse collection of descriptions.

Thirteen Ways of Looking at a Blackbird *(excerpt)*

I
Among twenty snowy mountains,
The only moving thing
Was the eye of the blackbird.

II
I was of three minds,
Like a tree
In which there are three blackbirds.

III
The blackbird whirled in the autumn winds.
It was a small part of the pantomime.

IV

A man and a woman
Are one.
A man and a woman and a
    blackbird
Are one.

V

I do not know which to
    prefer,
The beauty of inflections
Or the beauty of innuen-
    does,
The blackbird whistling
Or just after.

VI

Icicles filled the long window
With barbaric glass.
The shadow of the blackbird
Crossed it, to and fro.
The mood
Traced in the shadow
An indecipherable cause.

VII

O thin men of Haddam,
Why do you imagine golden birds?
Do you not see how the blackbird
Walks around the feet
Of the women about you?

—*Wallace Stevens*

6 Ways of Looking at a
    Butterfly

1. Look up
2. Look down
3. Look on a flower
4. In a tree, on the ground
5. Turn around
6. Look at me.

—*Tessa Barsalou, 2nd*

5 Ways of Looking at Time

1. A never-ending dream
2. Traveling to the future and
    past
3. Holding still to fly
4. Nights of staring at the
    moon
5. Days of gazing into space.

—*Phillip Gilpin, 6th*

2 Ways to Look at a Pig

1. Sloppy
2. Dinner

—*Zeke Smith, 6th*

20 Ways to Look at a History Test

1. Upside down
2. in the air
3. in the snow
4. at midnight
5. underwater
6. in the dark
7. at school
8. all ripped up
9. in the jungle
10. cross-eyed
11. at three o'clock P.M.
12. while eating ice cream
13. with glasses on
14. by a fire
15. while playing tag
16. while listening to music
17. while talking on the phone
18. while painting your nails
19. while watching TV
20. in someone else's hands.

—Misty Winteroud, 7th

10 Ways of Looking at a Zebra

1. When I look at a zebra, I get all dizzy.
2. If you go to the zoo, you'll find trees,
    bushes, grass, and a zebra.
3. I wish I could take an apple to the zoo
    and feed it to the zebra, but you're not
    allowed to feed the animals.
4. I want a pet zebra.
5. I would feed it hot porridge every morning.
6. I would give it spaghetti for lunch.
7. And a drumstick for dinner.
8. My family would move out of the house
    then my zebra would have its very own stable.
9. I would call her Emma.
10. And then it wouldn't have to live in a zoo.

—Julia Lee, 2nd

3 Ways to Look at a Rabbit

One. A ferocious beast ruining
    gardens across America and
    the rest of the world. Of
    course, he eats gardens
    to stay alive.
Two. A nice animal trying to
    stay alive of course he is
    ruining gardens all over
    America and the rest of the
    world.
Three. A nice beast trying to
    make a good but intimidating
    reputation for himself,
    in a world full of hunger and
    gardens.

—Vaughn Sandman, 5th

8 Ways of Looking at Life

1. Swaying in the breeze a
    willow whips. Is it life?
2. Wouldn't it be easier if I
    was a rock?
3.
4. Watch TV. There go two
    lives
5. Peach through life
6. From head to toe
7. Spider to human
8. The ways of looking at life
    will always be through
    mind.

—Penny Stenerson, 7th

12 Ways of Seeing Bluebirds

1. An outline of a bird in the sky but all you see
    is blue.
2. Blue in a tree? It must be a bluebird.
3. A pretty bird that doesn't do any good.
4. A shadow on your face, but then it's gone.
5. You ride along in the summer. A bluebird
    stands in the road.
6. The dentist's office has a bluebird decoration.
7. The great state of Idaho has a great bird of
    blue.
8. I see a bluebird in some people's eyes.
9. Peeking out from the leaves a beak and blue
    faces.
10. Flying in the sky defiant of gravity and the
    sun is a bluebird.
11. Resting in a tree the bluebird closes his eyes.
12. Gliding through the air I am a bluebird too.

—Jessica Dalrymple, 7th

USED TO / BUT NOW POEMS

This exercise is especially appropriate for very young children.

Establish a loose, humorous, imaginative mood. Introduce the idea of *used-to-but-now* to the class. Work out a sample list on the board with them, trying to make each line a surprise—not, for example, "I used to be a kitten but now I'm a cat." Many other connections can be established besides standard growth; logic can be transcended, as in the samples on the following pages.

Ask students to write their own poems. You might suggest that they use the shortcut of ditto marks, after the first line, for the "I used to . . ." and the "but now. . . ." Collect and read.

The idea of "used to / but now" is from Kenneth Koch's *Wishes, Lies and Dreams*.

I used to be afraid of the water,
  and the trampoline, and the
  first day of school.
Now I'm afraid of black widows
and avalanches while I'm skiing.
I'm afraid of the military and
old gold mines, and getting
lost in a mall.

—*Chris Anglin, 3rd*

I used to be afraid of clumsiness,
people with long fingernails.
Now I'm afraid of my mom falling
  in love and leaving me. And us
  moving away from all our
  friends.
I used to be afraid of my sister.
Now I'm afraid of things like
  surgery, drugs, and my mom
  getting remarried.
I used to be afraid of Frankenstein.

—*Marina Bartel, 3rd*

I used to be a can but now I'm
  recycled!
I used to be an egg but now
  I'm cracked.
I used to be a can but now I'm
  garbage.
I used to be the sun but now
  I'm the moon.
I used to be a horse but now
  I'm dogfood!
I used to be paint but now I'm
  a painting.

—*Becky Barsalou, 1st*

I used to be a kangaroo
but now I'm a golfer.

—*E. J. Infanger, 1st*

I used to be a letter but now
I'm a mailbox.
I used to be a rabbit but now
I'm a bunny.
I used to be a plant but now
I'm a flower.

—Bobbi Easton, 1st

I used to be an umbrella but
now I'm soggy.
I used to be a thought but
now I'm poetry.
I used to be dead but now I'm
alive.

—Ed Bowers, 1st

I used to be a kid but now I'm
a boy.
I used to be m but now I'm n.
I used to be an umbrella but
now I'm broken.

—Brody Miller, 1st

I used to be afraid of the toilet.
The blowdryer. I used to be
afraid of taking a shower. I
used to be afraid of being
home by myself. I used to be
afraid of Shadow when he
tried to bite me when I was
getting on the monkey bars. I
used to be afraid of the bus
driver in first grade. I used to
be afraid of boys with long
hair that would ride the bus.
Now I'm afraid of the bad
dream lady who lives under
the bed.

—Kira Phillips, 3rd

I used to be a bow but now
I'm untied.
I used to be a bee but now I'm
a honey.

—Lacy Wiley, 1st

I used to be afraid of my teachers
I was afraid of some people on TV
But now I'm afraid of guys that
ride
Motorcycles and carry
Guns behind their backs
And ask where a person is.

—R.J. Buster, 4th

I used to be a circle but now I'm blue in prison.
I used to be glasses but now I'm summer.

—Crystal Kearns, 2nd

I used to be afraid of the toilet because
I always thought it was going to send
the toilet people up to kill me & hospitals
because I'm afraid the doctors will kill me during
the operation.

But now I'm afraid of life in general.
I'm afraid of Death.
I'm afraid that tomorrow I will turn
around and face reality.

—Michelle McComas, 8th

I used to be afraid of the dentist, doctors, creaky old houses, elec-
trical outlets and appliances, running over any animal, using public bathrooms, my stepmother, being weird, different, haircuts,
knives, guns, arrows, teachers, someone under my bed, night-
mares that come true, bears, people with fake teeth, bald heads,
barbed wire fences, ickies in creeks, streams, etc., noises in the
middle of the night like firearms, losing my mom because of some
man, getting in another wreck, having more operations, high
schoolers, plaid colors, bellbottoms, men with large sideburns on
their faces, and getting lost.

But now I'm afraid of the people in the government, atomic and
nuclear bombs, not being a mature adult with wise decisions, dying, being lonely, irresponsible, loving, and poverty.

—Melissa Trueax, 8th

WATER POEMS

If it weren't for the rocks in its bed
The stream would have no song.
—Carl Perkins

Fishing, near-drownings, floods, aquariums, rainstorms, sprinklers, fire plugs, bathtubs, ponds, lakes, streams, oceans, dripping faucets, swimming pools, and swimming holes: whatever the circumstances, everyone has a story about water; it fascinates all of us landlubbers on planet Earth.

We first tried this exercise in a combined first and second grade class where it generated vast numbers of water-related memories. Every student wanted to tell his or her story. One girl in the class, for example, loved to climb up on the bathroom counter to watch her father shave. She pretended she was shaving too, scraping a finger along her cheek, poking out her upper lip with her tongue, and drawing off the soapsuds. One day she lost her balance and fell, stepping into the toilet. Her father told her to keep her foot in the toilet while he flushed it, which would rinse off her foot. She cried and refused, imagining herself sucked into the sewer and lost. Her father told her that no matter what, no matter how much water, he would never loosen his grip and she would never be torn from his arms. This example highlights a real fear among younger students (and amuses older ones); it's also an example of how poetry can involve ordinary things, with a twist of surprise.

This exercise needs very little introduction. Keep class discussion brief—you might just list sources of water on the chalkboard to jog students' memories and widen their choices.

Or you might read a model poem, such as Langston Hughes's "The Negro Speaks of Rivers" or Guillaume Apollinaire's "Pont Mirabeau."

Nate was fishing
and I
was a trout.
I looked like a rainbow
going through the water.
I was so beautiful
jumping through the air.
My mom and dad threw their
lines into the water to catch
    me
but I said NO.

—*Nathan Ware, 3rd*

If it wouldn't be for the mountains
we wouldn't have lakes if it weren't
for the lakes we wouldn't have any
    water
if it weren't for the cars how would
we get to places if it wouldn't be for
the world where would we live?

—*Michael Busby, 2nd*

The Falls

Water wriggles in the
song of spirit that falls
into a beautiful waterfall
that falls by a seed
the seed becomes a
tree of money and some
people came and with the
 money
on the tree they bought a
 store
and with the tree in the store
they made paper and the
 paper
went to Mrs. Olson's class
and one of the papers
went to Ed's desk
and he saw Sheryl
and he wrote a poem
called The Falls.

 —Ed Bowers, 2nd

At the swamp
I caught a frog
It had tiger legs.

 —Clint Dalrymple, 1st

W aves splash
A t the sky
T onight
E veryone looks
R ainbows
F alling
A ngels
L aughing
L ullabyes.

 —Libby Livingston, 2nd

River of No Return

One day I dropped my shoe
in the river. My shoe
disappeared in the mist.
I ran to my mom
and said, Mama Mama
I dropped my shoe in the
river. She said, you naughty
boy, you get that shoe.
But Mama. Now now it's
your fault.
So I went and sat on
the bridge. I watched and
 watched
and watched. I watched the
 sun
go down. Some ducks
flew by and fell in
and I floated away
and I found my shoe
in heaven.

 —Daryl Mudd, 5th

Go beneath the ice
on top of a roaring river
which is waiting to pull you
 under.
Its cold iron hand pulls
its voice is laughing while you
 are struggling
it cuddles you as you drift to
 death
not knowing that you are
 dying.
As it loosens its grip you fall
into the rhythm of the waves
and flow along with them.

 —Jessy Wiley, 4th

The Rain of Fragrance

As I walk on the desert a drop of rain comes down but not just any rain the
rain of fragrance as I still keep walking I hear voices of singing women and
still the smell of fragrance every time I see women pouring buckets of per-
fume into the air. At last I stop and I disappear into the rain of fragrance.

 —Luis Perez, 6th

181

WILLIAM CARLOS WILLIAMS IMITATIONS

Write on the board (or distribute copies of) the following poem:

This Is Just to Say
I have eaten
the plums
that were in
the icebox

and which
you were probably
saving
for breakfast

Forgive me
they were delicious
so sweet
and so cold

Then tell them the story behind the poem: William Carlos Williams, who was a doctor as well as a poet, arose before his wife Flossie one morning, went into the kitchen, and saw in the "icebox" (fridge) a bowl of cool, tasty-looking plums. He knew Flossie was looking forward to having them for breakfast, but temptation led him to gobble them up himself. Then he felt a *little* sorry and left her a note of apology.

Being a poet—and a poet who loved to bring small, daily reality into verse—Williams thought that the note could be a poem. He broke it up into short lines to show off its rhythm. It hadn't occurred to *anyone* before that time that such a homely detail, in conversational language, could contain the wonders of a poem. The poem is now quite famous.

Point out to the class how the *s* sounds in the last three lines help create a mouthwatering effect that changes the whole psychology of the poem—he's really more impressed with how good the plums tasted than he is sorry that he ate them.

Tell the students frankly that a difficulty with imitating this idea is that the poems tend to come out heavy-handed:

Hey, too bad I
kicked your butt and
poured beer down
your pants
but it was fun!

Ask them to get beyond the obvious joke and get that delicate twist in there, with a balance of sorry and not sorry. Also urge them to feel free to *depart* from Williams's language. The title can be altogether different, too—"Sorry, Sis, But . . ." or "Gosh, I Didn't Know."

Read a variety of student examples. Ask your students to write only one poem each, leaving only a short writing time.

Since, in the same classroom hour, you can probably do another Williams poem, ask the students to keep their papers and volunteer either to have them read aloud by you as you walk from desk to desk, or to read them themselves.

Then ask them to turn their papers over, and proceed to the second poem. Write the following on the board, also by Williams:

So much depends
upon

a red wheel
barrow

glazed with rain
water

beside the white
chickens

Mention that this poem presents a big change in tone from the first poem. Then discuss "The Red Wheelbarrow"—how its extreme simplicity makes it stand out. Discuss the meaning, which has little or nothing to do with the utility of wheelbarrows, but is really in praise of common things expressed in plain images—these are the ordinary objects Williams would have seen in a walk around his small New Jersey town decades ago. Talk up the beauties of neglected everyday sights.

Read them some student samples. Possible "lead-ins" can be "Parts of my day," "What's around," "When I look," etc.

There's a danger that students' poems may become mired in "pretty-flower" clichés—warn them about this, and suggest they might want to try for unexpected combinations.

Ask them to write. Collect and read.

I'm sorry I ate your lunch.
I'm sorry I ate your breakfast.
I'm sorry that I'm going to eat your supper.

—*Carlos Cintron, 4th*

I Am Sorry to Say

I shot a bird today.
The dog watched as the wind
    blew through its wings.
It landed in the field, its heart
    cold but warm inside.
The wind turned pink white
    and grey as the bird fell.

    —*Leslie Gwartney, 4th*

This Is Just to Say

Sorry for embarrassing
you at the dance when I
    poured spaghetti
on your white dress but it was
kind of interesting looking at
    you
while you were screaming at
    me
for doing that.

    —*Angela Knight, 11th*

My Back Lawn

A swing, porch, fence.

Time to go to bed. Oh! my
cat knocked down the tent.

Do I have to start again?

No. A dog, a lawn
and me.

    —*Mark Drew, 2nd*

This Is Just to Say

I loved
pushing you on
a swing

Especially when
you flew over
the fence.

    —*Amy Beth Milan,*
    elementary

I am sorry I
let your
sister spill the
juice but
it looked like
orange raindrops
falling from the
sky.

    —*Kerry Washington, 1st*

So much depends on

the cat on the
car

the father in the
chair

the skidmarks in the
driveway.

    —*Vic Petersen, 12th*

So much depends
upon

a clock

a window

a
map

and
darkness

  —*Wes Woodward, 4th*

So much depends on

Halley's comet
my black cat Blinky
eating the middle of an Oreo
cookie
my life of darkness
a flaming match

  —*Kim Knabb, 5th*

So much depends
upon
aluminum siding
Well

maybe not

  —*David Phillips, 8th*

WORD PAIRS

This exercise is suited to very young children.

Either by yourself or with another teacher or friend, write two words on each of a few 3" x 5" cards, to serve as examples. The words need have no connection with each other. They might well be "favorite" or fancy words that simply go together in an odd or funny way, such as:

BURIED   **HELIOTROPE**   **PENGUIN**
SMILES   **LIMESTONE**   **DUST**

The sample word pairs needn't be restricted to a first or second grader's vocabulary. Write the words in elaborate or colorful ways.

Bring a packet of blank 3" x 5" cards to class, and have on hand plenty of markers, pens, and pencils for various colors, shadings, etc.

Show the kids your examples. Ask them to take one blank card each, think of a favorite word, maybe check the spelling with you, and then write it artistically on the upper half of the card. When they have done this, have them trade cards with their partners and have each partner write a second word on the card—either an unrelated favorite or a playful response.

Collect, read aloud, and pass around.

If the kids don't follow your directions exactly, that's all right. Whatever result looks interesting is fine.

Then glue the cards on black construction paper, say two to a page, cocking them this way and that at various angles, and you will have a little book that can serve as a visually appealing testament to the students' creative feel for words and letters, and a reminder that words can be both aesthetic units and objects of creative play.

x-ref: CONCRETE POEMS

On Integrating Poetry and Standard English Classes

I look on poetry as a way to do things.
—Tina Olsen-Cooper, teacher

Neither of the authors of this book is an English teacher. We hope that our suggestions here may have the "outsider's luck" to be something new that really works well for you in the classroom.

Many of the writing exercises and tips in this book *naturally* integrate the poetic approach into regular language arts activities. The "I Remember" poem encourages students to write clear, detailed sentences; the haiku and the lune encourage focus on minute syntactical effects. But the chief help to good writing that the poetic approach provides is not to teach grammar (not directly, anyway), but rather to increase students' love of language. The basic idea is this: if you find excitement in writing, you'll be more likely to write attentively and abundantly. If you write a lot, with focus and energy, you'll get good at it through sheer involvement.

We recommend a many-sided approach, ranging from pure drills to "wild" poetry. And it may be that letting the kids in on your intent and strategy as a teacher (explaining that you want to work with language from various viewpoints, followed by a specific remark like "Today we're simply going to work with verbs—action words—and tomorrow we'll write action poems") will help boost student attitudes toward their work. They understand, for example, the role of rote physical exercise in sports when preparing for a game. When they enjoy the "game" of writing, they can see how verbal pushups and forty-yard language wind-sprints fit in.

In addition, even the driest drill can be enlivened with funny, beautiful, colloquial, up-to-date, colorful language. If the text you're using gives "Betty walked home with her dog" as an example including a prepositional phrase, change it to "Queen Elizabeth trotted upstairs with her yodeling armadillo." Far from distracting the students, such playfulness will energize student attention, get them working, and make grammar and syntax stick in their minds. The students will not feel that studying language is just isolated nitpicking. William Carlos Williams's "So much depends upon a red wheelbarrow glazed with rainwater beside the white chickens" can be studied as a sentence too; you and your students can make sentences to fit its form:

And everything develops
from

a bright, clear-eyed
kid

playing with word
music

among mind-mouth-
hand.

However, it's hard to teach kids mechanics *and* poetry at the same time and really do justice to poetry. It might be best not to try too hard, and not to label it "poetry," but simply to work in an in-between category you might call "Creative and Entertaining Ways of Studying English." Lively grammar exercises can benefit poetry and other writing skills if presented as just *one* aspect of language—not its be-all and end-all.

Revision ties directly into the standard English curriculum, but students usually have little appetite for it, at least initially. They tend to be satisfied when they write anything at all, especially in the first flush of their own voices (which often *do* have a certain charm and integrity), and then stop there. "Why mess up a good personal statement? This is really me!" They don't realize how much more "me" there is to bring out. Also, they have little sense of what—or how—to revise. But writing is above all a *process of discovery*. Writing over and over, one finds more each time that was tucked somewhere in the amazingly complex and commodious brain, just waiting to be tickled out: ways of saying things, closer focus, half-hidden memories. One technique is to have students put away their first drafts, re-do them from memory and further imaginings, and then compare. They can do this several times (perhaps with different nudges—toward physical description, feelings, sound, and rhythm), and stitch together the best version at the end. (See "Two Looks at Revision" for more on this.)

Of course, attempts have always been made to make English "interesting," mostly through the use of stories and other literature. But these efforts have mainly treated language as a transparency: a mere conductor of the plot, character interplay, symbolism, historical relevance, etc. This approach scants the capacity of language itself to astonish, as if beyond grammar there were nothing to say about language. So the language arts curriculum has typically leaped from pragmatic structure to subject matter, leaving a big gap—the creative. The poetic approach revives everything in the in-between *pleasure* of language that small children and poets revel in—that we all revel in, at least subconsciously, as we talk. And within that revived pleasure is also a means of expression and expanded truth.

When students regularly write *as part of the process* of learning about literature, they're operating in the educational tradition in which people learn by doing, as opposed to observing passively. This is the way people learn almost everything. Imagine a doctor who'd only read books about medicine. And we are all active in literature all our lives; we speak and in varying degrees we write. Of the sixty major and the many minor exercises in this book, a number can be adapted to almost any literature up for study. You can also invent your own writing exercises (see "On Inventing and Adapting Exercises"). Writing parodies is an excellent way of studying styles—you have to note exactly what the author's doing in order to play off it. Beyond these correspondences, general hands-on creative writing energy brings students much closer to an understanding of what great writers have done.

Students don't need an extensive historical and analytical introduction to poetry before they themselves learn to write it. It's not necessary, and can in fact be harmful and inhibiting, to overintroduce the subject of poetry. Kindergarteners do not study Rembrandt before they begin making their own paintings and drawings. (Of course, historical study *along the way* is of great value.)

In auto mechanics class, the car is not studied so much for its historical repercussions or for its symbolic significance as for its *use*—how to keep it running. The language arts could profit from this emphasis. Perhaps it's been merely a philosophical conceit—the separation of the "noble" mind from the "lowly" body—that has kept simple empiricism (hands-on learning) in the background of scholarship so amazingly long.

*　　*　　*　　*　　*

Some ideas on studying literature:

• Begin with contemporary literature and work back in time (though there can certainly be eddies in this current, such as fairy tales for the very young). Contemporary language is usually easiest for the kids to understand.

• When possible, play recordings of poets reading their own works; listen to them more than once.

• Pay close attention to rhythm and sound. Read (expressively) parts of a given poem over and over to show the physical attractions of the language.

• Discuss meaning (when you do) in a down-to-earth way that leaves room for a sort of multiple, spreading symbolism. This, rather than "hard-edged" one-to-one explanations, is usually true to the way the poet's mind works. Varying interpretations may well be valid.

• When interpreting, leave room for playfulness and unexplainable "dream" or subconscious combinations. Emphasize originality of syntax as a delight, as well as a device.

• Speak of authors' lives frankly and honestly—this humanizes them for students—but don't let biography override the author's work. Don't psychoanalyze the author.

• Try to put different types of poetry in perspective for the kids: for instance, much older poetry, with its conventions of "tight" structure and leisurely revelation, may be hard for students to take in at first. Sometimes they'll get used to it by hearing it a lot; sometimes *in addition to* the original language of an old poem, you can "translate" it into today's idiom. This will demystify both the poetry and the past for the students.

* * * * *

Here are some ideas for enlivening standard English instruction:

• *Substitution techniques.* Ask students to substitute their own adjectives for all the adjectives in a passage under study. Or ask them to substitute more particular, vivid verbs for all the verbs in a passage of their *own* writing. Extend this idea to other parts of speech.

• *Fourteeners* (see exercise). Ask students to rewrite a sentence in a number of different ways, such as rearranging word order (even into abstract permutations), altering vocabulary, adding details, substituting details for generalizations, delving "behind" the sentence, etc.

• *Concrete poetry* (see exercise). Have the class make visually oriented versions of words and phrases, creative pictorializations of sentence diagrams, etc.

• *Imitation of models.* You can (still) ask students simply to copy passages of great writing, which, oddly, can bring about an intimacy between the author and student. Or ask students to recreate a piece from memory; to write lists of the characteristics of a work and then write in that style; or to take notes in a specified time, then rewrite from the notes and make comparisons with the original.

- *Expanding simple sentences.* Ask the class to flesh out the picture of, say, "Jim walked up," until Jim's arrival has been extended into a whole story or poem.

- *Trade-off "games."* Have the students exchange their writings with one another, read them, and then write, say, ten questions that come to mind, as helpful criticism. Or have them try rewriting each other's pieces. Instruct the students to consider anything from grammar through the creative to the personal. (See "On Collaborations.")

- *Use of dictionaries, thesauruses, etc.* To encourage the habit of browsing through the dictionary, have your students play various dictionary games (see "On Quickies: Icebreakers and Fillers"). Ask them to find an idea for a poem by looking in a dictionary. Suggest methods of making abstract poems from dictionaries, choosing words randomly.

- *Detail exercises.* Have the class describe the minutiae of a food, a place, a car, etc., emphasizing whatever aspect of English studies you wish.

- *Tapes.* Ask students to talk on tape (relating, perhaps, an anecdote from their experience), then to transcribe and rewrite. Ideally, the freshness of speech will merge with the coherence and economy of writing.

- *Onomatopoeia exercises.* Have students write a description of a galloping horse that sounds like one, or give a splish-splash rendition of a six-year-old in the bath. They'll discover a sense of onomatopoeia much more extensive than they would in studying isolated examples, such as *buzz.*

- *Distilling lists of young tongue twisters.* Have your students make up their own tongue twisters (which amount to jammed alliteration, mostly). This creates an opportunity for revision—kids will see the need for it.

- *Chant techniques* (see CHANT POEMS). Try using chant techniques— that is, rhythmic repetition—for oral review.

- *Acrostics.* Teach vocabulary by means of acrostics. (See exercise.)

- *Haibun.* Have students include short poems in their research projects. (See HAIBUN.) Variation: any piece of student writing can end with a poem.

- *Parallel pieces.* Have students write short creative pieces paralleling the form of a passage they're studying. Using "I burn, I pine, I perish" from *The Taming of the Shrew*, high school teacher Mike Crosby has his class write about their own lives by replacing Shakespeare's verbs with their own.

• *Altered poems.* Have students play with existing poems by substituting words and phrases, even nonsensically. This in fact enhances rather than harms student attitudes to the original poem (this author still has a soft spot for Poe's "The Raven," which he burlesqued at age eleven).

• *Prose chopping.* If students break a passage of prose into free-verse lines, they'll get practice in feeling out the poetic line—and also a fresh, closer look at just what the prose is "doing."

There is no end to the possibilities. The point is that by introducing elements of creativity into what is often looked on as drudgery, much more learning and work can be accomplished, and with pleasure.

—*Jack Collom*

x-ref: "On Quickies: Icebreakers and Fillers"

On Teaching Students of Different Ages

The handy and surprising fact is that by and large these writing exercises need not be restricted to particular age groups. They work for people from five to ninety-five. Acrostics, lunes, chant poems, etc. are simply avenues of poetry and can be "driven on" with enjoyment and seriousness by first graders or high school seniors—or middle-aged career poets. Any exercise that combines a sense of freedom with a structure of ongoing suggestion can lead to a good poem. And the potential for poetry is in everyone; it's in the fact of being human and having language. Given the opportunity and a boost, students of any age can write poetry. "I Remember" poems, for example, validate and give an easy form for personal expression of memory—soulful and important and full of "sweet fact" for the tiny child as well as for the golden-ager.

However, there *are* differences in how one teaches different age groups. Very young children, for example, can't write fluently yet, or are just learning to. But a teacher can lead class collaborations with them, serving as scribe (and seat-of-the-pants editor). Big wild and woolly poems can be accumulated in this way, using virtually any of the exercises in this book:

On Poetry

Writing is quadruple fun.
And writing is plain fun.
Poetry walks inside a guy's mouth
& then it walks back out.
After that it walks into a cave
& then it walks back to the mouth
& then it comes out &
Goes into a lady's mouth.
Poetry is a rainbow
Floating in the sky.
And then poetry falls, & it looks like white skies,
Like the bones are white,
& a train sounds like a poem.
& you pick up a pot of poetry.
Poetry is like a blue sky.
The rainbow comes back up.
Then it switches channels
& somebody catches it with a net.

A rainbow scotch-taped on the sky.
Poetry is like a desk with no papers,
Like dinosaurs eating food off trees.
A desk looks like a train.
A shooting star comes down with the poetry.
A rainbow is like a blue waterfall.
A rainbow has Jesus.
& poetry is like rocks with gold in 'em.
& like belt buckles off a big moose.
Then you run to the other end of the
Rainbow & pick up the other pot of poetry.
& that continues it from way up there.
& a zipper falls down.
A waterfall sparkles like gold,
Like a car going up a rainbow,
& a tiger goes in a house and takes a shower.

—*First grade class, Salmon, ID*

Certain exercises, such as the lune, the acrostic, and short pieces using "I remember," can be *written* by most first graders:

Think of me
coloring a beautiful picture on
my baby brother.
—*Tara Sorensen, 1st*

S un shining
A nd a
R accoon eating
A pples
H igh up in the tree.
—*Sarah Wade, 1st*

Because very young children tend to have short attention spans, a session of thirty to forty minutes may be enough. Bringing a class of, say, fifth graders down to a kindergarten or first grade class and having them act as secretaries for the little ones can be marvelous, providing an outlet for the younger children's poems and for the older ones' sense of helpfulness. Another technique is to have young children combine illustration and writing; this helps make the act of writing more fun for them. However, it is advisable—unless you are doing concrete poems—to isolate the writing time lest they hastily scrawl a few words and then slip into the easier, more immediate activity of drawing.

We recommend the following exercises as especially good for children in grades K–2:

as individual poems

ACROSTICS
COLLAGE POEMS
CONCRETE POEMS
"FEELINGS" POEMS

"GOING INSIDE" POEMS
"I REMEMBER" POEMS
LUNES
"MY SOUL IS . . ." POEMS
ORIGINS POEMS
PICTURE-INSPIRED WRITINGS
ODES
"PRIMITIVE" POEMS
QUESTIONS WITHOUT ANSWERS
"THINGS TO DO" POEMS
USED TO/BUT NOW POEMS

as class (or partner) collaborations

ACROSTICS
CHANT POEMS
"FEELINGS" POEMS
"GOING INSIDE" POEMS
ON POETRY
OUTDOORS POEMS
PLACE POEMS
Q & A PARTNER POEMS
RECIPE POEMS
TALKING TO ANIMALS
THING POEMS
USED TO/BUT NOW POEMS
WORD PAIRS

Please treat these as suggestions. We encourage you to try any other exercises that intrigue you.

From the third grade on up, all the exercises in this book should be useful. All you have to do is use your judgment and adjust your vocabulary.

Naturally the vocabulary you use with your students varies according to their age. If the way you talk to fourth graders, for instance, is mostly on their level, then *some* richer vocabulary will entice them to rise to the challenge. You can make a wider range of English seem attractive to them, without arousing any "anti-intellectualism" they might feel. If your students refuse to use anything but their own colloquial language in their poems—and remember, poetry includes the colloquial—you can use your own approval of their street talk or country talk to disarm their desire to stick with it exclusively.

*   *   *   *   *

For older students, some of the exercises, such as Used to/But Now poems, are obviously "child-like," but you can still use them in a spirit of fun to warm up their imaginations.

Older students rarely show the immediate enthusiasm for poetry the young ones typically do. This need not discourage you. If high school students seem apathetic or negative, don't confront them about it. Focus on what you're doing and plow right ahead with it. Their "cool" may prevent them from *showing* their enthusiasm outwardly, but if their work is good, that's proof enough that they're "into it" and enjoying themselves. When their poems are read aloud, a sense of poetic accomplishment will be in the air, whether they acknowledge it or not.

If some of the older students try to shock you or their peers with their beer-can negativism, look past the content of their poems. Read and comment on the poems exactly as you would any others, complimenting rhythmic successes, energetic language, or any other good points. You can point out that your objections are not to their poem's shock value, but to its lack of originality.

Some older students insist on producing rhymed Hallmark derivatives, intending profundity in their generalizations ("life," "love," "joy," etc.). Little by little you can ask them to illustrate, to be more specific, more original.

Rock and rap lyrics may seem to provide a ready-made poetry avenue—no need to build enthusiasm from scratch. However, having the students write repeatedly from such models is usually a dead end, for the same reasons "greeting-card verse" is. Stripped of their wild music (and disregarding their social criticism), rock and rap lyrics are usually poorly rhymed lines slogging through a swamp of cliché. Exceptions exist, such as Laurie Anderson's and Bob Dylan's lyrics, but without musical expertise on a student's part there's no "open end" through which imitation can grow to good use.

Some people feel that high school poets should devote their attentions to such "dignified" aspects of verse as symbolism and philosophic utterance. We disagree. Teenage poets are much better off developing their own language texture and fineness of perception. Literary criticism and philosophical issues are best approached slowly and inductively. Poetry should develop from real speech patterns. So while it's true that high schoolers often want to speak or write using big statements, their need for the overall view can best be met by helping them make their grand gestures *with* step-by-step rigor and the proofs of their own experience: perceptual detail.

*   *   *   *   *

Here is a letter to an excellent high school teacher who sought more integration of the study and the practice of poetry.

Dear Terry,

To my delight, you've brought up, on behalf of your high school students and their education in literature, the topic of a divergence in attitudes and practices between the way poetry is handled in such a textbook as your McDougal, Littell *Literature* (Blue Level) and the way it's handled by Sheryl and me. Very worthy of discussion. Not altogether easy to *integrate* these views.

The difference between their way and ours is in part the difference between a study of the finished product (as in the textbook) and learning by doing (Sheryl and me). Vive la différence! But we think a shift in emphasis toward learning by doing (learning about literature from the writer's standpoint) is educationally vital, in addition to being lively fun.

It *is* OK, and more than OK, that one's approach to a field, such as poetry, be composed of widely varying facts and tones and emphases, from one time (class period) to another. This is just being true to the many-sided nature of things. We don't have to impose an artificial unity that always dominates our responses to "a poem" or "a tree."

The McDougal, Littell textbook provides a visually attractive study of a range of poems. Obviously, much work has gone into the poetry unit.

However, I have several important quarrels with their presentation (as I do with what might be called the "professor's view" of poetry in general):

1. It represents a heavy emphasis on the analyst's look at the finished product. It is far more accurate and useful to view poetry as a *process*. Contemporary writing theory backs me up on this.

2. In so emphasizing, the textbook shows the elements of a poem as if they were contrivances calculated for deliberately chosen effects. Of course, to a degree, this *is so* for poetry; however, the actual practice of poets is much more "by feel" than that indicates, *and* the attitude that such "lit crit" engenders among students leaves poetry *out of their reach,* something they can't do—the product, only, of specialized knowledge. They think they have to know all the references in classical mythology, or have a huge literary vocabulary, to write a poem. But these dense networks of hard-label expertise have been too dominant in art education. The "knowing" in poetry is perhaps more like woodcraft—facts fused to an intuitive flow.

In its emphasis on isolating and technically defining the elements of poetry, the McDougal text makes writing a poem seem an immensely complicated mechanical skill—removed from personal response. It's not at all that I wish to scant taking care and working at exactitude in poems—it's that a lot of this good carefulness develops naturally with practice. Sure, as a teacher you can and should point things out, but students already have a tremendous, untapped talent for language. Check out the poems, again, in our student anthologies. They may not be as formally consistent as those of May Swenson et al., but they're in some ways more exciting as works of art. The students' potential will likely stagnate if we overemphasize literary analysis.

Many of the poems in the textbook you're using do not represent the best in modern American poetry—nor what student abilities could emulate. The poems are clever, they tend to *illustrate* identifiable factors in poetry. They seem contrived. They are more accomplishment than exploration. They're formal in obvious ways. And they're selected for these reasons.

Let me discuss one: John Updike's "Ex-Basketball Player" (a poem I've often read to high school kids).

Pearl Avenue runs past the high school lot,
Bends with the trolley tracks, and stops, cut off
Before it has a chance to go two blocks,
At Colonel McComsky Plaza. Berth's Garage
Is on the corner facing west, and there,
Most days, you'll find Flick Webb, who helps Berth out.

Flick stands tall among the idiot pumps—
Five on a side, the old bubble-head style,
Their rubber elbows hanging loose and low.
One's nostrils are two S's, and his eyes
An E and O. And one is squat, without
A head at all—more of a football type.

Once Flick played for the high-school team, the Wizards.
He was good: in fact, the best. In '46
He bucketed three hundred ninety points,
A county record still. The ball loved Flick.
I saw him rack-up thirty-eight or forty
In one home game. His hands were like wild birds.

He never learned a trade, he just sells gas,
Checks oil, and changes flats. Once in a while,
As a gag, he dribbles an inner tube,
But most of us remember anyway.
His hands are fine and nervous on the lug wrench.
It makes no difference to the lug wrench, though.

Off work, he hangs around Mae's luncheonette.
Grease-gray and kind of coiled, he plays pinball,

Smokes thin cigars, and nurses lemon phosphates.
Flick seldom says a word to Mae, just nods
Beyond her face toward bright applauding tiers
Of Necco Wafers, Nibs, and Juju Beads.

First, I like this piece, though I don't think Updike is more than clever as a poet. He sets up a predictable situation paraphrasably and prosily—Little Tin God (high school star) is revealed as sadly inadequate in real life. The poem does little more than "flesh out" its stated theme. I.e., there's no unpredictable magic—the poem, once it's underway, does not involve new discoveries, just proofs of what's already apparent. *Anyway*, I do like it, for what it does and shows.

As you pointed out to me, "Ex-BB Player" is actually loose iambic pentameter, cunningly roughed up to a semblance of local talk. Your detailed presentation (to the class) was great. I wonder, though, if such focus on structure could be used alongside a do-it-yourself approach more accessible to high school kids.

For example, you could simply preface reading the poem aloud by: 1) showing in a line or two how it is based in meter—just for a minute or two and just to a sophisticated class; 2) noting how it speaks almost entirely through facts; 3) mentioning how the abundant use of place- and thing-names gives it much local flavor.

Then the oral reading—settling into the most gas-station reaches of one's voice.

And then, *with* the downhome tone strongly established, the flights of metaphorical language—"The ball loved Flick" and "His hands were like wild birds"—will seem to the students inevitable, not gratuitous. Again—the piece creates a solid base of observation, out of which imaginative wordplay *legitimately* arises. You can ask the students questions that, by highlighting (even humorously) the *extremes* of metaphors, demonstrate vividly how such metaphors work.

"Does this mean the ball literally has a crush on Flick?"

"Does this mean he had robins on the ends of his wrists?"

The students will be into the logic of the poem and patiently answer, no, he just had a way of making the ball come to him, of doing what he wanted. His hands were quick, went anywhere, skillfully, seemed to fly independently.

And then the dramatic (but *unstated*) climax, the last two lines, where the old brands of candy form mock bleachers of "bright applause," is terrific—illustrates how *image* makes a strong ending.

Concentrating, then, on:

- *illustration*, not generalization, getting the meaning across
- the powerful effect of using particular names

- the few standout metaphors
- the language of real speech
- the socko ending

hits the virtues of the poem.

And at *that* point, just one-third to half the way through the class hour, you could ask the students to write creatively—nothing too close to Updike's piece, not stanzaic, but a prosy or free-verse exercise such as the "I Remember" poem, using the thrust of Mr. U.'s down-to-earth nounwork and careful observation—with a sort of airhole for metaphor to leap out from.

Afterwards, for further study, one could return to "Ex-BB Player" and delve more thoroughly into rhythm and other niceties. Following which, each student could try an exercise at composing a solid blank-verse couplet.

Thus the students would get, at a couple of points along the way, when their writing energies could be expected to be fresh, the special learning that comes through hands-on endeavor. It would be within the sensibility of the poem under study—the attention to detail—but also within their present writing abilities.

But the textbook follow-up questions called "Getting at Meaning" are couched in low-energy explanatory language (reducing the experience):

Getting at Meaning

RECALLING
1. Where is Flick employed? Where does he "hang out" when he is not working?
2. What kind of basketball player was Flick?

INTERPRETING
3. Has Flick realized the expectations of his youth? Explain.
4. What are the "rubber elbows on the pumps"? Reread lines 10 and 11. What brand of gas does Berth sell?
5. What does Flick see in the tiers of candy behind the luncheonette counter?
6. Reread the opening stanza. How does Flick's life resemble Pearl Avenue?

CRITICAL THINKING
7. Is Flick a believable character? Are there people like Flick in the real world? Explain.

Developing Skills in Reading Literature

1. *Imagery.* One gas pump looks like a football player. What do the other pumps look like? What words and phrases help the reader to picture the gas

pumps? In the last stanza what words and phrases help the reader to picture Flick? What do these visual images reveal about Flick's character and personality?

2. *Simile.* What simile describes Flick's hands? What is similar between the way that Flick handled a basketball and the way that he handles the lug wrench? What is the major difference?

3. *Personification.* Find two examples of personification in this poem. What objects are personified? How does the personification add to the reader's understanding of these objects?

4. *Tone.* What is the attitude of the speaker toward Flick? Quote lines and phrases to support your answer. How does the title reflect the tone?

Developing Writing Skills

Writing Poetry. Write an additional six-line stanza for this poem in which you describe what Flick sees, hears, feels, and smells as he gazes at the racks of candy. You might describe Flick making a basket, the noise of the crowd, the shouts of the cheerleaders, the heat of the gym, or the smell of liniment. Create vivid images that communicate specific sensory impressions. Eliminate all unnecessary words and end the stanza with a strong final line.

They begin with a longish, distracting exploration of the poem's meaning, whereas the meaning is immediately obvious—it doesn't need explanation. Explication screws up the students' attention to the poem's key workings. This prompts the students to give mundane answers— "The gas is Esso, sir." Though Updike *builds* his emotional effect with facts, *responding* with mere facts wrecks the experience—makes it seem the purpose of the poem was to learn those facts. The "purpose" was to learn how to respond to one's *own* experience.

The questions don't really *invite* the student to write.

The questions are too directive; they reduce the act of the student to analysis only. Enough "learning" about the poem could be tickled out by rereading and by asking the students what stands out for them—get the students used to thinking for themselves, not just "Flick-is-employed-in-a-gas-station."

An even more graphic example, because there are fewer formal factors to hitch response on, would be the following poem by Imamu Amiri Baraka:

Ballad of the Morning Streets

The magic of the day is the morning
I want to say the day is morning high
and sweet, good
morning

The ballad of the morning streets, sweet
voices turns

of cool warm weather
high around the early windows gray to blue
and down again amongst the kids and
broken signs, is pure love magic, sweet day
come into me, let me live with you
and dig your blazing

Though it's a simple poem, there are surprise developments generated *during* it—the slow revelation that this is an inner-city scene, and the contrast between that picture and more traditional images one might associate with lyric cries of morning—the sudden inclusion of "broken signs"—the way "morning high" sits, the linebreak opening an ambiguity: two "high"s—the sense that syntax "melts"—the natural paradox morning has of "cool warm weather" forming another double presence in the poem—and the assimilation, at the end, of street talk *into* dawn lyricism with "dig your blazing."

Baraka has extended a pastoral ecstasy into slum streets, and you don't really need literary vocabulary to point out how that works.

I'm not saying "toss out literary vocabulary"; I'm saying, "de-emphasize it."

I hope you take my argument in good spirit. I'm eager to hear what you think. My argument is part of a lifelong quarrel with standardized texts—and what I really want is positive—livelier treatment of literature and more learning-by-doing.

I'd like to note that I believe thoroughly that you succeed in sparking interest in your classes in poetry by proceeding as you already do. I've seen you do it. If I may say so, I think your personality helps strongly to cut what might otherwise be a too-academic experience for the kids—helps make it real.

Best,
Jack

*　　*　　*　　*　　*

SUGGESTED ACTIVITIES FOR ADVANCED STUDENTS

(These are experiments—that well may lead to poems—intended to get you going, and to help you keep a fresh relationship with language.)

• Pick a random word or phrase and let your mind toss it about freely until some ideas have come up, then seize on one and begin to write. Try this with a word that has few connotations. (The word *so*, for example.)

- Try rewriting someone else's poem. (If you reproduce someone else's style, tone, ideas, way with words, even devices, you should be aware you're doing it.)

- Using language characteristic of one field, write about another. For example, use the technical language of astronomy or physics to write about childhood.

- Try to write exactly the way you think. This is impossible, but see how close you can come. Then try writing very slowly—one word per minute or a phrase every two minutes for an hour.

- Try every conceivable kind of collaboration. Any type of poem that can be written individually can also be tried in partnership. And you can add to that infinite richness: one writer is fed information by another and writes, each writer gives the other instructions, each makes lengthy critical comments on the other's segments—etc. (See "On Collaborations.")

- Structure a piece of writing by units of travel. For example, take a walk and write a line per block until you have an informal sonnet. Ride a bus and divide your writing by time or distance or stops.

- Keep a number of journals on various subjects, such as dreams, food, ideas about writing, and weather, to serve as source material. Try writing a journal in alternate entries with another writer.

- Type out one of Shakespeare's sonnets, or any other poem you like, double-spaced on a page. Try rewriting it between the lines of the original. At the very least, you'll be learning about the poem you like and why you like it.

- Take poems you think are very bad and study them. Try to write a bad poem. Study it and decide if it's really bad and how and why.

- Write a poem that refers only to your physical surroundings— only what you can see, hear, smell, feel, or taste. Perceiving the simple, "ordinary" things around you, and learning how just to mention or describe them, is central to all creative writing. Try this in different places.

- Write a number of pieces that express anger or rage. Compose a larger work from them.

- Write a work while looking in the mirror without using the word *mirror*.

- Take a book of poetry you love, and, going through it poem by poem, make a list of everything you can determine, small and large, of the writer's exact methods, and characteristics of his or her language.

- Take a piece of prose and break it into free-verse lines.

- Write a piece consisting solely of questions. Prepare by thinking only in questions.

- Experiment with as many traditional forms as you can, both to learn them and to gain experience working with details of language. (See "On Traditional Poetic Forms.")

- Plan, structure, and write a long work, trying to make it either so personal or so avant-garde in style or form that it's "new." Consider what in your opinion are the topics or attitudes "on the upswing" in the world today. What's the poem of the future?

- Read! Not only poetry, but classics, science, new ways of looking at the world.

- Try writing in a way you've never done before. Use a voice or voices completely foreign to you.

- Invent a new form.

- Write about daily things of the plainest kind—household stuff, jobs, eating, shopping, errands and tasks, etc. Use your own personal daily vocabulary to the fullest.

- Write many different versions of one event, using many different styles and forms.

- Add to this list whenever you find a new idea you'd like to try.

—Jack Collom

On Sound and Rhythm

The speech of children *is* songs of innocence and experience. Seven-through eleven-year-old kids (apprentice writers) have already had thousands upon thousands of hours of practice talking (and listening) that would constitute—in terms of pole-vaulting or violin-playing—world-class experience. They are *fluent* within their own vocabularies. Already, the rhythms of their speech resemble those of rather interesting jazz.

Children's language seems to have a built-in musicality: listen to their talk; it's frequently like a mountain freshet bubbling along over rocks, full of silvery arcs. This is the raw material of poetry. By contrast, we adults, though much larger in our references and vocabulary, tend to fall into verbal ruts and toneless abstractions.

And children take a special delight in odd or pretty sounds. Given the chance to write, they are very playful with the sonic side of language. Experts say their learning of new words is a process of wonder, laughter, and punning. What children may lack is a developed sense of artistic judgment, so that their poems often include startling successes in sound right next to bland or awkward passages. They tend to accept whatever comes into their heads.

So they have the potential for art right on the tips of their tongues. It is important that we recognize this "little genius" for poetry that children have—and not try to "muscle" them into adult standards of poetic discourse. Yes, they should develop mature language skills—but gradually, organically, while as much as possible maintaining (and developing and transforming) their own fresh poetic talents.

*　　*　　*　　*　　*

A few versifiers such as Shel Silverstein, Jack Prelutzky, and Dr. Seuss have become very popular with children. Deservedly so! They present ideas the kids can identify with, perfectly worked into clever, sprightly poems—for example, as in these lines by Dr. Seuss:

If we didn't have birthdays, you wouldn't be you.
If you'd never been born, well then what would you do?
If you'd never been born, well then what would you be?
You might be a fish! Or a toad in a tree!

I love Dr. Seuss! But ah, then the question arises, how to "use" poems like his in the classroom. Have kids take them as models, try to imitate the technique? No. Very few can make language flow and still fit such a meter. If they try, the results will highlight their weak points, not their strengths. A poem by Dr. Seuss is a fine gift from an adult to a kid, like a gold watch that the child can enjoy and learn from (and tell time by). It does not, however, inspire the kid to make a watch too. For that, we use freer forms of writing—freer senses of time.

In previous centuries of English-language verse, a *formal* sophistication, harmonized with an intricate set of rules, was more important than it is now. Few children (Blake and Chatterton were two exceptions) could master the complex skills needed just to "get in the door" of poetry. In those times, poetry only *began* when the requisite versification skill was there. That is, anyone could learn to versify like this:

The dog is walking now across the street;
He doesn't like the hardness on his feet.

This is perfect iambic pentameter, with a perfect rhyme—but not good poetry. Good poetry, then as now, requires the spirit, imaginative resources, and intelligence of utterance. These qualities arise in the sound of a poem as well as in its meaning. The talented sixteenth-through-nineteenth-century poet was musical, able to vary sound away from the simple limits of iambic pentameter, while still keeping its basic structure. Poets accomplished this through differing syllable lengths, caesuras and other pauses, clustering and separating consonants, vowel progressions, secondary accents, alliteration and assonance, and rhythmic emphasis, among other means. The great poems of our immediate heritage go far beyond their verse system—circling back, in a way, to the vivacity and unpredictability of speech. It's in the *variations* that poetry has always had its most intense life.

Here's a little song from Shakespeare's *Tempest* in which the spirit Ariel delivers some tough news to the Prince of Naples:

Full fathom five thy father lies;
    Of his bones are coral made;
Those are pearls that were his eyes:
    Nothing of him that doth fade,
But doth suffer a sea change
Into something rich and strange.
Sea nymphs hourly ring his knell:
    Ding-dong.
Hark! now I hear them—Ding-dong, bell.

- The curt trochaic tetrameter shows up clearly in line 2: OF his BONES are CORal MADE.
- In line 1, the alliteration of *f*'s helps impress on the listener the intended "snuffing out" of life.
- The initial spondee (*Full fath-*)—an accent formed of two "hard" syllables next to each other—emphasizes the severity of the announcement. *Father* and *fathom,* close in sound, underscore the father's fate.
- The hard *c* of *coral* harmonizes with the hardness of *bones.*
- *Those, are, pearls, were, his, eyes*—almost every sound in line 3 can be held in the mouth (not snapped off, as with many consonants)—the liquid *r*'s and *l*'s, the buzzy *s*'s—expressing the slow transformation of soft eyes to pearls.
- In line 5, the spondaic *sea change* stands out rhythmically as a variation (with no light syllables between), slowing down the utterance, drawing attention to itself.

And so on. No wonder the Prince replies, "This is no mortal business, nor no sound / That the earth owns."

Rhyme aside, all the magical sound techniques in the Shakespeare song work exactly the same in a poem by an untrained student (though the outline of the kid's poem may be more free-form). Example:

Music takes me
away from the broken record
life I live.

—*Jesse Thompson, 8th*

- The *m*'s in *music* and *me* join them, help the music "take" the *me.* These solid sounds suddenly soften in *away*—it feels "away."
- The *k* sounds in *broken record* ironically link it with *Music takes*—a broken record *is* music, but it's stuck. You can hear in its four syllables how it whirls around rapidly.
- The alliteration of *life I live* presents another sound, with soft, pretty tones—it *shows* the new life at the same time as it mentions the old.

In this century, the practice of poetry, while no less sophisticated than in prior eras, has been involved more consciously in making decisions directly based on everyday speech and on input from the subconscious mind. Within their limits of judgment and range of reference, kids can do this as well as—or better than—adults. They're in touch with the basic sparkle of language.

In its musicality, most contemporary poetry does not use a metrical system; its rhyme or off-rhyme is more scattered than organized. This scattered quality does not imply carelessness; it could be likened to the arrangement of leaves on a tree.

Here's a poem by a well-known contemporary American poet:

Mid-August at Sourdough Mountain Lookout

Down valley a smoke haze
Three days heat, after five days rain
Pitch glows on the fir-cones
Across rocks and meadows
Swarms of new flies.

I cannot remember things I once read
A few friends, but they are in cities.
Drinking cold snow-water from a tin cup
Looking down for miles
Through high still air.

    —Gary Snyder

Though this is a free-verse poem, many sound correspondences function in it, to "tie things up" and add expressiveness to what's being talked about.

- First, the taciturn tone is expressive of the situation—a lone fire lookout in wild country.
- The first two lines almost rhyme (have vowel rhyme—assonance) via the long *a*'s of *haze* and *rain*. *Haze* is further united to the descriptive elements of line 2 by alliterating with *heat* and rhyming within the line with *days* (twice).
- Note how the long *o*'s stand out in line 3, forming a sort of swing with the tough sound of *Pitch* and the hard *c* of *cones* at the end of the line.
- *Cones* begins a series of *k* sounds continuing in *Across rocks*—and expressive of those hard items.
- Then, with *meadows*, a softer, hummy, buzzy sound carries through line 5, just right for the soft insect-song scene.
- *Drinking cold snow-water from a tin cup* makes some very lively music (repeat it a few times, for the rhythm) out of a plain drink of water.
- In the last two lines, the long *i*'s of *miles* and *high*, as well as the slowed-down rhythm of *high still air*, emphasize the breathtaking height of the tower.

Alliteration, assonance, and rhyme are wonderful if they're not made too mechanical. In modern poetry they tend to be organic or serendipitous rather than schematized. It's just that the more trained the ear is, the more appropriate that serendipity's arrival. Similarly, with children rhyme usually functions best when it is natural rather than prearranged. Here is an example by a seventh grade girl:

P isces
I s my
S ign,
C ool
E very time. Can't
S top thinking why I'm so fine!

—*Ana Grullon*

The assonance and rhymes of the long *i*'s take place with a charming jazzy syncopation.

Asking students to use end-rhyme and meter will lead in most cases to stiffness and artificiality in their writing—in its content as well as its form, since the two are pretty much indivisible. We can evoke children's poetic potential with loose or variable forms (free verse), and it will find its own shapes in due time.

Though children already have a lot of aesthetic power in the "sound" aspects of their writing, they're not conscious of it as an approved commodity. So what can one do to make students more aware of language-as-music?

It starts with the teacher reading a lot of poetry. In doing so, you become familiar with the various "sounds" poets employ and can welcome new ones in your students' writing, just as a botany student, wandering in the woods, is excited by new plant combinations.

As workshop leader, you should try to choose sample poems that are strong in soundplay or musical quality. Remember, rhythm in speech or in modern poetry is bright and special more in its variations than in any regularity. As explained above, this is also true of metered verse. You should point out and repeat lines, phrases, and sections that are especially appealing—either in the pleasure of the sounds themselves or in the ways they lend emphasis to certain words. Once you're attuned to the happiness of variability, you can trust your ear for examples. It's basically a question of attentiveness.

Read poems aloud in class with verve and a strong, natural emphasis on the rhythm and sound.

As often as possible, point out, among your comments on the kids' poems, interesting or playful sounds they've created, or instances where sound supports—or intriguingly works *against*—meaning. If you make many comments on sound, sound will become important to your students.

*   *   *   *   *

Following are examples of felicitous uses of sound, with commentary.

B ouncing
A long
L ike the ground was just there to
L et it spring back into the air.

  —Juan Martinez, 7th

The rhythm naturally speeds up like the diminishing bounces of a free ball. Making the ball primary to the ground intensifies its free spirit. Also, the there/air rhyme amounts to a bounce from ground up.

O how beautiful is the ocean. Why don't you
C ompare it to the fish's swimming motion?
E ven in a fishtank you can compare
A fish's swimming motion. Even in a turtle
N otion, you can find a fish's swimming motion.

  —Percy Nuñez, 6th

The rhythm of the second and third sentences (starting with lazy dactylic waves) matches their content. Comparing the whole ocean to the motion of one of its parts (is a resident a part?) is a deep idea, taken further by the fishtank limit. And further yet, beautifully accompanied by a goofy, attention-drawing rhyme in "turtle/Notion . . . motion." Repetition and vowels—all swim.

Grenada coconuts, coconut water, rivers, crayfish, colorful blue
seas, seaside grapes, fresh walnuts, fish houses, beautiful
freedom, nice beach, mangoes, pears, oranges, cherries, funny
fruits and grapefruits.

  —Temelle Peters, 4th

The randomness of moves within the list gives a feeling of paradise-lying-around, the tropics. Read this poem aloud; the rhythm and soundplay are like a brook dancing down to the sea.

Typing Room

Click clack click clack as the keys go back
FGF space FGF space when the keys go back
The keys go back again and again and again
Sit back and straight
Fingers on the guide keys

Look at the chart
Pg 17 Supplementary Practice
When you finish put your hands on your
OK, let's start again
FGF space FGF space as the keys go back
As the keys go back

    —Jaye Slonim, 4th

Sophisticated sound abstract, mixed with other fact. The sound varies nicely between hard and soft (most strikingly in the move from line 8 to line 9). It's abstract but, paradoxically, concrete as no description could be.

        —Jack Collom

Using Great Poems as Models

The truth about poetry is that it has an actual effect upon the listener. A great poem can make the hairs on your neck stand up. Some poems can cause other powerful reactions, such as the desire to answer back by writing a poem of one's own. In the classroom it is essential to read the poem aloud to the students in a way that conveys the poem's energy and feeling. The best way to do this is to read the poem aloud to yourself many times. Allow yourself to get the feel of the poem's emotions and tone. Familiarize yourself with the sound and pace of the poem until you are comfortable reading it aloud, with a spark, really using your own voice. When the person reading the poem aloud likes and appreciates the poem, the effect is irresistible. You bring a lively personal force that children respond to and you show them that one doesn't have to use a stilted formal reading style but that *your own voice will suffice.* This teaches students to trust themselves and their own language: they will start having fun while learning, start experiencing the joys of creation, and approach their own lifetime of reading with a positive attitude. Even an expectant one!

Sometimes all you have to do is read the poem aloud a few times and students will light up and begin writing. The poem speaks directly to them and they know how they want to respond to it. It's a good idea to talk about the poem with the class. Ask what your students think of it, which aspects stand out for them. What about the poem is striking—or surprising? What in the poem would the students like to try? For example, "The Truth" (below) is written from the perspective of a four-year-old boy during the London blitz. He is in a sanatorium or hospital, and in the first two lines he is trying to remember what really happened to him:

> When I was four my father went to Scotland.
> They *said* he went to Scotland.

By italicizing the word *said,* the author (Randall Jarrell) is helping you to read the poem the way he'd like it to be read. I think every poet tries to put words on the page in an order that will best suit how they sound, thereby showing you how to listen to the poem. Jarrell's poem is written in a disjointed manner, with thoughts abruptly interrupted, then completed several sentences away. He recounts a confusing night of death and fire, like a dream except that it was light outside. *At night.* The boy talks out loud to himself, trying to reason out what happened, where his father went, and his sister. Because he has been lied to about their deaths he is not sure that his mother is really his mother, and is told that he is not himself. You can hear the frustration and understand why certain words throughout the poem are stressed, in italics, to be read a certain way. This poem almost instructs you how to read it aloud.

"The Truth" is a wonderful example of the power of language. Watch the faces of your students carefully when you read this poem. At first, they will be silent. Then many ideas and remarks will fly. Direct this energy to the poems they will write. The general writing idea I suggest for this poem is simply to write about the consequences of lying. Ask them to write about the first feelings that came to them when they heard the poem. What connections did they make with the boy and his confusion? Did any of the poem feel familiar, like they could have written parts of it? Suggest the class write about what this poem caused to happen in their imaginations and memories.

Another example of a great poem to use as a model is Ezra Pound's translation of Li Po's "The River Merchant's Wife" (below). First of all, you can tell your class that this poem was written hundreds of years ago, during the T'ang Dynasty. (Both Li Po and Ezra Pound—a great twentieth-century poet as well as a translator—have fascinating personal histories that students enjoy hearing about.) The poet uses metaphor to talk about feelings. Tell students how the poem is coming to them from another language and another world, and yet how it can move them. Simply spoken, yet old and mysterious, the romantic lyricism of this poem makes it a pleasure to read aloud: monkeys make sorrowful noise overhead. The different mosses by the gate have grown too deep to clear away. Paired butterflies already yellow with August are somehow painful to the wife. She is growing old, she says, and yet she is only sixteen, married already two years. Students are fascinated by information like this. It is an exciting poem. You can communicate this excitement to your class with a smooth, confident reading of the poem and discussion afterwards of its particulars. Talk about the poem as you would to a group of peers in a writing group. Give them encouragement to talk about poems by setting an example yourself. Tell them what the poem did for you. For example, in "The River Merchant's Wife" I hear the voice of a child growing up and experiencing a great love. There is the terrible implication that her husband is dead. The plainness of her speech makes the image of a girl even stronger. There is a yearning throughout the poem that pulls at my heart.

"The River Merchant's Wife" is a good model poem for the writing assignment of composing a letter to someone who is gone. Have your students describe a memory, or make one up. Writing letters is a natural way to begin poems: you can be direct and personal, and forget that it is a poem. "Forgetting yourself" in a poem is like flying. I highly recommend it.

Aristotle said that one of the two ways to learn is by imitation. Look at how poets write—learn from them. Learn to recognize each poet's individual techniques and tricks and common themes and, most of all, have fun. It's like when you're learning to dance—you get behind the dancer and copy his or her steps. That's how learning from great poems works.

Discovering which poets you like is a process of self-discovery. You are what you like. Then you can use what you've learned you love about poetry in your own poems. The value of a poem is what you choose from it, what strikes you. Discover your own standards and procedures for critical evaluation. Guide your students to do the same. Sometimes it is up to your sense of humor or insight to find something to remark upon in a poem that is not immediately clear to the reader. Sometimes it's the element of surprise—a memory of love, or a recognition of a shared history—when suddenly, the poem changes everything. People cannot write poetry together and remain strangers.

—Sheryl Noethe

The Truth

When I was four my father went to Scotland.
They *said* he went to Scotland.

When I woke up I think I thought I was dreaming–
I was so little then that I thought dreams
Are in the room with you, like the cinema.
That's why you don't dream when it's still light–
They pull the shades down when it is, so you can sleep.
I thought that then, but that's not right.
Really it's in your head.

And it was light then–light at *night*.
I heard Stalky bark outside.
But really it was Mother crying–
She coughed so hard she cried.
She kept shaking Sister,
She shook her and shook her.

I thought Sister had had her nightmare.
But he wasn't barking, he had died.
There was dirt all over Sister.
It was all streaks, like mud. I cried.
She didn't, but she was older.
     I thought she didn't
Because she was older, I thought Stalky had just gone.
I got *everything* wrong.
I didn't get one single thing right.
It seems to me that I'd have thought
It didn't happen, like a dream,
Except it was light. At night.

They burnt our house down, they burnt down London.
Next day my mother cried all day, and after that
She said to me when she would come to see me:
"Your father has gone away to Scotland.
He will be back after the war."

The war then was different from the war now.
The war now is *nothing*.

I used to live in London till they burnt it.
What was it like? It was just like here.
No, that's the truth.
My mother would come here, some, but she would cry.
She said to Miss Elise, "He's not himself";
She said, "Don't you love me any more at all?"
I was *myself*.
Finally she wouldn't come at all.
She never said one thing my father said, or Sister.
Sometimes she did,
Sometimes she was the same, but that was when I dreamed it.
I could tell I was dreaming, she was just the same.

That Christmas she bought me a toy dog.

I asked her what was its name, and when she didn't know
I asked her over, and when she didn't know
I said, "You're not my mother, you're not my mother.
She *hasn't* gone to Scotland, she is dead!"
And she said, "Yes, he's dead, he's dead!"
And cried and cried; she *was* my mother,
She put her arms around me and we cried.

—*Randall Jarrell*

The River-Merchant's Wife: A Letter

While my hair was still cut straight across my forehead
I played about the front gate, pulling flowers.
You came by on bamboo stilts, playing horse,
You walked about my seat, playing with blue plums.
And we went on living in the village of Chokan:
Two small people, without dislike or suspicion.

At fourteen I married My Lord you.
I never laughed, being bashful.
Lowering my head, I looked at the wall.
Called to, a thousand times, I never looked back.

At fifteen I stopped scowling,
I desired my dust to be mingled with yours
Forever and forever and forever.
Why should I climb the lookout?

At sixteen you departed,
You went into far Ku-to-yen, by the river of swirling eddies,
And you have been gone five months.
The monkeys make sorrowful noise overhead.

You dragged your feet when you went out.
By the gate now, the moss is grown, the different mosses,
Too deep to clear them away!
The leaves fall early this autumn, in wind.
The paired butterflies are already yellow with August
Over the grass in the West garden;
They hurt me. I grow older.
If you are coming down through the narrows of the river Kiang,
Please let me know beforehand,
And I will come out to meet you
                              As far as Chò-fù-Sà.

—Li Po (translated by Ezra Pound)

On Traditional Poetic Forms

People often view poetry in terms of its traditional, outward forms. But poems—and poetic forms—depend more importantly on their "inner life." Such well-known forms as the pastoral poem, satire, ode, epic, lyric, elegy, chant, concrete poem, collage poem, parody, and abstract poem depend more on content, tone, spirit, and language play than on their structural appearance.

Until this century, for hundreds of years, most of the poetry of the western world was in rhyme and meter. This meant a comparatively strict word-music. Meanwhile the rest of the world was making marvelous poetry too, in forms ranging from the complexities of the renga (Japan) to more flexible breath-based American Indian chants to intricate and variable African pygmy song.

While full of admiration and love for our English poetry heritage, and believing that students should read widely and deeply in it, we feel that it does not, on the whole, provide an appropriate set of working models for our time.

The standards of rhyme and meter do not constitute the basic nature of poetry; they represent the surface of a few hundred years in one small area of the world. English poetry was neither rhymed nor metered until the late fourteenth century. Styles of poetry are usually in dynamic flux (when they aren't, poetry suffers—long periods go by in which poets only produce carbon copies of existing modes). The dramatic poetry of Shakespeare's boyhood, for example, was quite different from what Shakespeare himself wrote twenty years later—so rapid were the shifts in late sixteenth-century England.

In the twentieth century, poetry in the western world has undergone radical modifications. With the advent of the Imagists before World War I, the leading edge of poetic practice shifted away from rhyme and meter. Many previous poets had already opened the way: one thinks of Blake's and Whitman's expansive lines, Baudelaire's and Rimbaud's prose poems, Mallarmé's use of white space around his words. Of course, poets such as Frost and Yeats continued in metered verse after that point, but for eighty years the main energy has been in the huge realm called "free verse" and in eclecticism—the use of styles and forms from around the world, and back in history. Many serious poets still do use rhyme and meter, but it's generally as an occasional *part* of their repertory, not as the "whole music."

This book does not concentrate on the traditional western forms. We've included forms we find most useful as models for elementary and secondary students.

Let us examine, as an example of a famous form omitted, the sonnet. This form originated in Italy in the thirteenth century and became a dominant poetic form in following centuries. A typical sonnet has fourteen lines and consists of an octet and a sestet (eight- and six-line groups, respectively). The rhythm is iambic pentameter and there is a pattern of end-rhymes. Most often the subject matter of a sonnet is philosophy or love, expressed in metaphorical language. The octet presents a situation or idea that builds to a climax, and the sestet lets it gracefully die away with a philosophic remove or a personal resolution. Sometimes the final couplet is used as a sort of summary punchline. The complex graces of the progression of thought are delicately merged with the metric requirements. The rhymes must not only be present but artfully placed in the flow of the poem. The *poem*, beyond its technical skeleton, is still a matter of spirit, expression, energy, "light and dark," and the many subtle and shapely *variations* in sound and sense that create an interesting, whole harmony. It takes the devotion and immersion of many years to bring all this off.

So a fully composed traditional sonnet is rarely within the reach of most schoolchildren. It's not good to have students write awkward travesties of verse and think it's the real thing (or have them sense that it's *not* and feel that poetry is out of their reach). In a finished poem, meter and rhyme should be done well or not at all. Student work in the traditional sonnet elements should be in the spirit of practice, like linguistic sit-ups.

But there *is* a certain attraction to the compact fourteen-line poetic utterance, with a shift partway along. Contemporary poets have been drawn to sonnets, writing them not with mechanical rules but with a delicate catch-as-catch-can pursuit of the basic spirit. One can have a talented group of students write fourteen-line free-verse poems with the first eight lines presenting an idea and the last six taking it in unexpected directions.

Here is an example of a modern sonnet as intricate, mysterious, and beautiful as those of Elizabeth Barrett Browning but freer in outward form:

Sonnet XVII

Each tree stands alone in stillness
After many years still nothing
The wind's wish is the tree's demand
The tree stands still
The wind walks up and down
Scanning the long selves of the shore
Her aimlessness is the pulse of the tree

It beats in tiny blots
Its patternless pattern of excitement
Letters birds beggars books
There is no such thing as a breakdown
The tree the ground the wind these are
Dear, be the tree your sleep awaits
Sensual, solid, still, swaying alone in the wind

    —Ted Berrigan

In this poem, one of a book-length series, Berrigan moves the mood along without metrics but with verbal gestures that resemble both wind and tree. Several of the lines are collaged in from poetry by John Ashbery, and Berrigan extends the collage sense throughout the other sonnets in his book by including, in varying orders, some lines over and over contrapuntally. Thus, each poem's shuttling of new and repeated lines is a microcosm of the whole book. Berrigan immersed himself in Shakespeare's sonnets for years, so that a sonnet feel comes through his own, no matter how personal and "modern" his adaptation. Paradoxically, the more poetry you read, the more original you can be in your own.

The point is that although many traditional western forms are not appropriate writing models for students, we *can* rethink and modify some of them for contemporary use.

And it *is* important for young poets today to read intensively the poetry of "our own" heritage and others. Part of a multi-faceted approach to reading and writing poetry is developing the ability to Read and Do Otherwise. That is, inspiration's products are often and legitimately very different from their sources. As language studies can and should be divided—punctuation one day and poetry the next—until they integrate, so poetry itself may be divided and integrated. One day students can study one of Shakespeare's sonnets or a poem by e.e. cummings (and do a tiny exercise, such as writing a single good line of iambic pentameter or making a typographic figure). The next day, they can write chant poems about local animals—perhaps after hearing African poems. More and more, the modern world forces us to approach a given subject from multiple perspectives; poetry certainly needs to be understood in this way, with a sense of options.

*   *   *   *   *

Two popular forms for school use are the cinquain and the limerick. I consider the cinquain too prescriptive. Filling out the tight little "tailed" pyramid, students lose track of their poems—the form takes over. Poetry is sometimes boosted by a formula, but should not be subservient to one. It could be argued that the haiku is similarly restrictive, but haiku poems emphasize line more than syllable or word count, thus encouraging speech flow. Their brevity and tradition of wit and image help insure them against syrupiness. Also, the sense of surprise has more elbow room in a haiku than in the two-syllable tailpiece of the cinquain. If you use the latter, use it to focus students on the atoms of language.

The limerick is a nifty form, but the traditional haw-haw and habit of starting out "There was an old something from somewhere" cramp it, reducing the likelihood of a good poem. Its toughest feature, though, for children, is the requisite rhythm; kids are just not able, in most cases, to master meter. And there's nothing clunkier than ill-done meter. Still, it's true that kids like hearing limericks, and you can use the form as a way of helping students understand rhythmic effects.

Both of these forms influence kids merely to answer their basic formal requirements. Partly it's due to the available examples—cinquains tend to high-flown posturing; limericks are mostly shaped jokes. There are, on the other hand, countless and various great haiku.

However, there are many traditions to follow. Certain poetic forms are terrific for kids. Acrostics and various concrete (visual) poems are thousands of years old. Chant poetry is perhaps the most ancient of all. Pantoums bring in a practice from a faraway culture. More recently, William Carlos Williams's "Red Wheelbarrow" and his "plums poem" (see WILLIAM CARLOS WILLIAMS IMITATIONS) are already traditions. Each of these, though, either by its nature or through current adaptations, has a large element of openness along with its formal requirements.

For teachers interested in looking into poetic forms, we recommend *The Teachers & Writers Handbook of Poetic Forms* (Teachers & Writers Collaborative, 1987). A good way to study forms is to write parodies of them.

—*Jack Collom*

x-ref: "On Sound and Rhythm"

On Poetry Units

In scheduling poetry sessions over a period of time, the main point is not to let the poetic spirit die. This doesn't mean that you have to push poetry all the time. Poetry, or any creative writing, should simply recur enough in class so that it's kept alive as a possibility in kids' minds, and is not overwhelmed by long stretches of the more standardized modes of writing. There is no single recipe for this.

We recommend that you have class periods—alternating (and sometimes mingling) with periods devoted to study of published poems—in which the students write their own poetry. Writing exercises or topics need not be directly related to the poetry you're reading. It's fine for you and your students to reach into the grab-bag of writing exercises and pull out something that has virtually no relation to what you're studying. Writing is writing, and you'll often find that two styles of writing you thought were completely different in fact complement each other surprisingly well. There's no reason not to read Whitman on Tuesday and then write acrostics or haiku on Wednesday. For one thing, this helps to relieve any tight feelings students may have about what poetry "has" to be.

It's also good to search for connections. See if the students surpass Carl Sandburg by writing "I Remember" poems. Follow a session on Shakespeare by having your class write dialogues using dense imagery. Write lunes after reading Emily Dickinson. Or make up your own writing assignments (see "On Inventing and Adapting Your Own Exercises").

You may want to have your students get used to writing poems a while before beginning to study "adult" poetry. In this case, you have several ways to go. You can string their writing sessions out, say once a week, over a long period and let the activity sink in in between. (The danger, of course, is it might sink out of sight.) Or you can jam it up into intensive sessions, writing poems many hours in a given week. The shock of such an intensive immersion in writing may well carry students into a new relationship with language—which is wonderful, but may also alienate some, especially those who can't easily get over a feeling of inadequacy with words.

As for how to choose a series of writing exercises, we recommend variety, even contrast.

It's good to begin with a down-to-earth assignment such as "I Remember" poems because it *immediately and by example* disabuses students of the notions they may have that poetry is: 1) rhymed; 2) cast in artificial English; 3) made of generalities; 4) on "lofty" subjects; and 5) imbued with sentimentality.

You can follow this loose, conversational exercise with a more controlled, formal exercise—one that's conducive to the imagination—such as lunes or acrostics.

The writing exercises in this book are designed so that you can alternate between their various qualities: emphasis on content (PLACE POEMS) vis-à-vis emphasis on form (CHANT POEMS); observation (OUTDOORS POEMS) vis-à-vis imagination ("GOING INSIDE" POEMS); expansion (any prose description) vis-à-vis concision (HAIKU). *And* you can combine such contrasts in one exercise (ACROSTICS *about* places, etc.). The point is to avoid creating the impression that poetry *is* . . . (something one can label).

The following suggested series is for a fourth grade class, but with light modification is suitable for students of any age:

1. "I REMEMBER" POEMS
2. ACROSTICS
3. "MY SOUL IS . . ." POEMS
4. PLACE POEMS
5. CHANT POEMS
6. LUNES
7. "GOING INSIDE" POEMS
8. CONCRETE POEMS
9. RECIPE POEMS
10. ON POETRY

This sequence covers most of the basics; it's good for a first exposure. Later you can follow up with more specialized exercises (DECLARATIONS, for example), and with exercises you invent yourself.

Just as, within a poem, odd juxtapositions can work well, odd jumps in a series of creative writing exercises can inspire remarkable student writing. Poetry cannot "be" a curriculum; it is rather an ongoing process. Don't worry too much about a logical sequence; the issue is that students are writing.

There's no reason not to repeat some of the writing exercises at a later point. You might try introducing a twist the second time around. In any case, it's interesting to observe how the students have developed or changed. But don't be disappointed if students' poetic abilities ride long plateaus or even seem to decline for periods—remember, you're largely just tapping what's already in them, and sometimes the first tapping will unleash an outburst of poetic force that's hard to match in every session thereafter.

In general, it's best to avoid a rigid poetry curriculum. As students proceed, a lot can be left to individual and informal evolution. Ultimately, the *reading* that young writers do is perhaps the best key to their development.

—*Jack Collom*

x-ref: "On Different Ages"; "On Follow-up"

On Inventing and Adapting Exercises

When you set about to invent a writing exercise (a wonderful thing to do, and something many teachers have done), consider the qualities you wish to bring out in your students' writing, such as

- Originality
- Imagination
- Observation
- Lively, flowing language
- Sensitivity to sounds, patterns, and variations
- Use of details from their own experience.

Your concentrating on these—rather than versification skills, positive or nice thoughts, correct English, the ability to generalize, and the like—will help apprentice students of any age to write creatively. In other words, you want to tickle out into articulate, written form the vitality that's already in them. A very open proposition.

At the same time, being children, they do need guidance. Most kids, left to their own devices, will be at sea without some structure or idea to help them get going.

Any subject matter is good for poetry, from a roadapple to the Big Bang. But poetry doesn't need a "subject"—it may most enduringly be "about" its own movements of language and thought. Subjects make an easy entrée, but the likelihood is that students will write mediocre poems if you ask them to tackle love, freedom, drugs and rock, parents, war, school, cafeteria food, cars, nature, pets, etc. It's best not to give kids a license for triteness. We all have a stock of clichés that leap to mind about these topics. An important role of poetry is to go beyond the knee jerk phrasings that attend such labels of experience.

The *structure* of the exercise can get the kids to "think about it differently" much more than exhortations do (though they too can help). One of the most popular approaches is to "acrosticize" responses (see ACROSTICS). Even a subject such as "My Summer Vacation" can become fresh this way—the random factor of the spine word's letters steers students away from hackneyed writing. They're nudged away from their "lines of least resistance" into something fresh.

Don't be afraid of "gimmicks"—a term that high-toned people sometimes use to denigrate devices that they feel are contrary to the "dignity" of poetry. The acrostic is a gimmick. The sonnet is a cluster of gimmicks. Demystifying poetry by exposing its gimmicks in class is all to the good. And if the gimmick has an openness to it, the magic of poetry has room to enter.

So, in a nutshell, all kinds of gimmicks and processes are fine for teaching creative writing, but make sure they leave plenty of room for the compositional genius of your students. If the exercise allows little more room for expansion than a crossword puzzle, it could work as a warmup, but is too confining to serve as a poetry exercise. In inventing an exercise, *think small, but think open.*

*   *   *   *   *

Here's a little sample description of the invention of several exercises. I first heard of the acrostic poem when I was past forty, but since then have grown to love it. I often write them and often suggest them in schools. Once, while toying with ideas for variations on the form, it occurred to me that instead of having letters-making-a-word down the left margin, one could use words-making-a-phrase. But then—would it "work"? Or would it be too restrictive? I decided it would work if I let students know that a lot of options for their "backbone phrases" were available ("titles, sayings, slogans, fragments, or just any bunch of words that strikes you"). I read them various samples to illustrate the point. I stressed the freedom of rhythm, line-length, etc. after the first word (in each line) is in place. A potential danger of this form is that student poems may merely echo or explain the backbone phrase. One doesn't want poems like:

> LIFE in all its facets
> IS really and truly
> FUN. Don't you think?

So I simply urge students to make their poem a definite slant *off* the basic statement or feeling of the backbone phrase, even a contradiction, and read them examples. (See ACROSTICS-FROM-PHRASES.)

Another example is INTERNAL RHYME. How the idea came I don't know. Again, the crux was in deciding if it would work. I thought, why not? It's a bit demanding, good for the advanced student poet. It's one of those little ways to encourage the union of form and freedom.

One more example: "CAPTURED TALK." Working in factories, I was charmed by the lively, down-to-earth talk around me (in my teens I'd spoken too much like a dictionary). I began jotting down verbatim phrases that appealed to me, informally editing (choosing) for sound and feel as I went. At first these were occasional notes; then they became distinct projects. My factory-mates were fascinated to read their colorful chitchat published as poems. By extension, it seemed good to assign students this sort of verbal collage.

*　　*　　*　　*　　*

Try to work together with other teachers to invent and disseminate writing exercises. There is no end to them! But any one person, no matter how inventive, will be able to make up only *some*, it seems. We've been happily amazed at how many good, new ideas—after years of constant searching for good ideas—have arisen from and with the teachers we have worked with.

All exercises don't work well for *all* poetry teachers. Personality and taste intervene. However, you can surprise yourself by trying one that doesn't appear, on the face of it, a likely prospect for you. When you're comfortable with teaching poetry, you can begin to experiment with ways of extending your range.

If you try an exercise you've made up and the student poems that emerge seem bland or derivative, don't give up—maybe it just needs a little tinkering. You might recheck the "Tips" section of this book; perhaps you'll discover one little "trick"—for example, a catalogue approach to nature poems that will get students beyond trite generalizations, or "writing around" an idea (in the "MY SOUL IS . . ." exercise)—that will make all the difference in the world.

*　　*　　*　　*　　*

We also encourage you to *adapt* the exercises you find in this book—or elsewhere—to suit your own needs. For example, the exercise titled DECLARATIONS uses a famous sentence from the Declaration of Independence as a beginning for personalized poems. One could pick sentences from a myriad of other sources to serve as catalysts for poems. One might be "Call me Ishmael." With a little background on *Moby-Dick* and the wandering nature of Ishmael, one could lead the students into narrative poems, multiple self-namings, ways to speak of their lives symbolically, and so on. Or "Don't give up the ship!" Students could write lists or chant poems on things and qualities not to be given up. (A related idea: several exercises suggest phrases that students can expand on over and over. You can try other phrases—"If I were rich . . . ," "Behind my secret door. . . ," etc.)

A few final tips:

• Even if some students seem puzzled by ambiguity in an exercise, given a little time, they'll be able to think their way into it. The teacher needn't rush in and program them to immediate activity. Many of the exercises here intentionally include an element of think-for-yourself challenge. It's good to risk a little student blankout in order to leave their creative capacity open. Some children may need, especially at first, additional smaller and simpler suggestions; these can be given during writing time. But sometimes when students ask for help they're really calling for attention, or just expressing their initial anxiety at not being told exactly what to do. A friendly "toughness" will allow them to enter the self-activating field of their own poems.

• Try to find ways to direct your students' attention to the *details* within any large theme (such as "happiness").

• Be open to results that are interesting but not what you expected.

x-ref: ACROSTICS; ACROSTICS-FROM-PHRASES; "CAPTURED TALK"; DECLARA-TIONS; INTERNAL RHYME; LIST POEMS; "GOING INSIDE" POEMS; "Using Great Poems as Models"; "On Quickies: Icebreakers and Fillers"; "On Teaching Students of Different Ages"

*　　*　　*　　*　　*

STUDENT-INVENTED STYLES

Some students invent their own styles, and regularly use them in their writing (see student samples below). We recommend that you heartily encourage this phenomenon. Usually, they'll expand their repertory in due time on their own. As with painters, who practice "problems" over and over, the experience will get them deeper into their material (language); this is all to the good.

If you feel, however, that a student is keeping himself or herself from making important developments or is using a "one-shot" gimmick in every piece—or if the student's style overwhelms or homogenizes all content—gently suggest other ways of writing *in addition to* (not instead of) the invented style.

A few observations:

• Miscellaneous, one-time-only devices (such as Theo Vander-schaaf's poem below, that creatively blends the immediate scene with something overheard) should be praised—tell students how and why their pieces work.

• Be on the lookout for works that may not succeed *in toto*, but contain fragments that may stand up as good short pieces on their own. Practicing poets often arrive at their poems by extracting such nuggets.

• Also be on the lookout for out-and-out experiments (such as the piece below by Beckey Fritz). They usually show (at the very least) a commendable thrust toward originality.

• Also look for off-task pieces—pieces that don't meet the guidelines of a certain writing exercise, but are good nonetheless (e.g., the lunes and haiku poems by students below, which don't satisfy the prescribed word or syllable count).

• The same can be said about the "misuses" of grammar, and even, at times, misspellings or odd punctuation. If students are deliberately breaking the rules, it shows that they understand them. Be sure you are not "correcting" a feel for using words differently—which is, after all, part of the constant refreshment of language that good poetry gives us.

—*Jack Collom*

This poem was written at a poetry reading in response to a poem on the extinction of the passenger pigeon:

Reading

Reading Reading Reading
the vast waterfall of words
Poetry is like the huge
cluster of passenger pigeons
When the guns fire the
words shoot at the audience
The pigeons fall the audience
claps.
When the people eat the
pigeons the audience will take
a break
When the pigeons have
their babies the audience
will come back
The reading starts the shooting
starts
Then the shooting and reading
end but we keep clapping.

—*Theo Vanderschaaf, 5th*

Following are some very short poems that violate the lune or haiku form but are nonetheless little gems:

A black stallion is black
And a sun is yellow and
It is all fancy.

—*Derek Linger, 2nd*

Every morning I see
a green and white pickup truck
that never moves.

—*Dennis Coles, 11th*

One day the sky became the sun and the class became pictures.

—*Jeremy Fairchild, 2nd*

Once I was sneaking up on a thing.
I didn't know what it was, but
all at once it bursted into rainbows and little floods.

—*Jimmy Hobbs, 2nd*

The next poem was written in response to the CHANT POEMS assignment:

One car two car go three
car go go go four car go
five car go down the road
we go

—*Beckey Fritz, 2nd*

The following poem is metered and rhymed, but the *style* is quite idiosyncratically developed—the galloping rhythm, high spirits, and walloping vocabulary. Praise such to the skies, while gently suggesting additional ways of writing.

Snüs

It splitters, it splatters, it plops on your dome.
It challenges lifestyles (a house ain't a home!)
It breathes with resistance, it slides down your cheek.
Gathers moss like a rolling stone, subtle and weak.
You're doomed to the Limelight; it stirs in your breast.
It hollows you out and builds you a nest.
The pipe-lines decay till they're nothing but rot.
The sewage, the spillage . . . all steaming and hot.
It's not what it seems like. It's nothing at all.
He straddles the goal-posts and strolls the South Hall.
A western scenario, waxlike and mean.
A "Regis Millette": ripe, sticky, and green.
Alphabetical order—they call you by name.

It snaps like a twig and then nothing's the same.
The surge of the aftermount shaves off your bones.
They stiffen, they're swollen—monotonous tones.
A spank it shall give ye if caught unawares.
You'll hustle and bump and cavort down the stairs.
A prize will be given in lieu of perspective.
Her father's a nuisance—an "armchair detective."
Blimey! The Blarney Stone up and surpassed,
and all of my houseguests were taken aghast.
It dribbles, it slobbers, wipes off of good leather.
A monogrammed tea-towel, let's pray for good weather!
These symptoms I've seen until death do us part.
My 98-dollar-receipt from K-Mart!
If wooing the musketeer made her a whore
she should ask for a job as cashier in a store.
Anything different to boost her morale.
It appears that the musketeer wasn't her pal.
As a matter of fact, he retreats from the past.
Read all about it! (I doubt it will last.)
Perhaps the peculiar and odd goings-on
contribute success to the mule and the fawn.
But speckled or spotted, because or in spite,
let's now dim the lantern and sleep for the night.

—*Pam Nelson, high school*

Here's an experiment using three-word lines:

I hear can
voice will I
ignored long ago
out my mouth
like a dance
from flowing rain
drops get wet
me underneath pain
fire, yet fire
to the grass
of home land
snows can set
mists new beyond
light shall set
free that I
seek to find

once cry trapped
in golden beams
set off new
of old destruction
mine blaze fresh
throughout my hands
can see I
two cry trapped
fields with o'er
ceiling cracked pink
fingers search black
peanut butter crackers
three cry cracked
oh cello god
can see I
face all face

through the once
one cry trapped
murmur, nonny, murmur
close the door
my mother said
you'll get cold
eyes were red
can't you see?
I screamed aloud
I turned away
lost my cloud

—*Darla Anderson, high school*

This last example inventively blends content and form:

There's always two sides to everything
Tһere's always two sides to everything

war, peace, sheepskin, fleece
war, peace, sheepskin, fleece

tame or wild, kid or child
tame or wild, kid or child

two sides to everything
two sides to everything

watches, clocks, straight or on the rocks
watches, clocks, straight or on the rocks

sides to everything
sides to everything

beard or mustache, charge or cash
beard or mustache, charge or cash

to everything
to everything

live, die, coast or fly
live, die, coast or fly

everything
everything

> —*Chip Coors, 7th*

x-ref: Deanna Smith poem, p. 40; Krista Prescott poem, p. 42; Russ Kluge poem, p. 61; Kelly Wagner poem, p. 117.

On Collaborations

Any kind of poetry can be written collaboratively. And there are some types of poetry that are strictly collaborative. So there's an even wider variety of approaches for partner or pass-around poetry than for the lone scribbler. Poets great and small have collaborated for millenia. Yet in the history of poetry very few collaborations stand out as memorable works of art; the lone writer has composed virtually all the really fine works. Collaboration can indeed result in delightful poems, but mainly it's fun and it's good practice.

What basically happens when you do a collaboration is that the burden of wholeness is removed from your shoulders. You are no longer responsible for the meaning of the poem. As you trade off, you note with renewed amazement how different your thought processes and speech rhythms are from those of your partner. Your attention is thus plunged into language as something to dance with, not just as the means of expressing your opinion. You don't have to worry about what to say; there's always something to respond to. You become conscious of your own "voice" as it adapts to, opposes, ignores, or imitates the other "voices" present in the poem. In many of the best collaborations there's a great wildness of verbal energy that the lone poet can scarcely approach.

When kids write collaborations, meaning tends to take a back seat, and the hope is that imagination rushes to the steering wheel in its stead. In actual practice, it may be chaos or, even less interestingly, flipness, haste, top-of-the-head scrawls (such as "Oh yeah?" and "You stink"). The cover of anonymity can at first liberate some of the most tedious iconoclasms of the young mind. Put another way, the surreal texture of many collaborations can confuse the participating poets, so they are reduced to a "so's your old man" type of articulation. Also, rhyme can become a refuge in such confusion. It's best to steer clear of it except in special cases.

A ready sense of play is perhaps the key to collaborating well. This flexibility of thought is not only a liberation; it allows the poet to see the poem as a field of exact choices. Partly it's the ability to be "crazy"—in the sense of the old workplace saying "You've got to be a little crazy around here to keep from going nuts." A proportion of playfulness keeps us in tune with how the world is. If your partner writes, "I saw seven geese in a green field," you weren't there—you follow it, but not from within that experience. You may be more likely to write, "Full of geysers, wearing golden crowns" than something consistent, like "Of grass that rippled like the sea." Trade-off poems can open up happy inconsistencies that amount to wide opportunity. They can initiate the young writer into an attitude that says, "I'm not using this poem to tell you something; I'm dancing for you."

But "craziness" is not the only desired result in collaborations. Underneath the best craziness is a deep thoughtfulness, as in Shakespeare's fools, who spout wisdom in disjointed forms. Indeed, sometimes two people can actually write a serious lyric together, and you should point out this possibility to your students. Between these two extremes is the most common good possibility—that a poem will result in which playfulness and seriousness illuminate each other.

Reading a few examples of collaborative poems with your class and pointing out their virtues—their sense of high energy, surprises, uniqueness, and fresh humor—will encourage students to do more than dash off the first wiseguy cliché that comes to mind.

Paradoxically, haste is sometimes the enemy of spontaneity. When your writing partner is eagerly waiting for you to finish your line, you tend to write before you have something "good." Simply urge your students to take their time. Advise them to jot down notes while they're waiting—good words and phrases that come to mind—so they won't get lost. Have partners do two poems at once so each is occupied more or less all the time.

Before students collaborate, you can try a warmup that tends to lead students into the fun of goofy associations (see the chapter called "On Quickies: Icebreakers and Fillers").

One way to encourage students to come up with surprising juxtapositions is to use the "Exquisite Corpse" method. Each writer folds his or her line over after it's written, so the next writer can't see it. A variation is to fold over all but a word or phrase. This is much like the drawings in which one person draws the head of a person or a monster and folds the paper before passing it on and the next person draws the torso without seeing the head, and so forth.

You can also have the whole class be one big collaborating entity—that is, each student begins a poem by writing one line (which can be left open as to length, or restricted to a certain number of words per line) and then passes the paper on. You can pre-establish the traffic flow. Each poem then circulates around the room. Thirty poems are weaving snake-fashion among thirty people. It's best to advise your students that if three or four poems accumulate on one desk, that student should pass a couple on *without* adding to them, so everybody always has something to do.

In the most common form of collaboration, however, two or more people alternately compose lines, using free verse. But any exercise in this book can be done by groups or partners. If you try it with a particular poetic form, it is best if the class is already familiar with that form. Here are some other options:

• Restricting each writer to three words per line results in a very distinctive snappy style, helping the kids learn about line and rhythm.

• Restricting each writer to one word per turn tends to change a collaborative poem to a story. This *can* be done with no attempt to create sense or grammar, but it's interesting and challenging for the students to come up with something that makes sense. Almost invariably a crazy tone creeps into the piece despite the most sober efforts, which helps everyone realize how fragile "making sense" is; it also helps students realize that any point in a poem is rich with choices. To keep a flow going, it's best that one person serve as secretary, so each participant can just tell his or her word to the group.

• A good exercise to get your class focused on language is to make collaborative poems of three words only—you write "hello," partner writes "red," you write "slice."

• In free-verse collaborations, try asking the class to follow a particular theme. This is a good technique for use with young children.

• With advanced students, try rhymed poems, simple sonnets, bouts-rimés poems,* sestinas, etc. You can also have students of all ages use drawings and collages, as well as poems that combine different poetic forms.

• Individual students can also "collaborate" with "the world" by interspersing their own lines with lines from outside sources (see COLLAGE POEMS; "CAPTURED TALK").

—*Jack Collom*

---

* *Bouts-rimés* is French for "rhymed ends." To create a bouts-rimés poem, one person makes up a list of end-rhymes. A second person uses the list to create his or her own poem.

x-ref: "CAPTURED TALK"; COLLAGE POEMS; Q & A PARTNER POEMS; A RUN ON IMAGINATION; "On Quickies: Icebreakers and Fillers"

Here are a number of sample poems that show some of the various ways you and your students can write collaborative poems.

Spring
a beautiful butterfly
 sits on flowers
bloom every
 spring I see
the blue diamond
 in the center
of the middle
 of the flower

—*Cheyenne Stone &*
Misty Winterowd, 5th

"Think and thought,"
said the bird
and the deer
together.

—*Essie Cleeves & Steve*
Bartlett, 2nd

The deer has
a few horns
to go with
its good luck

—*Adrian Jarshaw &*
Ryan Burns, 2nd

Paint splotches on time
stolen at the scene of the crime
red, yellow, and green
looking like a string bean
time ticking away by the minute
staring for an hour is the limit!
skiing down slopes of colored decades
people moving along wearing their shades
jumping jumps and hitting trees
then eating honey because of bees
all a symbol of feeling
the walls, the floor, the ceiling.

—*Treva Sorensen, Alicia Corbett, & Jenny Heckendorf, 8th*

Yesterday it looked like somebody had stolen the mountains,
and today it looked like somebody stole the sun.
Tomorrow maybe they'll steal the Earth
and the moon and the stars.
Where do they put all those things?
In a museum under the bed.
And who are "they"—these universe robbers?
They're peanuts, with ice cream on top.
And they have little red diamond brains
with a peanutbutter sandwich
for a face.
     When I need mountains, I
turn into a nose with pink spots on it.
That gets 'em every time.

          —*Josh Bielby, 2nd, & a teacher*

The yellow sun blazes
 Birds of North America are big and small
The stars shine in the darkness
Sun rays coming in the window at night
The flowers looking bright day after day
Bonnie bell lip smacker
The moon eerie and frightening

          —*Jacie Green & Tamara Stephenson, 5th*

The flowers are
dying in the
cold evil snow.
We stay inside
by the cozy
fireside, listening to
the warm crackle
of the fire.
The fire dies
as it gets
colder and colder.

          —*Darcy Summers & Shyra Scott, 4th*

On Quickies: Icebreakers and Fillers

Sometimes you might want to break the ice with a short warmup exercise to help lead up to a challenging main exercise or to perk up a sluggish group. Or perhaps your class has finished an exercise and you feel that stretching it out would spoil its effect, but there's still a little time left.

Here are short descriptions of some ten-minute "quickies."

• Call on a student to volunteer his or her initials. Be sure the volunteer won't be embarrassed if the class makes a few jokes with his or her initials. Write them on the board. Then ask for a trio of words that begin with those letters (assuming there are three). The words can make sense together or not. Think up examples yourself. Write the best ones on the board. The idea is to make word combinations that are appealing in some way, either by their humor—e.g., surprising juxtapositions—their beautiful or unusual sound as a trio, or their interesting collective meaning. Advise your students that each new trio should contain all fresh words:

BLM—
   Beautiful Lamp Management
   Blue Lion Mountains
   Babies Love Molasses
   Bag Lip Mud
   Bard Loses Melody
   Butterflies Lipsync Malevolence
   Bliss Lisps Missed . . .
   Be Lovely, Man!

If there's time, try to keep the list going long enough to show that ideas *do* keep coming. Then advise (or assign) the kids to make a long list from their own initials at home. They can either leave their lists in the original order or rearrange them for sound or meaning or interesting tone progression.

This warmup can lead right into acrostics, but also can lead to just about anything. It simply gets the students going; it focuses attention on language details and validates imaginative moves.

• Freewriting is a wonderful way to limber up. Some teachers begin every writing session with freewriting. Ask the students to write as fast as they can, without lifting pencils from paper, writing sense or utter nonsense for a few minutes. First read them a wild sample (you could make one up beforehand) to make sure they know that anything goes.

Freewriting can be directed toward a subject. For example, "Now let's freewrite all the words and phrases we can on the Battle of Gettysburg." Or it can be undirected.

The products of freewriting can be left as they are, or used as a basis for further writing (see, for example, the exercise called "PROCESS" POEMS).

• An in-class version of the game sometimes known as Fictionary goes like this. Before class, pick a word from the dictionary, a word nobody's likely to know. Try to select one that looks as if it could mean almost anything: avoid *-tion* words, words with recognizable roots, obvious scientific terms, and the like. If possible, choose a word with a surprising or colorful meaning.

Write the word on the board and ask if anyone knows it. When no one does, ask the students to write definitions (perhaps one good one each) for the word, having fun with their imaginations while also trying to imitate the language and form of a dictionary entry. You might want to read them a couple of examples from the dictionary before they write to remind them how exact definitions are. It's also good, before they write, to read the students a handful of made-up definitions.

Collect and read the students' work. You can include the real definition and ask them to guess which one is "right." A variant is to use a made-up word (such as *nepo*) rather than a real one.

• If students are familiar with acrostics or lunes—or any other short exercise—have them do it, as either a warmup or a filler. Such exercises can be slanted toward the main activity, or not. Acrostics are a great way to cap off a lesson.

• To get students into a topic or form, ask them to write lists of related words, facts, or ideas first. Urge them to be specific and seek out unusual items.

• Here's one called "Telephone on Paper," which was developed by Ms. Combs-Stauffer's high school class in Salmon, Idaho: "I handed the first sentence to a student and asked her to give it one read-through, then hand it back to me and write it down on paper as well as she could remember it. Then *her* sentence was handed to another student, and so on."

A white mouse sneaked into the bluebird house, ate some seeds,
    and curled up like an egg.

A mouse sneaked through a house and snacked up some seeds and
    ate them.
A mouse sneaked through the house and snuck into the bedroom.
A mouse sneaked through the bedroom then snuck.
Although the snake went in the bedroom it came out of the
    same room.
A snake came in the gameroom and ate all the candy.
A damn snake came into the damn gameroom and ate the food.
A clam snake came into the clam gameroom.
A clam snake came into the clam gameroom.

• Any specialty you have that has anything to do with language can
be useful. Do you know any Chinese? Write a few Chinese characters on
the board and ask the students to guess what they mean. Show them the
connections between a character's look and meaning. You can even *learn*
a little Chinese for the purpose. Or discuss visual aspects of English
words and letters. The letter A originally represented an ox. You can associate colors or other qualities with letters, as did the French poet
Arthur Rimbaud in his poem "Vowels." This sort of warmup could lead
into concrete poems (see CONCRETE POEMS), or simply serve as a device to
focus students on the visual aspects of language.

Do you know German? Ask the students to call out words or
phrases randomly for you to translate into German on the board. You
can use these words to construct a little poem or story, in German, English, or both.

You can even have them make zany mistranslations from poems in
languages they don't know.

• Do you know sign language? Its connections between body and
word fascinate students, and inspire them to write poetry more imagi-
natively.

• Draw maps or pictures as a warmup. This too helps ground the
writing that follows.

• Have them write mock want-ads.

• April Fools' poems are good in season, but encourage originality.

• Ask them to cut up writings (their own or others) and then to put
them together in new combinations—sensical or nonsensical.

• Do a brief session on word origins. The etymologies of words are often colorful and surprising, and really get the kids interested in language.

• Ask them to make up three-word poems (without relying on initials).

- Have them do short partner-poems of any kind (see "On Collaborations").

- Read aloud a poem you like (but unrelated to what will come after)—just to "fill the air" with the energy and good sound of poetry.

- Have a little open discussion on what poetry is (and might be).

- Have them do something physical—stretch or tap out a rhythm for a minute.

- Ask them to look out the window or at some object for a couple of minutes.

- From a list of prefixes and suffixes, ask them to make up (and perhaps define) new words: *heterograph*—a weird poem; *hyperology*—the science of excess.

- Have them describe facial expressions via metaphor and simile. With young children you can combine this with a guessing game.

- Have them make up "dream names" for themselves, for imaginary playmates, for children they might have.

- Have them come up with oxymorons ("jumbo shrimp") or invent their own.

—Jack Collom

x-ref: "On Inventing and Adapting Exercises"

Two Looks at Revision

Some poets claim they never revise. Others revise programmatically, exhaustively. Most poets fall somewhere in between. The basic problem seems to be that the spontaneity of the first draft will often catch a really poetic phrase or thought—but at the same time may cough up unconscious self-justifications, clichés, confusions, and other dull matters. You must examine each piece on a case-by-case basis; each poem has unique needs. Writing in demanding forms, such as the sonnet or the sestina, usually requires careful revision.

There's no good formula for when to revise. It's often hard to capture the delicate mood and flow you had while writing the first draft. Sometimes it's best to throw out whole sections and start over, sometimes it's helpful to let a piece "lie" for a while. After it has had a chance to "simmer," new ideas and phrases can kick in. Emphasize to the class that correcting a piece is *not* the same as revising it.

Revision is the act of becoming one's own teacher. The more poetry you read, the better your individual sense of a good or a bad poem; however, you must try (as poet or teacher) to remain open to expanding that sense.

Here are some tips for the revising poet:

• Keep your originals; you may want to go back to them.

• Read the poem aloud a lot. It's very important to hear how it sounds.

• Let the poem sit unlooked-at for a few days or weeks—or years.

• Shut your eyes and reimagine your poem. Try adding details, even if they're "irrelevant." Don't forget sounds, colors, weather, smells, dress, postures, movements.

• Try starting in the middle and adding the beginning later. It's often good to begin a piece with action or an image.

• Rewrite the poem without looking at the original. Let yourself go off in new directions.

- Eliminate low-energy excess. A small example: students often use the word *that* unnecessarily, thinking (that) they need it for correctness. But sometimes it stiffens the tone, weakens rhythm and energy, when automatically stuck into lines or sentences: "I believe that I am having a heart attack." Likewise, don't pile up adjectives relentlessly.

- Eliminate abstractions, unless they enhance a poem with irony or perspective. *The greatest originality is to be exact.*

- Let the writing sound like you talking—at your best. Don't strive for correct English as your chief aim. Don't feel you have to eradicate "weirdness."

- With colored pens, mark awkward lines, words, or phrases, then work with them. Different colors can make those spots more distinct and easier to work with.

- Also, try marking good ones, and extracting them. See how they look out of their original contexts.

- Direct your language toward particulars. Make the nouns and verbs as specific as possible (*eucalyptus,* not *plant; squinted,* not *looked*). If you catch yourself, say, trying to solve "love" in half a page, toss it.

- Don't justify or overexplain.

- Try numbering, categorizing, rearranging parts, especially for longer works.

- Some revision is done right along with the first draft, as you are writing. One technique, when you've written a word and immediately want to change it but can't think of one you really like, is to search your mind for *sound* correspondences. Alliteration can be a lead—"Hmm, if I write a short word starting with *m* here, it'll sound good." (This resembles the way that the letters of the spine word in an acrostic poem help spring new ideas.)

- Another approach to revision is to figure out exactly who's speaking (not necessarily just "you"), and to whom—and proceed from that understanding. Think of the poem's speaker as a character you're developing. Does the character sound wooden? whiny? boring? preachy? incomplete? Does the voice suit the poem?

- Revise by re-doing the linebreaks, to bring new emphases, new rhythms. You can try rewriting your current draft by using slashes (. . . / . . . / . . .) to indicate new linebreaks.

- Look again at your title (or lack of title). Titles can help cut poems "down to size" (which makes them better). They often work ironically or as a focusing device.

- How a poem concludes is very important. The ending can enchant ordinary material—or wreck a strong work. Here, above all, you should avoid anything that smacks of triteness. Usually an image, rather than a statement, will be solid. But even images can be clichés; try to make sure your ending doesn't remind you of any other piece of literature.

—*Jack Collom*

*   *   *   *   *

After the class has finished writing their poems, have them put their work away for a few days. Then, when it's time to work on revision, ask students to pretend that their poems were written by someone else, to look at the writing impartially. At this point, your doing an example on the board can be extremely helpful for students.

Tell them that this is their chance to make the poem perfect by adding or changing whatever they feel is necessary. Sometimes it's only enhancement—adding some descriptive words, replacing stale words such as *good, pretty,* or *beautiful* with more exact and meaningful ones. One technique I use is to draw a grave on the board and have the class help fill it with "dead" language and clichés. Tell them to look at every word and see if they can add a descriptive word to it or replace a tired or general word with a more precise one. Sometimes a student will decide his or her poem is finished, and the poem is actually fine as it is. But this is rare.

Use the professional terms *first draft, rough copy,* and *final draft.*

Tell your students to try to make their poems stronger, more direct, and more interesting. "Cut away the flab in a poem, the words that weigh it down." "Punch some holes in the muffler of a poem, so it roars!" "Make your poem fly like an arrow, not like a stone." Revision requires cutting away whatever words are not really important; it's great practice for students to decide which words are important and which are extraneous.

Remind the class how sometimes when you're angry with someone it takes a whole day of walking around talking to yourself before you get it straight and can express all your feelings. It works the same way with writing—you can spend days or weeks working out the fine points in a poem. You can go to sleep and wake up with a better idea. You can dream the lines you need in your poem. It's hard not to improve a piece of writing if you let your mind work on it as you go through the day. Suddenly, the right word or phrase will appear and save the poem.

Have your students try copying poems side by side with earlier versions. Then have them volunteer to read both versions and have the class decide which is better.

Have the kids exchange their poems with a partner and suggest to each other how to improve their pieces, using the ideas mentioned above—to make their poems stronger, more real, more honest, more engaging for the reader.

—*Sheryl Noethe*

See *Deep Revision: A Guide for Teachers, Students, and Other Writers* by Meredith Sue Willis (New York: Teachers & Writers Collaborative, 1993).

On Follow-up

Just as your energy is essential to the classroom, your response to your students' writing is crucial. Some students become very shy when they read their work aloud (or even when the teacher reads it); others look so unconcerned that they are hardly in the room. The teacher's response is what students have to measure their work by. Watch their faces when they read their poems aloud. Invariably they look first to the teacher for approval. Together you generate a momentum that can continue to enthuse the kids in every other area it touches.

The remarks you make about student poems carry a lot of weight. Look at the words and phrases in them, and see which ones dance out as unusual and original. Show the class your sensibility—what you appreciate, what moves you, what makes you laugh—and ask the students about their own responses to the poem. This discussion can show how differently each person can see a given poem—that no particular view is ever necessarily correct or incorrect. Just as each teacher teaches in a unique fashion, each person writes in his or her own way. Thus your responses to student poems should reflect the strengths of the particular authors.

If you can't find something to praise in the construction of the poem, look again for another quality: subtlety, wit, clarity of thought, or the simply-yet-perfectly-stated. It takes flexibility to appreciate many styles of writing. Here are some comments we make to students about their work:

> Exuberant, musical, dances across the page, full of rich ideas and irony. Each idea kicks up another like a string of firecrackers. Great movement of ideas, serious thoughts, wonderful command of language, rhythm that knocks your socks off, vivid, alive, fresh, great attention to detail.

Of course, you must be yourself and convey your own enthusiasm. It's fun to develop ways to talk about poetry, especially using adjectives you'd use to describe good food, weather, or a parade!

At the same time, you must be critical as well. Criticize constructively by drawing attention to the best lines and images, and compare them to the weak parts. By emphasizing what a student is doing well, you can allow clichés and derivative writing to wither away from lack of attention; the kids will get a much clearer notion of what poetic skills are, as well as how to develop them. Talk to the students as if you were talking to real authors—because you are! Discuss their images and dialogue seriously and respectfully, praise vivid and honest writing. Repeat their best lines back to them in a powerful voice.

Don't lose the momentum. Poetry can change students' feelings about themselves and the world. Weave the adventure of writing into all you and your students do. Don't stop at weekly writing sessions. *Write together every day.*

Use creative writing in all subjects. It's a great way to get students involved, and can enliven any subject. In one social studies class studying Canada, we wrote acrostic poems about that country. Students included their new vocabulary and knowledge of geography, combining them with the whimsy of the acrostic form. The class didn't feel tested. Instead they wrote with pleasure. Later, we wrote haiku about South America, using photographs from students' textbooks to come up with initial images. Again, the class showed what they'd learned in a context much broader than that of a test: they were able to include creative and descriptive language.

What about outside the classroom and afterwards? Here are some ideas for bringing poetry into the community at large:

• Publish anthologies of student poetry and artwork. It is extremely rewarding and inspiring for students to see their work in print. The anthology may be the single most important activity you can do as follow-up. (See "Eight Steps to Publishing an Annual Poetry Anthology" below.)

• Distribute student anthologies in businesses and stores in the community.

• Keep good student poems to use in following years. Younger relatives and friends of students whose works are read aloud will be excited and feel encouraged to write themselves.

• Display student poems on school bulletin boards.

• Try to arrange for a poetry column in the local newspaper.

• Send poems home to parents. Ask students to write partner poems with parents or with other kids.

• Student poetry readings are splendid. Make sure you publicize such an event well—plaster posters all over the neighborhood. Use students' "connections" to hang posters in local businesses and workplaces. At the reading, be sure to use a good sound system, so the kids can be heard.

- Bring in local poets and writers to the classroom; also have them give public readings elsewhere in the community.

- Start an adult writing workshop (or writing group) for both teachers and parents.

- Organize open readings, inviting students, teachers, parents, and interested bystanders to take part.

- Get your students and their work on the radio. This is easier to do if you're dealing with a small-town or university station.

- Meet with other teachers to trade ideas and lesson plans. In Salmon we had a regular Thursday group. Teachers discussed what they were doing with poetry and exchanged hybrids of various lessons adapted to particular classroom needs—from making math problem poems to sprinkling glitter over first graders before writing fantasy poetry.

In Salmon, we ended up, as high school teacher Terry Magoon put it, with "a community full of kids who think poetry is normal, poetry is fun, poetry is something real people do."

—*Sheryl Noethe*

*   *   *   *   *

EIGHT STEPS TO PUBLISHING AN ANNUAL POETRY ANTHOLOGY

1. Each participating teacher should select the best poems from each writing session. Then they should type them up and save them (preferably on a computer). If each teacher does this on a regular basis, a deadly year-end pile-up will not ensue. The final deadline should be around April 1, depending on the school calendar. Expect some late submissions.

2. Choose an editor-in-chief to make the final selection, taking into account production costs, etc. It's best if there is one person who has this central responsibility—with extra pay perhaps, or extra credits or prep time. This chief "editor," in consultation with others, should create a production schedule, establish deadlines and instructions for format, and find out about printing costs. (The editor should also send memos and reminders to all involved.) A small group of teachers—perhaps one from each school—could aid in collecting poetry and artwork. The members of this group can also represent their schools at meetings, and report back information.

A limit on the number of pages each teacher can submit should be set. This limit should be generous, with the understanding that budget considerations might necessitate further cuts. The final decision, of course, would belong to the editor-in-chief. (Some teachers feel that every student should be included in the anthology. This is, of course, impossible in a district-wide anthology because of size and cost limitations. One solution for those teachers is for them to put together their own classroom anthologies.)

3. Make sure to gather artwork for the book. Black-and-white line drawings usually work best, and they're also inexpensive to reproduce. Photographs are a great asset, of course, but they are not cheap. The illustrations need not relate directly to the text.

4. In Salmon we used desktop publishing for our anthology. Poetry was submitted on disk and, following the guidelines of the editor, high school students did the actual work of formatting and laying out pages. (Editing, first the responsibility of each teacher at each school, is still possible at this time.)

5. You can add artwork using the old-fashioned method of cut-and-paste. The first year in Salmon we reduced illustrations using a copier and then pasted them into the text. The next year we used our new scanner, which digitizes the original images, allowing us to translate them into computer files. The scanner also makes using photographs more feasible.

6. There are many different ways to do the cover. The first year, we silkscreened 800 covers in three colors. This was a gigantic undertaking involving many of the student poets. We used two paper stencils and had one stencil made from a transparency. We chose the type for the title (selected by vote in a teachers' meeting), printed it on a piece of paper, and used a thermofax machine to make a transparency. A local T-shirt shop then made a screen for us.

The next year the high school art class took responsibility for the cover. They created black-and-white line drawings to be scanned.

7. Ask various printers for estimates based on the number of pages and number of copies. *You will probably want the editor to find out prices fairly early on, in order to avoid any unpleasant surprises.* We took our print-outs to a copy shop and had about 1,000 copies of a ninety-five-

page anthology made for about $2,000. The printer copied, collated, and stapled the books for us.

8. Teachers should distribute a copy of the book to each student. It's good to offer copies to local businesses, stores, and the public library, as well as bars and cafes, where it can be available in a sort of reading-room fashion.

—*Dorrie Prange and Sheryl Noethe*

APPENDIX: MATERIAL ARRANGED BY SCHOOL SUBJECT

Many teachers—even social studies, math, and science teachers—have come to view writing as a main key to the learning process. Poetry writing gives students a fuller, more exciting, and more accurate learning experience. You can apply or adapt almost any exercise in this book to almost any field, with results that *personalize* the subject for the student. A good example of this is the exercise we call CREATIVE REWRITES. Another approach we recommend highly is using lively primary sources: in biology, for example, those by Charles Darwin, Rachel Carson, Stephen Jay Gould, and Lewis Thomas.

OF SPECIAL INTEREST TO TEACHERS OF SCIENCE AND MATH

"A Note on This Book and How to Use It"
"Tips on Leading Poetry Sessions"

Exercises:

ACROSTICS
ACROSTICS-FROM-PHRASES
ANATOMY POEMS
COMPOST-BASED POEMS
CONCRETE POEMS
CREATIVE REWRITES
DEFINITION POEMS
EARTH POEMS—THINGS TO SAVE
GEOMETRY POEMS
LIST POEMS
LUNES
ODES
ORIGINS POEMS
OUTDOORS POEMS
PICTURE-INSPIRED WRITINGS
"PROCESS" POEMS
RUBE GOLDBERG POEMS
QUESTIONS WITHOUT ANSWERS

RECIPE POEMS
TALKING TO ANIMALS
THING POEMS

OF SPECIAL INTEREST TO TEACHERS OF SOCIAL STUDIES

"A Note on This Book and How to Use It"
"Tips on Leading Poetry Sessions"

Exercises:

ACROSTICS
COLLAGE POEMS
DECLARATIONS
DEFINITION POEMS
"FEELINGS" POEMS
"GOING INSIDE" POEMS
HAIKU
HAIBUN
"I REMEMBER" POEMS
"I HAVE A DREAM" POEMS
"LAST WORDS" POEMS
ODES
ORIGINS POEMS
PICTURE-INSPIRED WRITINGS
PLACE POEMS
POLITICAL POEMS
PORTRAIT OR SKETCH POEMS
"PRIMITIVE" POEMS
Q & A PARTNER POEMS
RECIPE POEMS
"THINGS TO DO" POEMS

OF SPECIAL INTEREST TO TEACHERS OF MUSIC AND ART

"A Note on This Book and How to Use It"
"Tips on Leading Poetry Sessions"
"On Sound and Rhythm"

Exercises:

ACROSTICS
ACROSTICS-FROM-PHRASES
CHANT POEMS
COLLAGE POEMS
CONCRETE POEMS
DREAM INTERPRETATION
"FEELINGS" POEMS
"GOING INSIDE" POEMS
LUNES
METAPHORS
"MY SOUL IS . . . " POEMS
NAME-LETTERS STORIES
ON POETRY
PICTURE-INSPIRED WRITINGS
"PROCESS" POEMS
QUESTIONS WITHOUT ANSWERS
A RUN ON IMAGINATION
RECIPE POEMS
"THIRTEEN WAYS OF LOOKING" POEMS
USED TO/BUT NOW POEMS
WORD PAIRS

OF SPECIAL INTEREST TO TEACHERS OF ENGLISH

Everything! But particularly "On Integrating Poetry into Standard English Classes."

OTHER T&W PUBLICATIONS YOU MIGHT ENJOY

Moving Windows by Jack Collom. An in-depth guide to evaluating the poetry children write. "A landmark book . . . stimulating ideas that any teacher could utilize and wonderful examples of children's poems"—*Oregon English.* "First rate"—*Rolling Stock.* "Superb"—*Fessenden Review.*

Determined to See the Far Land by Theresa Mack. This 26-minute color videotape of poet Sheryl Noethe teaching poetry writing to deaf children shows how her method is relevant to all children. Moving and inspiring.

The Teachers & Writers Handbook of Poetic Forms, edited by Ron Padgett. This T&W bestseller includes 74 entries on traditional and modern poetic forms by 19 poet-teachers. "A treasure"—*Kliatt.* "The definitions not only inform, they often provoke and inspire. A small wonder!"—*Poetry Project Newsletter.* "An entertaining reference work"—*Teaching English in the Two-Year College.* "A solid beginning reference source"—*Choice.*

Poetic Forms. Ten 30-minute audio programs on ten basic poetic forms. "Informal, lively, and appealing. . . . Highly useful to teachers and to anyone who would like to try writing poetry"—*Choice.*

The List Poem: A Guide to Teaching & Writing Catalog Verse by Larry Fagin defines list poetry, traces its history, gives advice on teaching it, offers specific writing ideas, and presents more than 200 examples by children and adults. An *Instructor* Poetry Pick. "Outstanding"—*Kliatt.*

The Poetry Connection: An Anthology of Contemporary Poems with Ideas to Stimulate Children's Writing by Nina Nyhart and Kinereth Gensler. "An entirely indispensable classroom tool"—*California Poets in the Schools.*

The Writing Workshop, Vols. 1 & 2 by Alan Ziegler. A perfect combination of theory, practice, and specific assignments. "Invaluable to the writing teacher"—*Contemporary Education.* "Indispensable"—*Herbert R. Kohl.*

The Whole Word Catalogue, Vols. 1 & 2. T&W's bestselling guides to teaching imaginative writing. "*WWC 1* is probably the best practical guide for teachers who really want to stimulate their students to write"—*Learning.* "*WWC 2* is excellent. . . . It makes available approaches to the teaching of writing not found in other programs"—*Language Arts.*

•

For a complete catalogue of T&W books, magazines, audiotapes, videotapes, and computer writing games, contact Teachers & Writers Collaborative, 5 Union Square West, New York, NY 10003–3306, (212) 691-6590.

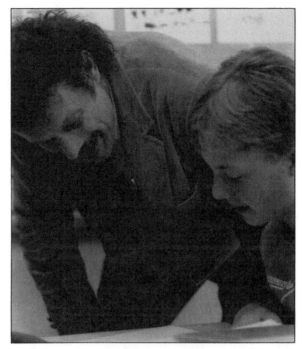

Jack Collom and student

Sheryl Noethe and student